United States perceptions
of Latin America

United States perceptions of Latin America

1850–1930

A 'New West' south of Capricorn?

J. Valerie Fifer

Manchester University Press

Manchester and New York

distributed exclusively in the USA and Canada by St. Martin's Press

Published by Manchester University Press
Oxford Road, Manchester M13 9PL, UK
and Room 400, 175 Fifth Avenue,
New York, NY 10010, USA

Distributed exclusively in the USA and Canada
by St. Martin's Press, Inc.,
175 Fifth Avenue, New York, NY 10010, USA

British Library cataloguing in publication data

Fifer, J. Valerie
   United States perceptions of Latin America, 1850–1930: A 'New West' south of Capricorn?
   1. United States. Western states economic policies, history, compared with South American economic policies, history.   2. South America. Economic policies, history, compared with economic policies of western United States, history.
   I. Title
   330.978
   330.98

Library of Congress cataloging in publication data
Fifer, J. Valerie.
   United States perceptions of Latin America, 1850–1930 : a 'New West' south of Capricorn? / J. Valerie Fifer.
      p.   cm.
   Includes bibliographical references and index.
   ISBN 0–7190–2845–0
   1. United States – Foreign relations – Southern Cone of South America. 2. Southern Cone of South America – Foreign relations – United States. 3. United States – Foreign economic relations – Southern Cone of South America. 4. Southern Cone of South America – Foreign economic relations – United States.   I. Title.
   F2217.F64 1991
   327.7308–dc20   90–39922

ISBN 0 7190 2845 0 *hardback*

Typeset by J&L Composition Ltd, Filey, North Yorkshire
Printed in Great Britain by Biddles Limited, Guildford & King's Lynn

Contents

Figures

Acknowledgements

Grateful acknowledgement is made to the staff of library and archive collections in South America, the United States, and Britain who have afforded me every assistance during the preparation of this book. I should like particularly to thank Ricardo José Giancola, Head of the Centro de Estudios Históricos Ferroviarios in Buenos Aires; Norma Vera Bustos, archivist at the Museo Histórico Nacional in Santiago de Chile; and Thomas L. Welch, Director of the Columbus Memorial Library, and Myriam Figueras, Special Services Librarian, at the General Secretariat, Organization of American States, Washington, D.C.

I am also most grateful to staff of the American Geographical Society and the National Geographic Society for answering specific queries so promptly, to the cartographer Gillian Tyson, and to the University of London Institute of Latin American Studies for the stimulating environment it provides for research and discussion. Finally, and especially, I thank my husband for his encouragement throughout.

J. V. F.

Introduction

The Temperate South was widely regarded as the setting for spectacular new growth in South America in the second half of the nineteenth century. This book focuses on the changing United States perceptions of the region between 1850 and 1930. In a period of increasing European commercial penetration of Latin America, the United States had begun to seek a more active political and economic role in the subcontinent. American attitudes to the Far South, however – a region also referred to by Americans as the Southland or the land below Capricorn – acquired a double edge. This study sets out to show that US perceptions of Temperate South America were not merely the perceptions of a United States rehearsing a general policy of special hemispheric relationships and 'backyard' economic and political interests; they were also the perceptions of a United States actively engaged in the economic and political development of its own trans-Mississippi West. The experience gained there influenced assessments of the South American South.

By 1850, the United States had secured a continuous 1,500-mile boundary on the Pacific Coast, and begun to organize the first comprehensive regional surveys of the trans-Mississippi West. These Pacific Railroad Surveys marked the beginning of a major adjustment to the USA's arid and semi-arid environments, and to stronger political and economic linkage to the West Coast. There was to be a rapid switch from the early development model of the Eastern States based on river, canal, rail and lake transport, to a Western development model based almost exclusively on the railroad. In 1850 there was still no railroad west of the Mississippi River; even in 1860, only one had reached the Missouri. The mood and timing were right, therefore, for a broader continental perspective encompassing the whole of the

Americas. In addition to the Pacific Railroad Surveys, Congress also commissioned a series of exploratory surveys across South America in the early 1850s, and these strengthened the perception of a 'New West' south of Capricorn – a familiar juxtaposition of cordillera and pampa, bounded on the west by the Pacific and on the east by a navigable river system opening into the Atlantic, a possible future Mississippi–Missouri of southern South America. A Western-style development model was envisaged for the Temperate South; like the trans-Mississippi West, it was a region awaiting European investment capital backed, for maximum benefit, by the application of American technology and know-how.

The emphasis both on the potential for rapid progress and the perceived physical similarities between the two areas characterized US assessments of the Southland in the 1850s and 1860s, a view enhanced by the positive steps towards frontier colonization being taken in Chile and southern Brazil, and by Argentina's apparent determination to adopt the United States development model of railroad expansion, immigration, and the promotion of new economic opportunities in the interior. The farther one travelled south, it was argued, the more one was in touch with the new growth points in South America, a region perceived as being comparatively unburdened by the deadening weight of Hispanic colonial tradition, and without the large concentrations of Indian and *mestizo* population that characterized the Highland Tropics. The Temperate South represented 'Progressive Spain' – the real land of opportunity. The Southern Cone states of Argentina, Uruguay, and Chile, together with southern Brazil and Paraguay, were the 'New West' south of Capricorn, and both they and the United States would benefit from that fact.

Perceptions began to change in and after the 1870s as North American observers increasingly voiced the opinion that achievements in the Far South were being exaggerated, perspectives limited, and that opportunities for a more soundly-based internal economy, particularly in the key state of Argentina, were not being seized. United States commentators looking for a 'New West' in Argentina in the late nineteenth and early twentieth centuries concentrated on the huge neglected region *beyond* the Humid Pampa, that forgotten world beyond the margin of the wheat–alfalfa crescent bounded approximately in the west by the 20-inch rainfall line. Argentina's failure to tackle seriously its own 'New West' in the dry lands of the west and south was regarded as an irretrievably lost opportunity for promoting long-term economic growth, and a new sense of national pride and identity. Americans familiar with their own West deplored Argentina's willingness, despite statements to the contrary, to allow the bulk of the country to waste away in isolation and remain content instead to overpraise the achievements on the Humid Pampa. In the light of their own growing experience in the American West, United States engineers and developers were often the most concerned of all with the unused or undervalued potential of the Dry Pampa, the Andean foothill zone, and the broad valleys and low dissected plateaux of Patagonia. The persistent neglect of the capacity of these areas for large-scale irrigated agriculture, more intensive ranching and forest management, hydroelectric power, selected manufacturing sites and new towns – indeed for any sustained development programme, however modest its initial stages, was consistently criticized.

Railroads were the basis of the United States regional analysis. 'On the plains and in the mountains the railroad is the one great fact', observed a New Yorker making his first trip across the American West in the early 1870s, and as the key to national expansion and consolidation in the post-Civil War period, Western America's 'one great fact' assumed responsibility not only as the carrier but also as the pioneer in selling land, attracting settlers, promoting industry and agriculture, and creating new business. Since Americans placed so much emphasis on railroads as regional developers in the trans-Mississippi West, it is in this context that Argentina's failure to do the same was most heavily criticized. Amid general condemnation by American observers of the restricted landowning opportunities for small farmers in the Southland, this study underlines the fact that, in particular, the United States perceptions of neglect and abuse by British and Argentine interests of a land-grant railroad policy were measured against American knowledge and expectations of the system following its successful introduction into the Midwest and the Far West after 1850. While some of the United States criticism of the British railway companies stemmed solely from commercial rivalry, it is a mistake to dismiss it all on this basis. Argentina was to be the setting for a crucial early dispute on the merits of American, as opposed to British, railway technology and style of operation. Argentina's continuing dependence on the European money market, strongly reinforced by its own tastes and preferences, led to the adoption of the British system, and to the costly, conservative approach to railroading that Americans regarded as totally unsuited to frontier expansion. Worse, it was considered to have inflicted lasting damage to the economic integration of the Southern Cone.

Along with the call for more progressive and coherent land and transport policies, the need for transcontinental railroads was continually stressed by the United States between 1850 and 1930 in its analysis of the Southland's regional development. Unlike the situation in Anglo-America, however, improvement of transport and communication between the Atlantic and Pacific coasts never became a unifying political and economic issue in South America. In the opinion of the United States, the failure to build and promote a series of transcontinental railroads in the only part of South America where such development was ever feasible had serious consequences. Of course, in dismissing the physical problems for railroad construction posed by the Andes as being greatly exaggerated, the United States at the same time underestimated the political obstacles to a genuinely transcontinental perspective. The USA was slow to appreciate the durability of the Chile–Argentine boundary, and its divisive effect on the prospects for integrated development in Temperate South America. The anticipated mobility of the Southland's settlement frontier did not occur. Despite some impressive statistics in parts of the region, the dynamics of immigration remained extremely weak. Expanding waves of new settlers did not advance and take matters into their own hands with regard to boundary adjustment; unlike frontiers in the tropical deserts and the rain forests, those in the Temperate South were effectively never changed by war, annexation, arbitration, or purchase. Argentina might be called 'the United States of South America' but its Oregon and California continued to lie in Chile, and its manufacturing belt in Western Europe.

America had brought its own 'New West' within the framework of the industrial revolution and big business in the second half of the nineteenth century. At the end of the primary frontier phase, the freeing of domestic resources hitherto absorbed in opening the West, coupled with the need to find new markets for investment and for manufactured goods, strengthened the perception of another 'New West' south of Capricorn as a major field for United States economic expansion. Counterbalancing the Atlantic seaboard, an important baseline for entry to the Southland in the early twentieth century was to be the Pacific Coast. It was Chile after all, not Argentina, that lay due south of New York. The Panama Canal was nearing completion; if the opening of South America's first transcontinental railroad in 1910 marked the first in a series of such lines, a start could be made on establishing 'backdoor' linkage of the Plate River markets to the West Coast through a revival of the overland routeways – new growth corridors for American enterprise, and a means of invigorating the still moribund interior of the Southern Cone. Even before the effects of the First World War reduced European trade dominance, the United States was making inroads into the Southland, which, despite sixty years of 'growth', and the prosperous image projected, was regarded on closer investigation by North Americans as astonishingly under-developed. The widely held perception of the 'transformation' of Argentina into a modern state was difficult to justify. There had been few of the familiar 'Western-style' developers in the Temperate South who as part of the USA's great frontier movement had helped to open and publicize the trans-Mississippi West. As one widely travelled North American reported at the turn of the century: 'When one compares its possibilities with its performance, except for a few, very limited exceptions, one gets the impression in South America of a vast continent almost literally going to waste.'

The United States had played a minor role in the Southern Cone during the nineteenth century, and the subsequent speed of change was dramatic. 'The Americans have come down late in the day,' observed a British resident in Buenos Aires in 1917, 'but they know how to make up for lost time.' Embarked now on a huge fact-finding exercise, a new wave of businessmen, travellers, publishers, geographers, economists, and engineers explored the Temperate South in the 1920s and 1930s in a new mood of realism. They found a commercial frontier for American manufactured goods and a resource frontier for United States industry, but they did not discover any widespread or deeply-rooted optimism about the future of the Southland, nor a hopeful and stimulating environment for individual effort. 'There is great opportunity here for Yankee enterprise,' wrote one of them, 'but it is not the Land of Opportunity we have at home. ... One thing for sure, it is not the American West fifty years on.'

1
The new pathfinders

In the early 1850s, the United States Government carried out the most ambitious, far-reaching series of land surveys of the New World since the days of the *conquistadores*, more than three centuries before. This second-stage exploration broke fresh ground, however, since in their speed and detailed documentation these new continental surveys authorized by Congress were unmatched by any earlier reconnaissance of the Americas.

Accurate, comprehensive fact-finding by trained observers was the order of the day. Once gathered, the information had to be made available for public debate. As a result, in a burst of energy between 1853 and 1856, the field notes, statistics, maps and sketches of explorations stretching from the Canadian border to the fringes of Patagonia were not only painstakingly sorted and written up but also printed and widely distributed – voluminous reports on the Pacific Railroad Surveys across the trans-Mississippi West, on exploration of the Amazon Valley, on Chile, on journeys across the Andes and the Argentine Pampas, and finally on the regions drained by the Plata river system as far north as Brazil, Bolivia and Paraguay. Workers in the Capitol struggled to find more space in the storerooms for the thousands of extra copies immediately ordered by the House and the Senate for nationwide distribution and discussion. Newspapers, magazines, scientific societies, and many chambers of commerce summarized each report as it appeared, and wasted no time in widening the debate.

For the explorations in South America, the US Navy took on the role of the US Army in the trans-Mississippi West, so that it was naval officers who made both the river and the overland surveys in the southern subcontinent. The significance of their findings goes beyond the wealth of material presented on the tropical and temperate regions of South America, and the determination to fight European commercial competition there. The reports also reflect rapidly changing transport technology and growing regional conflict within the United States itself. If the Amazon expeditions of Lieutenants Herndon and Gibbon (1851–52) and the Plata–Paraná–Paraguay surveys of Lieutenant Page (1853–55 and 1959–60) represented the traditional 'waterway school' of development, the expeditions of Lieutenants Gilliss and MacRae (1850–54) through Chile and Argentina revealed the possibility of opening a 'New West' by rail – another trans-Mississippi West – smaller in scale, but with the familiar sequence of western mountains and eastern plains set between the Pacific and Atlantic Oceans. Above all, here was a region ready and waiting for a transcontinental railroad.

Growing sectional interests within the United States were apparent in the expeditions north and south of Capricorn. Closest to home, the resources and perceived opportunities in Amazonia were associated with the aspirations of the Southern States – a tropical extension to the Mississippi basin's economy that would create a huge, diversified trading area focused on the Gulf of Mexico. By 1850, however, the Mississippi River had also become pivotal to both Northern and Southern interests in their struggle for control of the West. The Mississippi might be the great unifying waterway cradling centre and south, but it was also the baseline from which the new transcontinental railroad would strike off for the Pacific Ocean, opening the way along the selected parallel for North or South to seize the initiatives in California and the Orient.

Thus the Mississippi beckoned in two directions – west and south. The desire to maintain the integrity of the Mississippi network was fundamental to the 'waterway school' of development. Indeed, Mark Twain's assertion that 'the basin of the Mississippi is the body of the nation' was backed by the fact that, by 1850, the basin contained more than 60 per cent of the total national territory, and the bulk of the United States immense agricultural and industrial resources. Here was the 'natural' North–South linkage that could split the otherwise indissoluble union of East and West. Traditionalists favoured the idea. Colonial and national expansion in the eighteenth and early nineteenth centuries had been shaped by the waterways, later in conjunction with roads and railroads. Tidewater, Great Lakes, rivers and canals had established an initial circulation of 'natural' movement in the United

States which had its origins in the concept of free and uninterrupted navigation on the high seas.

It was in that connection that the Mississippi had immediately become the most politically sensitive boundary in the newly independent United States, despite its distance from the main centres of population. Under the terms of the treaty with Britain in 1783, the river became the western boundary as far south as 31°N, but with Florida and the Gulf of Mexico still in the hands of Spain, the United States had no south coast. When Spain closed the Mississippi to United States navigation in 1784, Alexander Hamilton's political realism became a rallying cry for the survival of the Union: 'Free navigation of the Mississippi to the sea is of the first moment to our territories to the westward; they must have that outlet, without it they will be lost to us.' The stages by which Spain's restriction was modified and eventually removed dominated 'Western Waters' diplomacy for the next twenty years, until the whole problem was swept away dramatically in 1803 by the Louisiana Purchase. Steamboat transport began on the Mississippi in 1811, revolutionizing the network's efficiency and greatly enlarging its continental influence. Within a few years, the continued determination to make the Mississippi–Missouri an all-American waterway was decisive in the new Great Britain–USA Canadian boundary negotiations of 1818–19. The final agreement ran the line from the Lake of the Woods to the Stony (i.e. the Rocky) Mountains along the Forty-ninth Parallel, and thus kept the boundary north of the Missouri River and well to the north of the source of the Mississippi. Although the latter's precise location was still unknown, it was to be safely enclosed within United States territory.

The Amazon surveys

The vigorous attempt in the early 1850s to persuade Brazil to open the Amazon to free navigation represented the climax of the United States 'waterway school' strategy, and a logical extension of Southern policy to promote increased trade between the Mississippi river ports, the Gulf of Mexico, the Isthmus, the Caribbean, and Amazonia. Not that the 'waterway school' concentrated exclusively on maritime and riverine transport. Since the beginning of the nineteenth century, the concept of the integrity of the Mississippi basin had been extended west into arid and mountainous regions where the rivers themselves were unnavigable. In 1803, Thomas Jefferson's instructions to the Lewis and Clark expedition had followed 'waterway school' tradition, emphasizing the importance of finding a *river route* to the Pacific in order to balance and extend the Mississippi network, sea to sea. But the Missouri–Columbia river routeway, having proved impracticable, was abandoned by the 1820s in favour of a National Road; in turn, by the 1840s, the idea of a Pacific Railroad had gained wide acceptance, nowhere more enthusiastically than in parts of the South. Thus, plans for a southern transcontinental railroad to capture the California traffic and develop Texas and the Southwest, as well as support for a Panama Railroad, were also crucial elements in the 'waterway' scheme for an integrated transport network designed to boost Southern industry and commerce, and to stimulate the economic and political growth of the port cities.

Lieutenant William Lewis Herndon's instructions from the Navy Department in 1850–51 'to proceed across the Cordillera [from Lima], and explore the Amazon from its source to its mouth' had originated with Matthew F. Maury, Superintendent of the National (Naval) Observatory in Washington, D.C., and an ardent promoter of Southern expansion. Indeed, Maury's influence was far wider than his professional title would suggest, since he lectured and published tirelessly, and was closely involved in advising politicians, agents and journalists on various projects to advance the sectional interests of the Southern States. As a distinguished oceanographer, and a key figure in the 'waterway school', Maury was personally responsible for masterminding the official Naval expedition to Amazonia, an investigation he regarded as more significant than any other undertaken by the United States in South America.

Maury's enthusiasm for giving the South, and especially New Orleans, new 'frontdoor' opportunity in Amazonia was sharpened by signs of a numbing decline in the port's 'backdoor' trade. Chicago had completed the Illinois and Michigan Canal in 1848 and immediately began to draw off the Mississippi–New Orleans freight traffic via the Great Lakes and their connections. The Illinois and Michigan Canal was a particularly unwelcome latecomer to the 'waterway school' so far as the South was concerned. In the Upper Mississippi Valley, it could clip one to two weeks off the time taken to reach the northeastern markets, while the canal's success in snatching business from St Louis, and even in diverting northward part of Louisiana's sugar and molasses trade, sent a shudder through the Delta region. A second, greater threat had also appeared. Even before the canal was opened, plans for the first railroads in Illinois were under way. By 1855, nearly 3,000 miles of railroad were focused on Lake Michigan, and 100 trains a day were rolling in and out of Chicago. The South watched what had been an overgrown village before 1848 spurt to a population of 28,000 by 1850, and explode into a combined lake port and railroad centre of more than 100,000 by 1860. As Maury emphasized in the South's influential *De Bow's Review*:

The enterprise of Illinois has created another mouth to the Mississippi, and placed it in Lake Michigan. Much of the produce that formerly touched at New-Orleans on its way to market, now goes through that canal; ... articles are turning about and flowing upstream.

It is as idle, I say, for the people to rest quiet, and expect the proper lines of steamers to come to them, as it has been for them to rest quiet upon the advantages which the Mississippi River gave them, while all around them was enterprise and activity. Other cities and sections tapped the Mississippi valley, and sent rail-roads there for their own benefit and advantage. ... *We must extend the commerce of the South and West by sea.* The Amazon river-basin is but a continuation of the Mississippi valley .... In short, as a commercial matter, the free navigation of the Amazon is the question of the age.[1]

Such conviction was shared by William Herndon, Maury's brother-in-law, and a resourceful, dedicated fellow-Virginian who had commanded a vessel on active service in the Gulf during the Mexican War. With the route through Amazonia left to Herndon's discretion, he assigned Lieutenant Lardner Gibbon to undertake the Bolivian portion of the survey, and then proceeded to follow the main course of the Amazon himself for more than 3,000 miles through Peru and Brazil. Permission for this and all other United States exploration in South America had been sought on the time-honoured basis of conducting a scientific expedition. Despite the often narrow terms of reference, however, such surveys were expected to return laden with facts, figures, and impressions on just about every aspect of life in the region. Herndon and Gibbon wasted no time, given that neither Maury nor the Secretary of the Navy had minced words about the importance of the expedition. The orders were to obtain the fullest possible information on both the present condition and the estimated potential of the entire Amazon basin: 'the navigability of its streams; the number and condition, both industrial and social, of its inhabitants, their trade and products; its climate, soil, and productions; also its capacities for cultivation, and the character and extent of its undeveloped commercial resources, whether of the field, the forest, the river, or the mine'.[2]

As Herndon travelled through the heart of Amazonia, surrounded by 'miles of rivers rolling on in silence and neglect', his eye was on its future potential. The geographical and commercial complementarity of the Amazon and Mississippi basins had enormous possibilities, he decided, but everything would depend on improved transportation. The sheer length of the Amazon, so daunting to some, presented no intrinsic problems to a naval officer provided the river was open to efficient steam navigation. Herndon, like Gibbon, saw a vast internal waterway system laced through the Tropics, awaiting only freedom of navigation, steamboat fleets, new settlement, and commercial enterprise. Amazonia could not be realistically assessed in isolation. The internal waterways were not to remain a closed world, swirling similar products around a huge South American inland lake. They had to become part of a greater *continental* circulation. Herndon was impressed by the unique opportunities here for the United States, for the Central and Southern States in particular, since the northern gateway ports for this immensely expanded water-borne economy would be New Orleans, St Louis and Cincinnati, not the ports of the Atlantic seaboard. 'We, more than any other people, are interested in the opening of Amazon navigation. ... The trade of this region *must* pass by *our* doors, and mingle and exchange with the products of *our* Mississippi valley.'[3]

With Lieutenant Gibbon responsible for exploring the Madeira and its headwaters, Herndon supplemented his own findings on the Amazon with the latest local reports on the navigability and resources of the major tributaries, including the upper and middle Ucayali, Juruá, Japurá, Negro, Tapajós, and Tocantins. Everything now hinged on a successful outcome to the pressure being placed on Brazil by Britain, France and the United States to open the Amazon to free navigation. But while Brazil welcomed the optimistic tone of the Herndon–Gibbon investigation, it firmly rejected the arguments for establishing an international waterway – unmoved, in particular, by Maury's assurances that opening the Amazon to foreign steam navigation was 'a policy of commerce', not 'a policy of conquest'.

Herndon was depressed to learn on his return to Washington, D.C. in the summer of 1852, that Brazil's only response to the United States expedition had been to grant (in August 1852), in association with

Peru, an exclusive thirty-year privilege for steam navigation on the Amazon to a Brazilian citizen. This was the worst possible outcome, Herndon complained. Instead of keeping alive the possibility of opening the waterway,

> Brazil has effectually closed the Amazon by her De Souza contract, ... though I very much doubt if the contract will endure. The Brazilians are so little acquainted with river steam navigation that De Souza will run his boats at great cost ... and, even *with* the bonus of $100,000 per annum, I doubt if the trade of the river for several years to come will support the six steamers that he contracts to keep on the line.

Six steamers! – when Herndon envisaged an Amazon 'furrowed by a thousand keels'.[4]

Herndon's conclusion that Brazil had failed (or declined) to recognize steamboats as a tool, rather than as a symbol of development, was endorsed by the British Minister in Rio de Janeiro: 'The scheme for sending a steam boat once a month up the Amazon to the frontier of Peru ... is better calculated to close than to open this splendid river, and is justly considered rather as a reward given to a Government contractor ... than an enlightened measure of improvement.'[5] But ever-sensitive to European and North American encroachment, Brazil preferred Brazilian solitude to foreign-dominated commerce, particularly commerce meshed with the southern United States. Herndon's vision of 'waking up' the Amazon Valley with 'the steamboat, the plough, the axe, and the hoe', helped by the introduction of large estates, Southern planters and Southern slaves, did not endear him, nor any of the 'waterway school' of developers, to the Brazilian Government.[6] Despite unflagging promotion by Maury during the 1850s of a great Mississippi–Amazon reciprocal trading area, the project was dead in political terms, both in Washington and in Rio. The US Navy Department turned its attention elsewhere. The failure to secure free navigation on the Amazon was a major blow to Southern interests, a setback to those with hopes of new perspectives and new diversification in an expanding Southern economy. There would be no time to test the reality of the dream. Ironically, Brazil was not persuaded to open the Amazon until 1867, two years after the defeat of the Confederacy.

The Plate Basin surveys

The official US naval expedition to the River Plate was meanwhile being organized in a mood of much greater optimism. Not of course by those for whom Amazonia held a special place in the South's sectional politics, but certainly for general 'waterway school' adherents. The reason for this optimism was that unlike the obstacle caused by Brazil's continued closure of the Amazon, the Plata system had been opened to free navigation by the Argentine Confederation and Paraguay in 1852, and by Uruguay a year later, and was incorporated in commercial treaties signed in 1853. In fact, recognition of Paraguayan independence, and renewed diplomatic relations with Argentina after the downfall of Rosas by Britain, France and the United States, had been conditional *inter alia* upon the securing of free navigation on the Paraná–Paraguay system.

The United States responded swiftly, becoming the first foreign state to investigate in detail what this unknown waterway had to offer. The planned exploration was also urged forward by the newly formed American Geographical and Statistical Society, which chose to make the La Plata expedition its first crusade. A Memorial was sent by the Society in New York to the Secretary of the Navy, underlining the fact that

> at least one quarter of the whole of South America is now, for the first time, within the reach of our enterprise, offering positive and far more profitable results than we have gained or can gain from many old countries where, at a large expense, we have kept up formal diplomatic arrangements, and where our squadrons ride at anchor in courteous idleness.
>
> The marts now opened to us in South America ... are as yet almost without limit. The commerce of our country has but to enter them to be enriched.[7]

The need for 'the axe, the saw, and the steam-engine' made its customary appearance in this, as in virtually every official US publication and newspaper editorial on South America's most pressing requirements at this time. Preparations for the Navy's La Plata expedition were widely publicized, and reports emphasized two points: the more progressive attitudes to regional development likely to be found in the southern portion of the subcontinent, and the importance of preventing powerful British and French commercial interests from seizing the initiative in this newly available portion of

America's own backyard. The exploration was placed under the command of Lieutenant Thomas Jefferson Page, and the steamer *Water Witch* left Norfolk, Virginia in February 1853, bound for Montevideo and Buenos Aires.

The first object of the expedition, Page noted, was 'to explore the rivers, and to report upon the extent of their navigability and adaptation to commerce, ... but my instructions covered a much wider field. I was ordered to penetrate into the interior of the countries of La Plata, to examine their agricultural resources, and, consequently, the probable extent to which commercial intercourse might be desirable.' Page was also instructed to make botanical and geological collections, record astronomical, meteorological, and topographical data, and sketch or photograph (daguerreotype) the scenery and the local Indian population.[8]

Page undertook the overland surveys into the interior so conscientiously that he and his officers eventually covered some 3,600 miles by river and 4,400 miles by land. The expedition ascended the Paraná–Paraguay as far as Corumbá in Brazil, and explored the navigable portions of the Uruguay, Salado and Bermejo. A second expedition in 1859–60 extended the exploration even farther up the Paraguay River into Mato Grosso and south-eastern Bolivia, as well as into the swamps and shallows on the upper Bermejo and the Pilcomayo. Like Lardner Gibbon, who had followed the Mamoré–Madeira waterway into the Amazon, Page was anxious to find a navigable outlet for eastern Bolivia, since in January 1853, Bolivia had issued a decree opening all Bolivian rivers draining into the Amazon and Plata systems to world commerce. For good measure, Bolivia had also identified several of its river settlements as 'free ports'. This freedom-of-navigation announcement was commended by the United States, but it remained entirely theoretical so long as the navigability of the rivers remained unknown, and political opposition to a free outlet to the Atlantic for Bolivia persisted in Brazil, Paraguay and Argentina.[9]

In fact, Page had little encouraging to report about the navigability of the rivers on the extreme northern fringes of the Plata basin, although the Bermejo was regarded as having a promising future provided ignorant landlubbers stopped launching unsuitable vessels into it, and allowed a few experienced riverboatmen to take a hand. 'I strongly advised,' wrote Page,

> that the steamers required for the navigation, especially of the small tributaries of the central rivers, should be procured in the United States;

for, apart from a national feeling, and without reflecting upon the skill of the English ship-builders, I do not hesitate to assert that in no part of the world has the construction of boats of small draught been carried to the same extent or brought to such perfection as in the United States.[10]

Referring to the country between Salta, Jujuy, Orán and Tarija, Page noted that while nothing could bring navigation to the door, good roads to a selected river-port would allow 'the successful navigation of the Bermejo to divert trade into the channel which Nature seems to have made for it'.[11] Here was the authentic voice of the 'waterway school', a voice which continually regretted meeting many in Argentina and Paraguay who regarded the opening of the Plata system only as a political gesture, not as a practical move. Page struggled to combat the sense of irrelevance to their everyday lives with which people dismissed improved river transport. Anticipating, for example, a welcome at one typical riverside community deep in the interior, he was exasperated to find that 'the approaching Carnival was a more important event than the arrival of the first steamer'.

Lack of interest in river navigation stemmed mainly from lack of experience, Page's survey team decided. As Lieutenant Murdaugh noted:

These countries have an extensive system of natural canalization in the streams that course through the interior provinces. Yet ... how carefully they are avoided as means of transportation or communication, while the ox-wagon, the vehicle of centuries, moves lazily on – so slowly that at a distance an observer can scarcely detect its movement; carrying comparatively little, and consuming time, money, and labor unnecessarily.

Page spent long hours in discussing the commercial value of the United States waterways, emphasizing to the sceptics just how much trade could be carried by river: 'When I told them of the floating palaces carrying millions [of tons] of freight over our interior water-courses, with a draught of only two or three feet, they looked as if they thought I was entertaining them with a "yarn".'[12]

The USS *Water Witch*, around 400 tons, had a draught of nine feet, and once the expedition reached Asunción, additional steamboats of around 2' draught were either built or chartered so that the major tributaries could be properly investigated. Lieutenant, later Rear-Admiral Daniel Ammen supervised this work, noting that although in some respects the Paraguay River resembled the Mississippi, fundamentally the truer comparison was with the Nile, because of the controlling factor of seasonal high and low water levels.[13] Well prepared now for both river and overland travel, the crew of the *Water Witch* divided and pushed ahead to complete one of the most extensive expeditions deep into foreign territory ever undertaken by the United States up to that time. 'We are opening, I sanguinely hope,' wrote Page, 'a new path to commerce and civilization.' Provided the inland waterways were worked efficiently, there was no doubting the range of tropical and temperate products awaiting a wider market. 'I have been filled with amazement at the resources of these "riverine" provinces. ... What a land of promise to European emigrants!'[14]

Of all the regions explored, however, Page reserved his greatest enthusiasm for the Rosario–Paraná sector. Rosario, 200 miles from Buenos Aires and nearly 400 miles from the ocean, not only offered the first high, solid ground along the shoreline going upstream, it was also the starting point for the projected railroad to Córdoba, 250 miles to the north-west. The route was surveyed in 1855 by the United States engineer, Allan Campbell, who, Page reported, 'pronounces it not only practicable, and offering a profitable investment of capital, but as one of the most effectual modes of developing the resources of the fruitful provinces of the West'. It would be an iron bond between east and west, Page added, promoting trade, strengthening the political fabric, and ridding the country through which it passes of predatory Indians.[15] There were exciting parallels to be drawn between this region and the great river-port of St Louis, Missouri, where the first few miles of railroad into the trans-Mississippi West had only just been laid in 1852.

Rosario had been given fresh impetus by Buenos Aires' refusal to join the reorganized Argentine Confederation led by General, later President Urquiza, after the defeat of Rosas in 1852. Rosario was declared the official Argentine port of entry, its future rosy with new opportunity to articulate modernized north–south river transport with western railroad expansion. Rosario's population had trebled in size to around 12,000 between the time of the arrival of the *Water Witch* in 1853 to its departure at the end of the expedition in 1855. The change in Paraná city, capital of the new Confederation, was equally dramatic:

When we first visited it, a noiseless inertion seemed to pervade all things; before our departure, ... an air of bustle and life quite 'American.' The saw and hammer were busily plied in every street, and they were preparing for use, not only the hardwoods of the country, but American pine. Even in the short period which had elapsed since the opening of the rivers, this lumber had worked its way six hundred miles in the interior, not only against the currents of the river, but the prejudices of the people, who had previously imagined no woods, for any purpose, equal to their own. Pine was not only extensively applied for doors and window-sashes, but, as flooring, was actually superseding tile and brick.[16]

The growth of Rosario and Paraná in three years, Page reported with obvious satisfaction, is not surpassed even by the strides of some of our own Western cities.

Page was already having second thoughts about Paraguay. President López had proved unpredictable and much less reformist than Urquiza, a leader who was actively encouraging the modernization of Argentine society, including free navigation and railroad construction, and who linked the political future of the Argentine Confederation to economic recovery and progress. By contrast, in the space of twelve months, the *Water Witch* had escorted the new US Consul to Paraguay, Edward A. Hopkins, both in and out of Asunción, together with whatever goodwill had previously existed between the two states. Hopkins had made the first of several visits to Paraguay in 1845; he later registered (in Rhode Island) the United States & Paraguay Navigation Co., and then returned as Consul in 1853 ready to set up a sawmill and cigar-making factory a few miles downriver from Asunción. Growing hostility between López and Hopkins put paid to the project, while relations between Paraguay and the United States worsened after López imposed new restrictions on the expedition that were unacceptable to Page, and the *Water Witch* was fired on by a Paraguayan river-fort in February 1855. Apart from López's volatility, however, in the opinion of the US Minister to Asunción in the 1860s, Hopkins had been a disastrous choice as America's official representative. Scarcely anyone more unsuitable could have been found to carry the flag, declared C. A. Washburn. Hopkins was enthusiastic and persuasive, but 'unhappily, he was of so arrogant and overbearing a disposition that no one could act long with him in any enterprise, so that, though ... the initiator and promoter of important and useful works, his withdrawal from them was essential to their ultimate success'.[17]

No wonder Page and his fellow officers found the noise and bustle at Rosario and Paraná to be a breath of fresh air. 'Associating, as we are apt to do, stagnation or a retrograde movement with all things in the

interior of South America', Page wrote in 1855, the healthful, progressive aspect of the Rosario–Paraná zone was both pleasing and
astonishing. Here was a region where 'immigration and the friction of
trade' would awaken a spirit of enterprise among the people, and, he
added crisply, 'teach them that time is money'. The prospect of new
wharves, with faster, cheaper loading, was already attracting New
England shipowners to Rosario – a promising start, Page observed, 'to
be followed, I hope, by hearing that the waters of the Paraná are
covered with vessels bearing the Stars and Stripes'.

Although Page was a Virginian, a colleague of Maury, and in due
course a staunch Confederate, his strong belief in the 'waterway
school' of development was never narrowly identified with Southern
sectional interests. In terms of commerce and colonization, the Plate
basin was of course more distant than Amazonia, but Page's positive
assessments of central Argentina's potential were greatly influenced by
his own keen interest in the American West, and by the need to
encourage European immigrants and yeoman farmers to the New
World. Like his namesake, Thomas Jefferson, Page saw an important
role in westward expansion for small landowners tilling their own soil.
Page also had numerous social and professional contacts with Boston
merchants and traders, and liked their brisk, businesslike approach to
competition and the search for new markets. President Urquiza's co-
operation and enlightened attitudes to progress in Argentina were
warmly welcomed – Americans regarded him thankfully as 'a man of
the times'. With improved transport and a tide of immigration, Page
concluded, the future of this region around the River Plate 'will only
be surpassed by the growth of the United States'.[18]

The Chilean surveys

While Page and his party were extending their investigations in the
Paraná–Paraguay region, Lieutenant James Melville Gilliss was back in
Washington, D.C. putting the finishing touches to his Chilean report.
Based in Santiago, the main expedition had completed its fieldwork by
1851; the report was submitted to Congress in 1854, and published in
six volumes the following year. Although officially established as the
US Naval Astronomical Expedition to the Southern Hemisphere, a
three-year study which had received strong recommendation from the
American Philosophical Society and the Academy of Arts and Sciences,

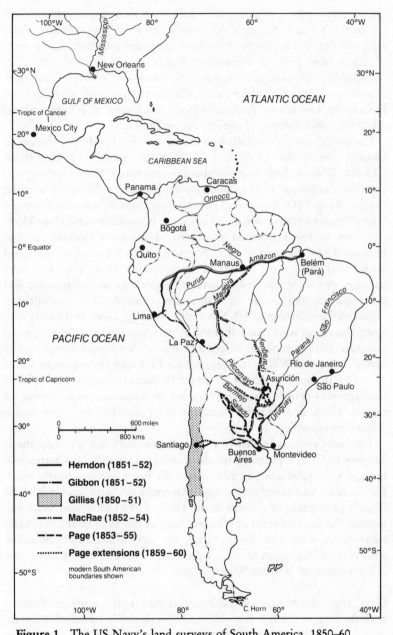

Figure 1 The US Navy's land surveys of South America, 1850–60

Gilliss was instructed to obtain the fullest possible 'useful information' on southern South America. As a result, the first two volumes present long and detailed accounts of the landscapes and commercial prospects of Chile and part of Argentina. Volume I is entitled *Chile: its Geography, Climate, Earthquakes, Government, Social Condition, Mineral and Agricultural Resources, Commerce, etc., etc.*, while Volume II contains Lieutenant Archibald MacRae's *Report of Journeys across the Andes and Pampas of the Argentine Provinces*.

Earlier US naval exploration in and around the Pacific and Antarctic Oceans during the 1830s and 1840s, most notably by Lieutenant Charles Wilkes, had been primarily concerned with charting sea channels, harbours, and victualling ports for use by American whaling vessels. After 1848, however, Chile attracted special attention from the United States because of the sudden surge in traffic around Cape Horn en route to the California goldfields. Thousands heading for San Francisco saw the west coast of South America for the first time, and found that their most favourable impressions of it, after a stormy passage, remained the deep, sheltered anchorage at Talcahuano, and the sunshine and bustle of Valparaiso. Central Chile had already attracted the attention of US Navy officers in the 1840s as the only area along the entire west coast of South America showing genuine signs of progress. 'Valparaiso, and indeed all Chili, shows a great change for the better', reported Wilkes in 1845, having first seen the region in 1821–22, while in January 1851, Lieutenant William Herndon left Gilliss in Santiago to begin his own exploration in Amazonia with a tinge of regret: 'Chili, in arts and civilization, is far ahead of any other South American republic.'

The most striking feature of Gilliss's report on Chile is the emphasis he gives to Chile's potential for development through transcontinental linkage with Argentina, in addition to the more obvious north–south Pacific coast and valley connection. Assessing the 'how' and 'where' of Chile's next phase of growth in the 1850s, Gilliss identified three key factors: the development of selected Andean passes to establish Chile's trade links with the River Plate; the agricultural and industrial potential of the Concepción region; and the pioneering aims and achievements of William Wheelwright.

First, from the fringes of the Atacama desert (the northern frontier with Bolivia) to the Bío-Bío valley, Gilliss assembled detailed information on the characteristics of eight trans-Andean passes, and drew attention to those that deserved to be better known than the traditional Uspallata and Portillo routes. Relatively few crossed the Andes at all, Gilliss discovered, and scarcely any except a few *vaqueros* and predatory Indians crossed south of the River Maule. But the eradication of Indian attack should remove the only obstacle to trade – 'Passes by the Planchon and Antuco must become the great thoroughfares to the Atlantic ... to Buenos Ayres, Montevideo, or the mouth of Rio Negro.' A start should be made as soon as possible, 'and when commerce justifies it, the distances, elevations, ... and character of the country, all designate these as the highways on which money should be expended'.[19]

Second, the relative ease of the Antuco passes (between 5,900 and 6,900 feet above sea level), and their approach from the Laja and Bío-Bío valleys, enhanced the outstanding commercial potential of Concepción. Despite the earthquake hazard, the town (population 10,000) and its deep-water port of Talcahuano were unmatched for future diversified economic development. Climate, varied soils and topography gave the surrounding region a remarkably broad agricultural base, which, if brought into high levels of productivity, Gilliss observed, would be 'capable of supplying all the wants of the entire population of Chile'. Added to this were the industrial resources, including copper, gold, coal, timber, and water-power. The region had excellent opportunities to attract immigrants and to challenge the dominance of Santiago – perhaps the latter was the real hindrance to its development, Gilliss suggested. American-built flour mills were already in operation; next should come sawmills, woollen mills, coalmines, and a Talcahuano–Concepción ship canal. The natural market was Buenos Aires, and the relative ease of the trans-Andean connection, and the complementarity of east–west trade between these two contrasted Pacific and Atlantic port regions excited Gilliss's imagination. Given 'one or two enterprising and intelligent capitalists' to set the ball rolling, the location and resources of the Concepción area made it perhaps the best placed zone in South America for diversified growth.[20]

Third, Gilliss was obviously cheered by his contact with William Wheelwright, 'our enterprising countryman', who was currently improving the water supply of Valparaiso, and planning to install gas lighting there. As part of his numerous West Coast improvement schemes, Wheelwright was also busy building Chile's first railroad, from the port of Caldera to Copiapó in the northern silver and copper mining district. For this enterprise, which was backed by the London-based Anglo-Chilian Mining Co., Wheelwright had formed a new company and gone to the United States in 1849 to secure the services of two well-known New York civil engineers, the brothers Allan and Alexander Campbell, together with a team of construction workers and mechanics. The locomotives and rolling stock were made in the United States, the iron rails imported from Britain. Begun in 1851, the fifty-mile line was completed by the end of that year, with a further 160 miles proposed or under construction. Significantly, Wheelwright planned to make the Caldera–Copiapó railroad the first section of a 1,000-mile transcontinental line to Argentina, with terminals at Rosario and Buenos Aires. Gilliss and Wheelwright inspected the Atacama area together in 1851, Gilliss relishing the 'go-ahead' atmosphere that the sailor–trader from Newburyport, Massachusetts was injecting into the desert wilderness.

Wheelwright was making full use of the Campbells' engineering skills in the early 1850s. With Alexander left to supervise the completion of the Caldera–Copiapó railroad, Wheelwright had sent Allan Campbell south to survey the routes for Wheelwright's proposed Valparaiso–Santiago railroad, and the Talcahuano–Concepción ship canal, along with other feasibility studies in central Chile. The energy and optimism that Wheelwright was bringing to the region prompted the American Stagecoach Co., owned and managed by B. F. Morse, to introduce a daily stagecoach service between Valparaiso and Santiago in advance of the railroad. 'Yankee stages and Yankee drivers', reported a visitor to Chile from Ohio in 1855, agreeably impressed.[21] Railroads and steamships provided the twin thrust of William Wheelwright's development strategy. Years of commercial experience on the west coast of South America had convinced him of the need for a regular steamship line, and with concessions obtained from Chile, Bolivia and Peru in 1835–36, Wheelwright went ahead to found the Pacific Steam Navigation Co., chartered in London in 1840 with British investment after this determined Yankee entrepreneur had failed to attract sufficient financial backing in the United States. In 1845, Wheelwright secured a much-needed mail contract, and the line was extended to run from Valparaiso to Panama. By 1847, success was assured, and Wheelwright's earlier reputation as a 'wild Yankee visionary' had been transformed into that of a 'perceptive New England pioneer'.

Wheelwright had created the Chilean port of Caldera. Despite the advantages of a good sheltered anchorage and easy access, Gilliss observed, 'when Mr. Wheelwright first landed ... there was neither house nor hut of any description'. So impressed was he with the speed of development there, Gilliss commissioned a sketch of Caldera in 1852, showing the new railroad, mole, warehouses, machine-shops, housing, offices, and custom-house. He included it with his report, adding the caption: 'Caldera just two years after the American engineers landed there in 1850!'

New ports, new railroads, new bridges, new wagon roads – Gilliss was searching for evidence of the frontier transport revolution so familiar to many North Americans. A new, double-span trestle bridge over the Maypú River – good! ... designed and built by an American engineer – even better! Roads being cambered, culverted and ditched – excellent! ... a happy accompaniment to that splendid trio, 'the axe, the saw, and the steam-engine'. Gilliss's travel report through central Chile is filled with notes on the agricultural possibilities of the region, provided that the proposed Valparaiso–Santiago railroad was completed and extended, markets expanded, and irrigation and flood control canals engineered along the base of the Andes. Time and again, Gilliss found himself 'in the midst of a most fruitful district; enterprise alone is wanting to render it prosperous'.

There was a dignified grandeur about Santiago, but although the streets were crowded at certain times of the day, the paradox was that the city lacked 'bustle': still in some ways 'like an overgrown country village through which there are few travellers, and but occasional intercourse with the rest of the world'. Valparaiso, by contrast, was full of strangers, one of the indispensable keys to progress.

Valparaiso was awaiting fresh harbour improvement by Wheelwright, and Gilliss emphasized the need to improve selected ports and hinterlands north and south of Valparaiso so that Chile did not remain synonymous with the core cluster pegged to Santiago. By the end of 1851, Gilliss was already warning that the honeymoon period of Chilean exports to the goldrush settlements in California, especially wheat, was virtually over. Supplies from Oregon were increasing, while the ubiquitous Yankee traders sailing from Boston and New York were no strangers to the West Coast. By kiln-drying his flour before loading, 'if the Yankee has not effectually excluded the product of Chile from the California market, his clipper-ships have rendered him a formidable competitor for its profits'. Moreover, Valparaiso's lucrative port taxes and victualling trade were also in trouble. Improvement in clipper-ship construction had put an end to Valparaiso being the port of call for nearly every ship doubling Cape Horn, a boost it had enjoyed from 1849 until the early part of 1851. 'Now,' Gilliss reported, 'the voyage direct to San Francisco is made in less average time than was formerly occupied in that to Valparaiso. ... Clipper-ships, with their thousands of passengers for California, dash by the ports, no longer leaving their treasure in payment for refreshments. ... *It has already become as rare for ships to call, as it previously was for them to pass by.*'[22] The Panama Railroad (built 1850–55), would further increase the isolation, Gilliss warned. All the more reason why Chile must press ahead urgently with internal development, get the basic infrastructure into place, attract more immigrants with the sort of industry and energy already being shown by German colonists at Valdivia, expand the domestic market, and promote transcontinental trade with Buenos Aires.

It was with this last end in view that Lieutenant Archibald MacRae was ordered to cross the Andes and the Pampas, and to report on the topography, meteorology, drainage, mineral and agricultural resources, and the social conditions he found en route. Crossing the Uspallata Pass, MacRae passed herds of cattle and mules being driven west into Chile, along with a small mule train laden with smuggled tobacco whose owners, MacRae later learned, failed to elude the Chilean custom-house officers. The Lieutenant pressed on to Mendoza, the old oasis settlement in the Andean foothills of Argentina that had originally been colonized from Chile. MacRae found an impressive range of crops around the town (population about 9,000) – wheat, corn, alfalfa, flax, grapes, peaches, melons, figs, olives, and plenty of livestock: 'the want of a market is the great obstacle to agriculture'. As he made ready to cross the Pampas, MacRae assessed the modes of transport currently available to travellers and freighters. There were just two categories to choose from – bad or worse: heavy stagecoaches (*galeras*); slow, large-wheeled ox-wagons; small, two-wheeled carts; mule trains, and saddle horses. These would have to be replaced, but that was no problem. There was talk in Mendoza of a railroad to Rosario: 'Nothing is wanted but timber and money,' MacRae noted, 'the country being highly favorable.'[23]

Like Gilliss, MacRae brightened at any sign of bustle. In one settlement along the trail, much to his surprise, he found a New York merchant doing a thriving business in a well-stocked general store, and his success seemed to have rubbed off on to the neat, compact little town. There was much more traffic as MacRae neared Rosario: 'The country was alive with trains of ox-carts and mules, going or coming. ... Altogether it was a very enlivening scene, reminding us, in an unmistakable manner, that we were approaching civilization.' Like Lieutenant T. J. Page, who steamed into Rosario a few weeks later in the *Water Witch*, MacRae found his own impressions on the landward side of the Paraná river port equally encouraging; 'the most modern-looking town on the road. With the exception of huts on the outskirts, the buildings are all of brick and mortar, and for one falling to decay there are ten being built.'[24]

MacRae proceeded to Buenos Aires and Montevideo before returning to the United States. In August 1853, he sailed again for the River Plate to make the trip back to Chile once more, adding variations to his earlier route, and selecting the Portillo Pass over the Andes. In crossing the Cordillera, MacRae had followed in the footsteps of Charles Darwin, whose notes MacRae carried for reference and comparison. In March–April 1835, however, Darwin had gone east over the Portillo Pass and returned via the Uspallata. All told, MacRae reported in his final review, the transcontinental journeys between Chile and Argentina had revealed no serious impediment to growth, provided new transport, new settlement, and new energy were introduced. 'Both ends of the road talk a great deal about the dangers of crossing the Pampa', MacRae added. There was the risk of Indian attack of course, but, on balance, he felt the dangers from any source had been greatly exaggerated. Sensible precautions would see you through.

Assessment

What conclusions did the United States draw from its 16,000-mile reconnaissance of the South American interior?

First, that there was indeed a huge potential in agricultural and mineral wealth, and that unquestionably this should be developed. Resources should not be left in idleness – an economic argument and a moral judgement that runs through every report. Gibbon condemned 'neglect', Gilliss castigated any signs of 'apathy', Page looked for some sense of urgency in implementing plans to disturb the 'death-like silence' of the interior. For South America as a whole, Herndon summarized the economic and moral attitudes of them all in a single sentence: the belief 'that this glorious country may be made to do what it is not now doing – that is, contribute its fair proportion to the maintenance of the human race'.

Second, given the determination that America, not Britain, should take the lead, the United States displayed a much greater interest in the development and future commercial potential of the Temperate South of South America than of Amazonia. Brazil's refusal to internationalize the waterway meant that, apart from the extremists in the 'waterway school', the United States moved to cut its losses. In one respect, the Amazon project and the rhetoric that accompanied it were becoming increasingly associated with Southern sectional interests, and thus dismissed by many in the North. But there was also a growing feeling among Southerners themselves that their existing stake in the American West would be more rewarding, and certainly more crucial to their political and economic future. At the Great Southern Convention at Charleston in 1854, for example, where Maury kept up the pressure with a series of vigorous speeches on the 'rights' of free navigation and the intransigent attitude of Brazil, some delegates emphasized that Brazil should not be pushed too far. Brazil was the largest market in Central and South America for United States exports, and far and away the biggest source of US imports from the same region – well over half of the total, with a substantial share of Brazil's coffee and sugar handled at New Orleans.

The 'obsession' of Maury and his supporters with the colonization and commercial development of Amazonia touched off a growing backlash in the South. *De Bow's Review*, sympathetic with Maury's aims, nevertheless reprinted an article by a Southerner published in the *National Intelligencer* which called for attention to be given closer to home: why look further afield? '*Thirty* millions of acres of unimproved lands lie within the States bordering on the Gulf of Mexico.' Readers were reminded that sugar, cotton, tobacco, and rice could all be cultivated *here* with much greater ease and profit than in the Amazon Valley, along with excellent crops of oranges, lemons, bananas, pineapples, figs, and a wide range of other tropical and subtropical products. Texas grazing land was first rate, indeed Texas and the Southwest was the future corridor of progress, through which the railroad would inject new business, and funnel the trade of California and the Orient. The writer criticized the tendency to downplay the disadvantages of Amazonia: 'While the medicinal plants of the Amazon country are more plenty, so also is the necessity for them.' There was no doubt about the preferred destination for those who felt they had to go to South America: 'A large number of whites have passed by the mouth of the Amazon and proceeded to the south temperate zone ... Chili, South Brazil, and the Argentine Confederation.' That was where the sub-continent's future lay.[25]

Commercial interests in the United States underlined this preference for the Temperate South, although not as part of an anti-Maury lobby. Chile and Argentina reproduced most closely the physical conditions with which North Americans, or enough of them at least, were familiar. Topography, terrain, climates, and vegetation had much in common with parts of the trans-Mississippi West, and offered the best scope for American-style economic development – railroads, including transcontinental railroads, steamboats, freight wagons, trestle bridges, lumber mills, irrigation works, and port and urban improvement. Clinching the argument, the Temperate South would be the only region able to attract large-scale European immigration. Like the area north and north-west of the Ohio, there would be expanding pioneer communities in the Southern Cone needing the nuts and bolts of everyday living. New markets would be opened for American tools, machinery, and manufactured goods.

The United States was so much more *practical* than Britain in adapting technology to local conditions. Great emphasis was laid on the importance of the existing know-how in the United States, and on the conviction that many of the problems of development in the Temperate South were common to the American continent as a whole. The United States had not only already shown what could be done, it was also currently and very actively engaged on its own frontier expansion – a point that would be made by the North with even greater force after the Civil War.

The Temperate South of South America, in other words, had immediate potential. There would be growth in the noisy, pioneering American way, the familiar din of axe, saw, and steam-engine, not the paralysing silence of resources forever untapped. Unlike Paraguay, stifled not so much by its interior location as by closed minds, Chile and Argentina in particular appeared to share similar objectives to those of the United States when it came to the ways and means of achieving sustained economic progress.

Above all, in reaching these conclusions the United States favoured perception of the Temperate South was strengthened by the assumption that this was the region that would turn words into action. With the strategy outlined, development would automatically follow. It was not a question of *if*, merely of *how quickly* it would be achieved. In this respect, it is important to view contemporary events in the continent as a whole, and to set the reports of the surveys carried out by the US Navy in South America alongside those of the US Army engineers in the trans-Mississippi West. In February 1855, Secretary of War Jefferson Davis laid before Congress the printed reports 'of the explorations and surveys [authorized in March 1853] ... to ascertain the most practicable and economical route for a railroad from the Mississippi River to the Pacific Ocean'. Five major explorations had been undertaken, and the instructions regarding the geographical and scientific information to be collected had been virtually identical with those for the South American expeditions. Decision and action on the trans-Mississippi reports would complete the work of exploration, mapping, and fact-finding. A rapid follow-through from initial enquiry to the identification and completion of key improvements was automatically assumed. As Davis reminded the House of Representatives in a statement that summarized the United States approach to the development of new lands, whether in North or South America:

If the results of the explorations made under these instructions do not furnish the data requisite to solve every question satisfactorily, they at least give a large amount of valuable information, and place the question in a tolerably clear light. We see now, with some precision, the nature and extent of the difficulties to be encountered, and, at the same time, the means of surmounting them.[26]

Notes

1 M. F. Maury, USN, 'On extending the commerce of the South and West by sea', *De Bow's Southern and Western Review*, XII, 1852, pp. 384, 389, 393, 396.

2 W. L. Herndon, USN, *Exploration of the Valley of the Amazon*, Washington, D.C., 1853 and 1854, I, p. 24 (Vol. II by L. Gibbon, USN, 1854).

3 *Ibid.*, p. 190.

4 *Ibid.*, pp. 366–7, 371.

5 H. Southern to the Earl of Malmesbury, Rio de Janeiro, 7 September 1852, *F.O. 13/294*, Public Record Office.

6 Herndon, *Exploration*, pp. 190, 281, 341.
7 'Memorial of the American Geographical and Statistical Society to the Secretary of the Navy', New York, 11 May 1852, reprinted in *Bulletin of the American Geographical and Statistical Society*, I, 1852, pp. 66–72.
8 T. J. Page, USN, *Report of the Exploration and Survey of the River 'La Plata' and its Tributaries*, Washington, D.C., 1856; also *La Plata, the Argentine Confederation, and Paraguay*, New York, 1859, pp. 25–6, 567–9.
9 J. V. Fifer, *Bolivia: Land, Location, and Politics since 1825*, Cambridge, 1972, pp. 98–100, 170–8.
10 Page, *La Plata*, pp. 444–5.
11 *Ibid.*, p. 701.
12 *Ibid.*, pp. 289, 225.
13 D. Ammen, USN, *The Old Navy and the New*, Philadelphia, 1891, p. 256.
14 Page, *La Plata*, pp. 186, 104, 97.
15 *Ibid.*, pp. 73, 350.
16 *Ibid.*, p. 86.
17 C. A. Washburn, *The History of Paraguay, with Notes of Personal Observations, and Reminiscences of Diplomacy under Difficulties*, Boston and New York, 1871, I, pp. 353–4.
18 Page, *La Plata*, pp. 40, 445.
19 J. M. Gilliss, USN, *The U.S. Naval Astronomical Expedition to the Southern Hemisphere during the Years 1849–'50–'51–'52*, Washington, D.C., 1855, I, p. 11.
20 *Ibid.*, pp. 59–63.
21 *Three Years in Chili, By a Lady of Ohio*, Columbus, Ohio, 1861, p. 73. Records a journey between Valparaiso and Santiago made in Sept. 1855.
22 Gilliss, *The U.S. Naval Astronomical Expedition*, pp. 235, 509, 240 (my italics).
23 A. MacRae, USN, *The U.S. Naval Astronomical Expedition*, II, pp. 16, 54.
24 *Ibid.*, pp. 38, 41.
25 'Our Gulf States and The Amazon', *De Bow's Review and Industrial Resources, Statistics, etc.*, XVIII, 1855, No. 1, pp. 91–3, No. 2, pp. 364–6.
26 *Report of the Secretary of War on the Pacific Railroad Surveys, 27 February 1855*, Washington, D.C., House Executive Document No. 129, XVIII, Part I, 33rd Congress, 1st Session.

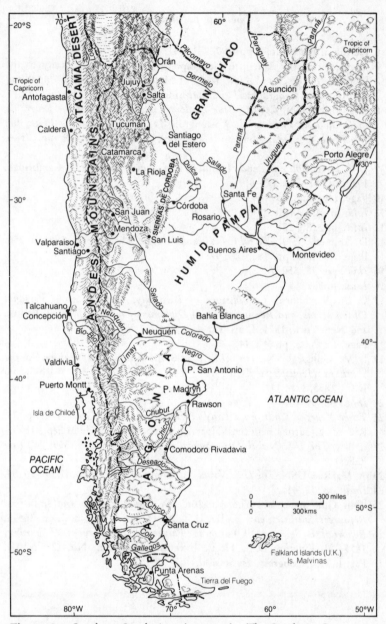

Figure 2a Southern South America: terrain. The Southern Cone states (Chile, Argentina, Uruguay) comprise more than 80 per cent of the Southland – the land below Capricorn.

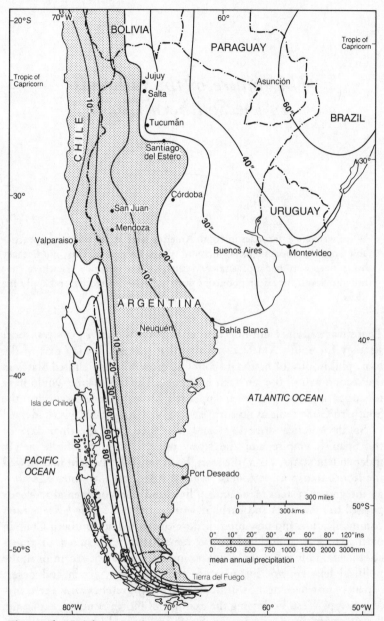

Figure 2b Southern South America: mean annual precipitation. North American observers saw scope for a major development of that part of the arid and semi-arid zone (stippled) which lies adjacent to the great water surplus region of the southern Andes.

31

2
The failure of the railroads in the Southern Cone

> Wheelwright's enterprises in South America were all regarded as impracticable until they became facts. Incredulity was his great enemy, not because his conceptions had not already been put into practice elsewhere, but because South American countries were not ready to receive and apply the ideas.[1]

There was certainly nothing new in William Wheelwright's transport strategy for South America, nothing that was not already part of the basic philosophy of national economic growth in the United States in the second half of the nineteenth century. The fact that he would have to adopt a more piecemeal approach to his grand design for the Southern Cone came as no surprise to a New Englander who had lived in South America since 1823 and witnessed both the final days of the Spanish empire and the slow, uneven progress of the newly independent states. From the start, however, Wheelwright had viewed the future transport pattern of South America on a continental scale – an integrated system of steamship lines and transcontinental railroads pegged to new ports and harbour works, and tied firmly by telegraph communication and new interior development. The Southern Cone in particular was considered to be remarkably well suited to transcontinental railroads – the distances involved were not exceptional, the political barriers not insuperable, and the steep terrain and desert expanses nowhere near as difficult over long stretches as in the trans-Mississippi West. Following the example of North America, economic development in depth in the Southland would depend not only on enlarging the existing seaboard cities, but on creating new opportunities for the isolated, sparsely populated interior. This meant faster Atlantic and Pacific interchange, substantial European immigration and enlarged internal markets. While fellow-Yankee Henry Meiggs remained essentially a trans-Andean railroad builder, William Wheelwright was indisputably a transcontinental man.

Initial proposals

Wheelwright immediately brought a new perspective to transcontinental movement in the Southern Cone by discarding the traditional Santiago–Buenos Aires overland connection, such as it was, and promoting instead a much longer north-west–south-east diagonal routeway through the heart of the region. After completing Chile's first railway from Caldera to Copiapó in 1851, however, and extending it to the mountain mining centres of Paballón and Chañarcillo, Wheelwright could get no further support for his plan to push the rails right across the Andes into Argentina via the San Francisco Pass, and continue them to Córdoba, Rosario and the River Plate.[2] The preliminary mountain survey commissioned by Wheelwright had been completed as far as Fiambalá on the east Andean slope, some 350 miles north-west of Córdoba, but Chile considered the enterprise too vast and impractical. Better opportunities lay closer to hand on the Pacific Coast. Fully occupied with extending its territorial claims northward into the guano zone, and before long, into the nitrate regions of the Atacama Desert, Chile had no interest in opening a new trade route to the River Plate, nor in waiting for any long-term advantages that might accrue to the Chilean economy from development of the Argentine interior. Buenos Aires would reap the initial benefits, probably at Chile's expense.

Wheelwright continued to press his case, exhorting President José Joaquín Pérez of Chile to avoid the narrow view of the transcontinental railroad as nothing more than a cheaper, faster method of maintaining the existing trade – mainly Argentine cattle trailed to the markets of Chile and Peru. *New* business would be created; *new* branches of commerce would spring up. And aside from the increase of trade, Wheelwright continued, 'we should reflect how much Chili and the Argentine Republic would gain from strengthening their relations and increasing their intercourse ... sister republics will be almost like one state in defence and in mutual development'.[3] Here was a vigorous early voice in support of the 'one state' strategy for the greater part of the Southland, a plain message from an experienced North American long resident in the region that the Andes must shake off their image as a 'natural' political divide.

Such statements of principle concerning east–west linkage sparked no enthusiasm in Santiago, where Chile's escape from isolation, even extinction, was seen to depend on northward expansion to challenge the power of Peru. Wheelwright was well versed in the commerce and politics of the West Coast. He resolved, therefore, to move to Argentina and tackle the problem of building the transcontinental railroad from the other end. By this time, Wheelwright's original surveyor, Allan Campbell, had completed his surveys in central Chile and also departed for Argentina. There, as a strong supporter of Wheelwright's South American transport strategy, Campbell accepted a commission from the Argentine Confederation to survey a line of railroad from Rosario to Córdoba, and he submitted his report to the Urquiza administration in November 1855 (see below, page 41). Like Lieutenant T. J. Page, USN, Wheelwright was greatly encouraged by Campbell's findings, and by the favourable official reception of his report.

By 1857, Wheelwright had been formally invited by the Argentine Confederation to organize financing for the Rosario–Córdoba railroad, and to prepare more detailed specifications for the concession. In doing so, he was to come into conflict with British railroad interests in Buenos Aires and expose the fundamentally different approaches of Britain and the United States to the style and cost of railroad construction, and to the type of role railroads should play in the development of new lands. The setting for the conflict was the Argentine Pampas, where the gulf between British and American attitudes to railroad expansion on the frontier was always complicated by local politics, and by the influence of the European money-market. But the rapid adoption of the British rather than the American approach to nineteenth-century railroad development not only worked to Argentina's lasting disadvantage; it also blighted the longer-term economic and political growth of the whole of the Southern Cone.

Such critical assessment of the rail system south of Capricorn was common among experienced United States observers by the early years of the twentieth century, and despite accusations to the contrary, it was a generally disinterested one. The judgement took full account of what had been achieved, and recognized that many derived complete satisfaction simply by measuring the dramatic increase in railroad mileage. But the full potential of the railroad had been seriously neglected, and explanations for the neglect based on the social and political preferences operating in the Southland neither excused nor improved the situation. At the end of the railroad boom, a visiting North American railroad engineer touring the Southern Cone in the 1920s was asked to comment on the region's railroad network. Did he not agree that it was an impressive sight, both on the map and on the ground? 'C'est magnifique,' he replied, 'mais ce n'est pas la guerre.'

The early divergence of British and American railroad technology: the United States adapts to the needs of the frontier

British businessmen travelling through the United States in the first half of the nineteenth century were frequently displeased by the railroads' rough, 'unfinished' appearance. British engineers on the other hand, on transatlantic fact-finding tours, often commented more favourably on the construction and performance, emphasizing the economy and general efficiency of American railroads which showed remarkable adaptability in servicing a mobile frontier, and a readiness to promote and respond to change.

'American railway engineering meets the wants of a rising community,' wrote David Stevenson, a Scottish civil engineer in the late 1830s; 'it is adapted to local circumstances and limited funds:

> At the first view, one is struck with the temporary and apparently unfinished state of many of the American works, and is very apt, before inquiring into the subject, to impute to want of ability what turns out, on investigation, to be a judicious and ingenious arrangement to suit the circumstances of a new country. ... It is vain to look to the American works for the finish that characterises those of France, or the stability for which those of Britain are famed. ... But it must not be supposed that this arises from want of knowledge of the principles of engineering, or of skill to do them justice in the execution.

Stevenson dismissed the common European criticism of shoddy workmanship in the United States:

> Although the works are wanting in finish, and even in solidity, they do not fail for many years to serve the purposes for which they were constructed, as efficiently as works of a more lasting description. ... The great traffic

sustained by many of them, notwithstanding the temporary and hurried manner in which they are finished, is truly wonderful.[4]

The principle of concentrating effort and precision only where it mattered was also applied to the rolling stock. The first engines used on American railroads were imported from Britain, and, given limited domestic supplies, iron rails continued to be imported from England and South Wales on a regular basis at least until the Civil War. But in a significant design revolution, British locomotives had been replaced by more powerful American models as early as the mid-1830s. Four of the new locomotive works were in Philadelphia, the largest that of Matthias Baldwin. Stevenson reported his findings: 'Baldwin requires very high finish in those parts where good fitting and fine workmanship are indispensable to the efficient action of the machine – cylinders, pistons, valves, journals, slides. But external parts such as connecting rods, cranks, framing, and wheels are left in a much coarser state.'[5] The 1830s also saw the development in the United States of two other important new features in rolling stock design – *equalizing levers* which kept the load uniformly distributed on the driving wheels so that locomotives could remain on the rails even when the track was rough and uneven, and the *four-wheeled swivelling truck*, or *bogie*, which allowed locomotives, cars and wagons to negotiate sharp curves. Curves of 1,000-foot radius became a common feature on American railroads. Indeed, curves with as short a radius as 300–400 feet (occasionally as little as 200 feet) were used. Sharp curves demanded reduced speeds, but passenger cars and freight wagons equipped with bogies could manage them so readily that rolling stock was successfully extended from thirty to forty-five feet, and even to sixty feet in length.

Americans had quickly abandoned what they came to call the 'English-style' of railroad-building. 'It was soon clear,' recalled an engineer on the Baltimore & Ohio Railroad, 'that the money wouldn't last.' Construction work on the B&O began in 1828, the company initially adopting the basic features introduced in England with the opening of the Stockton & Darlington Railway in 1825. Officials from the Baltimore & Ohio had visited England in 1828–29 and examined all the new railways, both finished and under construction. They returned greatly impressed with British railway engineering – level or near-level gradients over long distances; long, deep cuttings and tunnels to avoid steep climbs; well-ballasted track with only the gentlest of curves;

and, not least, finely finished bridges and viaducts of stone, brick, or iron.

The task ahead: the early influence of a voice from the West The Baltimore & Ohio Railroad had appointed Colonel Stephen H. Long as senior engineer and surveyor, an army officer who was already famous as an early explorer of the Far West. In 1817 he had been sent to examine routeways in the Upper Mississippi region, and in 1819–20 had commanded a major government expedition to the Rocky Mountains. By the early 1820s, Long had extended his knowledge of the trans-Mississippi West still further with detailed survey work on the plains. At this point, however, his interests and activities were to switch dramatically from trail to rail. In 1827, Colonel Long was assigned by the War Department to act as consulting engineer to the Baltimore & Ohio Railroad Co., where he quickly established his reputation as an authority in the new field of railroad engineering. Long's experience as an explorer and surveyor in the American Far West, so rare at that period, was thus applied to the planning and construction of the United States first major railroad, which was now about to pioneer this new technology into the trans-Allegheny West. Colonel Long's appointment at this stage was crucial. He brought a continental perspective to the work, helped to clarify the vision of future railroading in America, and underlined the need for faster, cheaper construction than that practised in Britain.

While his civilian colleagues at the Baltimore & Ohio crossed the Atlantic on their fact-finding tour, Colonel Long remained in the United States, unmoved by the praise for English-style railway engineering to which he was treated on their return. Had they lost their senses? 'The fact that railroad construction suitable for Great Britain ... might not be so practicable for pioneer America, apparently did not occur to them.' Before resuming his army duties in 1830, duties that were interrupted over the years by railroad consultancy work elsewhere in the States, Colonel Long published a series of field reports on routes, gradients, curvatures, and bridges which culminated in his seminal study *On the Principles which should govern the Location and Construction of Rail-roads.*[6] Long stressed that although prepared specifically for the Baltimore & Ohio, his findings would in future be applicable to railroad expansion throughout the United States. 'In this country, where the field for improvement is unbounded, ... the safest mode will be that which consists with the greatest economy of construction.' If it is cheaper to go the long way round than to cut and fill, he argued, do it. Improve later.

In his mind's eye, Stephen Long had already run the railroad into the Far West. America's railroad expansion could not be permitted to saunter slowly through the Alleghenies; the distances beyond were too immense and labour costs even then about twice those in England. Appalled by unnecessary waste, Long was emphatic about the need to abandon stone bridges immediately in favour of wood. Both these materials were available locally, so that it was time and cost that dominated the argument, not availability. Long listed some of the advantages of wooden bridges: they avoided serious frost damage; they were quicker to build, easier to repair, more readily adjusted after the ground had settled, cheaper to relocate when necessary, and easier to brace if the weight of traffic increased. 'Prime cost is so much less than that of stone bridges: the interest on the additional capital required for the latter is sufficient to keep wooden bridges in complete repair.'

Initially, however, the Baltimore & Ohio's 'English-style' supporters carried the day, influenced by Britain's lead, and also by the United States existing canal technology. Long's 'Western ways' were rejected as the B&O directors ordered the building of stone bridges of carefully dressed granite blocks along the first twelve miles of the line – with one exception. Colonel Long was to be permitted to design and erect a wooden bridge some five miles outside Baltimore. This was Long's opportunity and he seized it. 'The bridge was entirely in fine white pine,' recorded the railroad's historian a century later, 'a delicate-looking affair to the layman ... and yet Long's bridge, costing but $1100 [c. £220] to erect at that time, stood well to the task it was to bear.'[7] That bridge, and the reasoning behind it, helped to set the course of history in American railroad construction.

The efficient and imaginative use of wood in the United States impressed British engineers, who left it to the uninformed to dismiss wooden bridges as amateurish, and high trestles as dangerously frail. Edward Watkin examined railroads in the Eastern and Midwestern States in 1851, and praised their concern only with what was 'practical and essential'. Watkin deplored the amount of money that was poured unnecessarily into British railway architecture, not least into bridges:

Splendid bridges, costing on the average perhaps £3,500 each – *the cost of a mile of ordinary railway in America* – are now standing by the hundred on

English railways, ... over roads [he added bitingly] that in some cases are only passed over once a month by a milk-cart. I know of one bridge, for an unimportant road on a branch line in England, which has cost £20,000.

But all this, Watkin concluded resignedly, was only one of many examples of the massive style of railway engineering which Britain preferred:

We have made our rails strong enough for any possible weight of engine; our drainage capacious enough to remove any conceivable flood; our cuttings and embankments with slopes which defy the chance of slips; our bridges firm enough for many times the weight that can ever come upon them; and our tunnels with a solidity worthy of works of such magnitude, – not forgetting their huge stone 'faces', seen only by our engine-drivers, but equal to the architecture of the catacombs.[8]

Watkin and like-minded critics had ample support from American railroad men, who emphasized their different approach:

The English engineer ... defies all opposition from river and mountain, maintains his line straight and level, fights Nature at every point ... and builds his matchless roads. On the other hand, the American engineer ... bows politely to the opposing mountain range, and passes round the base. ... He is well aware that the directors like rather to see short columns of figures on their treasurer's books than to read records of great mechanical triumphs in their engineer's reports.[9]

Only those British railway engineers who had visited the United States became fully aware of how well 'American rough and ready' could compete in the New World with the substantial and costly style of British construction. Time and again in the forties and fifties, British railwaymen were told by their American counterparts that the philosophy of instant 'permanent way' was a bar to future improvement. Many Britons were impressed by the argument: 'The American plan of putting up with "what will do",' said one, 'leaves the door open for invention.' Building costs on the first six miles of the English-style Baltimore & Ohio Railroad had averaged £12,000 per mile, the next six miles even more, but the lesson had been learned. By 1837–38, Stevenson noted, the average construction cost of railroads in the United States was only £4,942 per mile.[10] By 1851, with a total of 26,000 miles of railway (all east of the Mississippi, and including difficult terrain in the Appalachians and New England), average construction costs were still only around £7,000 per mile.[11] Captain Douglas Galton, RE emphasized the point in his Parliamentary *Report on the Railways of the United States*, underlining the advantages of the American system's speed and flexibility in opening new land. The average railway construction cost per mile in Britain at this time was £35,000 – five to six times as much as in the United States.[12]

British engineers rejected the argument that comparisons between the two countries were invalidated by England's extra expenses – high land values; high, often exorbitant rates demanded for compensation and right-of-way; Parliamentary fees; faster trains; and the almost universal system of double-tracking, when, in the United States, only one-sixth of the total mileage was double-tracked. There was general agreement that these formidable 'extras' added an average £5,000–£6,000 per mile to the cost of railway construction in Britain. Indeed, the broad-gauge Great Western Railway had cost nearly £7,000 per mile in land and compensation alone. But when all was said and done, Edward Watkin concluded:

> The excessive cost in our case, and the smaller cost in the case of the United States, has proceeded rather from the different spirit and temper in which the railways were conceived by their promoters, and treated by the Legislature and the public, in the two countries, than from any other cause.[13]

'What do you want from a railroad?' conflicting British and American attitudes to railroad development in Argentina in the 1860s

William Wheelwright arrived in Argentina in the mid-1850s determined to bring American-style railroading to the Pampas. Enthusiasm for transcontinental railroads was sweeping across the United States, and Argentina's belief in the railroad as the single most important instrument of modernization and economic growth was already established. It had been publicized by the political philosopher, J. B. Alberdi, and enshrined in the Constitution of the Argentine Confederation in 1853. Born in Tucumán, deep in the interior, Alberdi underlined the railway's unique ability to create a new Argentina. In a powerful and much-quoted political tract, he argued that the railway would conquer distance, and unite the littoral with the continental interior more effectively than any government decree was capable of doing. Railways alone would enable immigrants to penetrate the empty lands long neglected by Spain. Railways were the key to genuine political and commercial expansion, and in order to build them quickly, foreign capital would be needed to boost meagre local resources.[14]

Earlier short-lived proposals and reforms in the 1820s under Rivadavia had shown a strong European influence, but in the post-Rosas period, support was explicitly given by the Argentine Confederation to the United States development model, with its emphasis on railroads, on immigration specifically linked to the colonization of new land, and on the need to welcome, rather than resist, change and experiment. Although railways were given priority, Buenos Aires' refusal to join the Argentine Confederation (1853–61) meant that two separate lines were planned, one to start in Buenos Aires and the other in Rosario, the main port on the River Paraná. British merchants in Buenos Aires were the first to sponsor a railway and apply for a concession from the provincial government in 1853, the *Ferrocarril al Oeste*. Work began in January 1854, and the first six miles had crawled into a western suburb of the city by August 1857. By 1860, a mere twenty-three miles of track were in operation, interest among individual Argentine capitalists in backing the project had evaporated, and the provincial government was left to increase its own stake in the railway, in addition to having provided the right-of-way and tax exemptions on imported equipment. In December 1862, Buenos Aires province purchased the *Oeste* outright. The fact that British merchants and London-based capital had given the initial impetus to Argentina's first railway resulted in the virtually all-British element that was introduced into its construction and operation; the contractor, work-force, rails, original rolling stock, station materials and other ancillary equipment all came from Britain.

Meanwhile, 200 miles away, the Argentine Confederation concentrated on the more ambitious 250-mile Rosario–Córdoba Railway, for which Allan Campbell had submitted his survey and estimate in November 1855, adopting the American approach throughout. As a railroad engineer with first-hand experience in the north-eastern United States and in Chile, Campbell had found the Pampas to be a region simply waiting for the railroad – one of the easiest environments in the world. Between Rosario and Córdoba, 'probably no railway of equal length has yet been built over so smooth a surface, ... or where fewer physical impediments are met'. There would be no difficult grades, no tunnels, no extensive cutting and filling, and only two major bridges and four short ones. The alignment was remarkably direct – in a total length of 247 miles, 240 were straight, while the remaining 7 miles contained no sharp curves at any point. Most of the work could be done using local labour; superintendents and mechanics would be hired overseas, but contrary to what he had been told beforehand, Campbell found no need to import the entire work-force. Thus, apart from imported iron and rolling stock, the main expense would be the supply and haulage of timber ties along certain sections of the route.

The estimated cost per mile was £4,000 ($20,250) – a sum, Campbell added, 'which may to those who are only acquainted with the costly railways of Europe, appear to be a low, perhaps an inadequate estimate'. Campbell was no stranger to English-style railroading, and dealt firmly with the criticisms he knew would be made. Money would be spent where it was needed: 'While it will be well to economize in every proper way, *avoiding expensive stations and all unnecessary outlay*, ... the estimate is intended to provide for a substantial work.'[15]

Creating business on the American frontier was always double-edged – the *expansion* of existing traffic where appropriate (in this case, trade by pack-mule, cart, and stage along part of the old colonial trail between Córdoba and Buenos Aires), and the *introduction* of new economic activities made possible only by the greater speed and power of improved transport and communication technology. Campbell considered both aspects in estimating future revenue on a railroad that was designed to open quickly and be enlarged and embellished as business increased. Increased business was thus the lifeblood of the line, and the prospects were good. It was a land-grant railroad (currently $1\frac{1}{2}$ miles each side of the track), to which immigrants and their freight-generating capacity would be drawn; it was also a trunk route, well placed to develop trade to the north and west of the country.

By the early 1860s, the higher cost of transport and materials for what was now to be known as the Central Argentine Railway led Wheelwright to increase Campbell's estimate of £4,000 per mile to £6,000 in his concession of 5 September 1862, and to £6,400 per mile in that dated 19 March 1863. Even so, Interior Minister Rawson and the new Argentine Congress were persuaded by Wheelwright's arguments. The estimate was regarded as realistically costed – higher than the cost of similar track in the United States before the start of the Civil War, but with allowances made for the differences in location, and for the lack of existing facilities and expertise in Argentina. Detailed comparative reports on American railroads were made available, in addition to the material originally submitted by Campbell. Average US construction costs of around £7,000 per mile in the 1850s were known to include the cost of imported rails, and to take account of more expensive work in Appalachia and New England. But many efficient railroads in the United States had been built at no more than £3,000–£4,000 per mile, even less in some cases. Contrary to the charge from British merchants that construction costs for the Central Argentine were grossly underestimated, Wheelwright was planning exactly the economical, no-frills type of railroad that the United States had been perfecting for thirty years. The Rosario–Córdoba railway would be the first section of the trunk line Argentina needed so desperately; moreover, it would possess the outstanding characteristic 'which distinguishes the American railway from its English parent, ... that is the almost uniform practice of getting the road open for traffic in the cheapest manner and in the least possible time, and then completing it and enlarging its capacity out of its surplus earnings, and from the credit which these earnings give it'.[16]

Wheelwright's concession for the Central Argentine Railway was welcomed by the United States Resident Minister in Buenos Aires, Robert Kirk, as an enlightened and 'certainly very liberal' award on the government's part, since (under Articles XV and XX)

> the Government guarantees to the company in the working of the line an annual interest of 7 per cent on the fixed outlay of £6,400 sterling per mile for a forty-year period – satisfying each year the difference between this interest and the nett proceeds of the line, whenever the latter should be less; but if, afterwards, the proceeds shall exceed the interest, such excess shall be applied to reimburse whatever sums the Government may have so paid.[17]

The 7 per cent guarantee had first been formally introduced into the Central Argentine's concession of 1862, and was to take effect, section by section, as the line was opened to public traffic. Calculations would be based on the proceeds per mile after 45 per cent of the annual gross receipts had been deducted as working expenses.

All material and equipment imported for the construction and sole use of the railway were to remain duty-free for forty years, while following the practice of the United States, mail was to be carried free of charge, and military personnel and baggage at half price. In an even more significant adoption of the latest American railroad policy, in addition to free right-of-way, the Argentine Government doubled the width of the original land grant to three miles (one league) on each side of the line for its entire length from the outskirts of Rosario to those of Córdoba, with only two small interruptions around the existing villages of San Jerónimo (Frayle Muerto) and Villa Nueva. As the United States Minister emphasized, *'the lands are bestowed to the company on condition of populating them*, and the Government agrees to facilitate and protect the introduction of immigrants by the company, and to allow it to build churches and schools'. Not least among the provisions for rail extension and branch lines, Kirk drew attention to Article VII, in which *'the Government allows the company the right to prolong the railway towards the Andes by the most favorable route*, with the same rights, privileges, and exemptions respecting the line from Rosario to Córdoba, *but without the guarantee'*. All in all, Wheelwright's concession for the Central Argentine Railway was considered to have produced a very American-style package, with two significant exceptions – the nature of the government guarantee on investment, and the absence of the 'checkerboard' pattern of lots held alternately by the government and the railway within the land grant.

Funding for the enterprise would have to come from Europe, mainly from London. Potential British shareholders assessed railway investment both at home and abroad as a business proposition, not as a selfless exercise in regional development. Investors needed to be convinced that a railway's earnings would be large enough from the outset to guarantee a profitable return on their capital. Some regions of the world encouraged greater optimism than others, but there was nothing certain about Argentina's prospects in the 1850s and early 1860s, and many investors regarded the risks as too great, even in the Buenos Aires area. Government guarantees of the type now offered by Argentina were not unusual – they were already a normal feature of railway investment in Russia, India and Brazil, for example, though not in the United States. Although the 7 per cent guaranteed interest rate was considered necessary to attract early railway investors to Argentina, it remained to be seen what effect it would have in instilling a sense of urgency to cut costs, or in keeping the railway hungry for new business.

As for the land grant, Argentine landowners and many in Buenos

Aires regarded it as an unwelcome innovation, particularly if it was to mark a permanent break with the tradition of extensive private landholding, establish the practice of compulsory purchase, and encourage the spread of small yeoman farmers. The land grant was dismissed by its critics as an isolated desperate measure – the only inducement that an impoverished interior had been able to offer to a railway concessionaire hoping to attract investors into the up-country wilderness. Wheelwright and the small American community in Argentina, took a much more positive view; the land-grant railroad had emerged in the 1850s in the United States as the greatest single pioneering agent for settling and developing the Midwest, and that was exactly how the Americans viewed the role of the land-grant railroad in Argentina.

'President Mitre is working heaven and earth to people his deserted country, and drive it ahead', Kirk informed the State Department approvingly. Wheelwright had acquired about 1,400 square miles (*c.* 900,000 acres) in the land grant to the Central Argentine Railway, and he proposed to establish towns and colonies at 8–10 mile intervals along the 247–mile line. As in the United States, speed was essential. Allowing for delays caused by the interior location, at least ten miles of railway were to be completed within eighteen months of ratification, and the entire line within five years unless other delays beyond the company's control intervened. The gauge stipulated by the government was wider than Wheelwright thought necessary for this, or any rail system. He had pioneered railroad construction in Chile using standard gauge, but for the Central Argentine it was to be 5′6″, the broad gauge already chosen for the existing short lengths of railway in the province of Buenos Aires, as well as in parts of Chile, Paraguay and Spain. It was known to railwaymen on both sides of the Atlantic as the 'Spanish gauge'.

British merchants in Buenos Aires, meanwhile, led by the wealthiest among them, Edward Lumb, had also succeeded in 1862–63 in acquiring a concession for a new railway – the Buenos Ayres Great Southern. What made this an early turning-point in the Southland's railway frontier strategy was that in addition to the forty-year tax exemption, the provincial government had also agreed to a 7 per cent guarantee over the same period on a capital investment of £10,000 per mile, i.e. £3,600 per mile more than Wheelwright's concession. Beyond right-of-way and servicing areas, there was no extensive land grant to the Great Southern, and in truth neither the British merchants nor their backers wanted one. The tracks of the initial 71-mile stretch from Buenos Aires to Chascomús crossed the properties of landowners willing to yield right-of-way, and supportive of this or any other line that would increase their land values; but they were reluctant to become involved in investing in the railway companies or in encouraging them to diversify their activities. The American railroad development model had little appeal to British and Argentine business interests in Buenos Aires province, despite the scope that remained there for its application. Better that Wheelwright be left to pursue his Yankee ways north from Rosario, well away from Buenos Aires, although *porteños* would have no objection to speculating in his land grant if the opportunity arose.

Wheelwright was in no mood to stay out of range and confine his activities to the Central Argentine Railway. His transcontinental railroad project had never been permanently pegged to a terminus at Rosario; once political unification had been achieved, the Atlantic gateway was to be at Buenos Aires, specifically at the proposed new, deep-water port of Ensenada, thirty miles downstream. With this in mind, Wheelwright moved quickly and obtained a concession for a short railway to run from Buenos Aires to Boca, the small port on the banks of the Riachuelo, with branches to Barracas and Ensenada. Not surprisingly, Wheelwright immediately ran into conflict with Edward Lumb and his associates, who had assumed that the concession for the Boca and Ensenada Railway would be awarded to the Buenos Ayres Great Southern Co. As one of the Southern directors, John Fair, complained: 'Mr. Wheelwright ... was endeavouring to poach on our preserves, ... which we thought extremely unfair, as this southern district of the Boca was so manifestly and geographically within our "sphere of influence."'[18] But poach he did, and then, adding insult to injury in the eyes of the Southern's directors, Wheelwright declared, in response to a query from the Buenos Aires provincial authorities, that if need be he could build the line to Chascomús more cheaply than the £10,000 per mile agreed – a figure Wheelwright considered preposterously expensive given the seaboard location, easy terrain, and potential traffic in the province. Of course it was possible to lavish £10,000 per mile (soon to be increased to nearly £11,430 per mile) on building an English-style railway, but why be talked into such unnecessary extravagance?

Furious with Wheelwright, the Southern's directors fell back on the argument that Wheelwright had seriously underestimated his own costs. *Properly* constructed railways, they had been told by their English advisers, required far more money spent on them to produce a soundly engineered, reliable line. Was a United States-style railroad really the way to launch what promised to be a major example of British industrial technology? All those curves and trestles on the US system had given their railroaders a 'hairpin and matchstick' mentality. Thus the seed was sown to an anxious Argentina that the American approach, typified by 'that meddling Yankee' Wheelwright, resulted in makeshift construction and shoddy workmanship; it meant cutting corners and making do.

Sir Morton Peto, contractor for the Great Southern and one of its major shareholders, became an influential figure in the debate. He had an established reputation for large, dramatic structures, and his fondness for massive engineering projects was strikingly displayed in many of Britain's railways, dockyards, bridges and viaducts. Peto was highly critical of the 'very imperfect' construction of United States railroads, quick to catalogue their faults as he saw them, and aghast to discover that 'not only the whole cost of maintaining the roads, but a very considerable proportion of the cost of their construction, has, in the case of the majority of the lines of America, been thrown *upon revenue*'. This was not the way to secure immediate and adequate dividends, Peto emphasized, whether in North or South America. In his opinion, the United States approach to railroads was unsatisfactory on many counts, and clearly inappropriate for Argentina. In such an atmosphere, key officials in Buenos Aires were eventually persuaded to support the Great Southern's costly programme; the idea of a national showpiece was appealing, and, since the point had been raised, Argentina's capital city certainly did not want its newest railway to be inferior to any of the Chilean lines. Work began in March 1864, and the seventy-one miles to Chascomús were completed in December 1865.

The Southern's directors were pleased with the 'fast speed' of the construction, although this was scarcely the case – an average of only three miles a month under easy conditions. As Wheelwright had observed earlier, the seaboard location eliminated further transport delays into the interior on the imported material, the terrain was virtually level, and the mileage limited. An added advantage had been the peaceful local conditions which allowed the work to proceed without interruption. The generous initial funding, and the Great Southern's popularity among investors, had provided ample working capital from the start. 'The line is nearly a dead level with few curves,' wrote a British observer in 1868, 'the stations well built and commodious, and of a very durable nature. . . . To look at the sheds, which are divided into compartments, and all numbered, you might fancy yourself at one of the warehouses of the London Docks.' The bridges were 'fine' and 'handsome', and the railway's general construction 'without doubt one of the best and most substantial permanent ways in the world'.[19]

The Great Southern had made a 3 per cent return on investment in its first year, 5 per cent in 1867, over 7 per cent in 1868, and 11 per cent in 1869. By 1869–70, having doubled the traffic on its seventy-one mile line, the Great Southern negotiated the cancellation of the 7 per cent guarantee.

It did not, however, repay any of the money received in the early years under the government guarantee, despite the contractual agreement to do so. Indeed the company demanded and received arrears of payment of the guarantee for the period when the return on capital was still below 7 per cent. The Great Southern considered its strategy to have been entirely vindicated. It had been able to establish the railway on a sound footing, investing in additional infrastructure and rolling stock in the crucial early years without risk to the shareholders, given the government's existing credit agreements. Even in abandoning the guarantee, the company had replaced one type of financial support with another; the Southern secured a future subsidy from the provincial government of £500 per mile for rail extensions built with government approval. Shareholders were now blandly informed at their half-yearly meeting in London that profitable lines could in future be built at a cost of £4,000 per mile, not the £11,000 per mile of the original section.[20] 'Those were grand old days,' recalled one of the directors with reference to the 1860s. 'The British community of Buenos Ayres was a compact, small but powerful community, not one-tenth of what it is today, nevertheless of immensely more influence and representation.'[21]

Wheelwright meanwhile had departed for London to secure financial backing for the Central Argentine Railway. Whether railroads were built in the 'English' or the 'American' style, the money still had to come from Europe. Wheelwright paid a price for his views on the expensive construction by the Great Southern, and for securing the Boca and Ensenada Railway concession – worse still, for holding on to it in the face of powerful Southern opposition. Having challenged British interests in their own Buenos Aires backyard, Wheelwright became the target of abuse, his 'blunder' and 'foolishness' becoming before long his 'irregular conduct', 'complicity' and 'megalomania', in the opinions of those sympathetic to the British enterprise. Although the dispute has been represented merely as a clash of personalities, it can perhaps more usefully be seen as part of the early showdown between US-style and British-style railroad development in the context of Argentina. Wheelwright was unperturbed by the invective but angered to discover that Great Southern interests had persuaded Baring Brothers by the end of 1863 to question Wheelwright's integrity and withdraw their financial support from the Central Argentine Railway project.

Despite this setback, however, Wheelwright was not readily dismissed by the rest of international community as an irresponsible Yankee; he was a well-known entrepreneur, widely respected for his achievements in South America. In London, he was successful in attracting the enthusiastic support of the distinguished railway contractor, Thomas Brassey. By the 1860s, Brassey had already built railways in Europe, the Crimea, India, Australia and Canada, and during a recent visit to the United States had been much impressed by American methods of extending new lines through undeveloped regions. Fast, low-cost construction, trestle bridges, and land-grant railroads all appealed to him, especially as some of the needlessly expensive work he had become involved in on the Canadian Grand Trunk Railway was still painfully fresh in his mind. Wheelwright and Brassey thus met for the first time in London at a propitious moment, both quick to grasp the main issues and pleased to discover a genuine agreement over the planned style of construction of Argentina's first trunk railway. 'As to the cost of the road,' Wheelwright confirmed to Brassey, 'I know enough of railways in South America to give an opinion founded upon experience; and if we do our work as we should, that is with a close attention to economy, you will find all the calculations will be fully and completely realized.'[22]

Wheelwright's concession from the Argentine government now became the framework of the new Central Argentine Railway Co., which was incorporated in London on 10 March 1864 with a capital of £1,600,000, divided into 80,000 shares of £20 each.[23] The project had acquired 'the halo of British protection', as Wheelwright put it; Brassey, Wythes & Wheelwright were the contractors, and accepted from the railway company one-half of the land grant in part-payment for the contract price.

The sense of urgency to get the Central Argentine Railway open and operational as soon as possible produced an American-style line that looked crude when compared with the Great Southern. In the field, however, supervising progress and talking to travellers, Wheelwright himself rarely failed to impress visitors with the point that his 'get going, improve later' philosophy would in the long run be more appropriate for the task ahead than the Great Southern's 'begin as you mean to go on'. Characteristically, the Great Southern was already at work on its prestigious new terminal station in Buenos Aires at a cost of over £200,000. In stark contrast, the Central Argentine's 'gateway' station at Rosario was still, in 1868, 'a few disjointed wooden sheds in an open plain, ... the terminus of a line already carried 158 miles into the interior; but all this is merely temporary', the visitor added cheerfully, as he followed the rails into the 'rough and ready wildness' of the backland. The first two way-side stations were 'mere mud huts' but were soon to be replaced; at Cañada de Gómez, where Wheelwright's son-in-law had recently established a large wheat and livestock farm, and a new town was planned, a substantial brick station was in place. Villa Nueva (Villa Maria), more than half-way along the trunk line to Córdoba, was the temporary end-of-track. 'I went over the railway station works, and found evident signs of considerable traffic, even with an unfinished line. ... A commodious brick ware-house has been built and works on a large scale are in course of erection, which will greatly facilitate the traffic now carried on. In fact, all was bustle.'[24]

Wheelwright had installed a steam sawmill and was exploiting a large stand of timber some fifteen miles from the line, for ties, and for his wood-burning locomotives. Expensive coal imports had now been dispensed with, telegraph wiring was nearing completion, and there was a spirit of optimism about the region. The combination of the railway and the land grant had great potential.

> Seeing is believing, and if shareholders who are sceptical as to the future could take a trip out here to satisfy themselves, they would be quite re-assured on this point. ... The Rosario and Córdoba line is considered to be ultimately destined to cross the entire country to Chili, and thus to form a highway for the traffic between the Atlantic and the Pacific.[25]

The United States Minister in Buenos Aires monitored progress on all Argentina's railroads, but showed particular interest in the Central

Argentine, uniquely isolated from the capital city, and galvanized by 'the energy and indomitable perseverance of William Wheelwright'. Kirk had recently received from the State Department a set of the remarkable twelve-volume work on the Pacific Railroad Explorations and Surveys across the trans-Mississippi West, which had been published by the Federal Government between 1855 and 1861 at a cost of over $1,000,000. He presented the set to President Mitre as a reminder that both countries shared the vision, and the task, of constructing transcontinental railroads.

Wheelwright kept Kirk apprised of his forward planning for the extension of the Central Argentine Railway from Córdoba to Tucumán. It was from this section of the line, at Horquetá junction, that Wheelwright intended to run his transcontinental line north-westwards to the Chilean port of Caldera. He had sent his surveyors on ahead to select the Córdoba–Tucumán route soon after construction of the line began at Rosario, and by May 1866 he had examined their report. The terrain presented no obstacles, Wheelwright informed Kirk; 'a railroad through the Northern Provinces will be the greatest boon that can be conferred upon them'.[26] In 1867, at the request of the Minister and the American community in Buenos Aires, Wheelwright – 'a 70-year-old ball of energy and one of our most respected and influential fellow citizens' – agreed to act as the United States Commercial Agent in Rosario. He placed his nephew, Samuel Wheelwright, in charge of the day-to-day supervision on the Central Argentine Railway, and prepared for fresh struggles in the attempt to keep Argentina's mind on the real job in hand, which was to concentrate on extending the trunk railroad and on protecting new settlers.

Argentina was now increasingly involved in the war with Paraguay, a deplorable distraction, Wheelwright informed the US Secretary of State, with President Mitre flattered into the position of commander-in-chief of the combined armies of Brazil, Uruguay and Argentina.[27] The momentum of frontier expansion in a region already peripheral to *porteño* interests could not survive major interruption, Wheelwright stressed; the war absorbed national revenue, increased overseas borrowing, and frittered away valuable time. With the withdrawal of the army units, Indian attacks on the new colonists increased, and the murder of three English settlers near Frayle Muerto received wide publicity. The regular loss of livestock through Indian raids was a more persistent problem, and caused many to abandon the land in the late 1860s: 'We had thought that the Government would protect us,' said one recent arrival, 'but General Mitre was too much occupied with the Paraguayans to pay any attention.' Anyone thinking of coming to Argentina was cautioned against 'the temptation to fix himself outside the older settlements and be, in the truest sense of the word, a Pioneer'.[28] Withdrawal of the army units also permitted unrest to flare in several interior cities, while 'wild gaucho' rebels from Santa Fe raided supply bases belonging to the Central Argentine Railway, fired on installations, tore up sections of track, and burned one of the bridges. Immigration faltered, new investment dried up, and work on the railway was suspended for several months through lack of funds. While the Great Southern was able to increase its earnings in the late 1860s in the comparative safety of Buenos Aires province (where trade was virtually unaffected by the war with Paraguay), the Central Argentine lost much of its dynamism in the final push to Córdoba. As Wheelwright had feared, the unwanted distraction of the war broke the rhythm of the frontier just when the twin thrust of fast railroad construction and land-grant settlement were being put through their crucial initial paces. In some ways, Argentina was forever to suffer the consequences of those wasted years.

None of these misgivings was voiced at the official opening ceremony of the Central Argentine Railway in May 1870. The national government had stepped in to subscribe the capital required to complete the line to Córdoba, and William Wheelwright, now aged seventy-two, was present at the inaugural festivities. It was almost exactly a year since the historic Golden Spike ceremony in the United States, at which the Union and Central Pacific had been joined in the West to form the first great transcontinental railroad. No archbishop had blessed the line that day in Utah, but the North American imagery was otherwise well in evidence at Córdoba. 'Before long,' said the United States Minister at an accompanying celebration, 'the locomotive will scale the Andes, in the same manner as the great Pacific Railway now traverses the North American continent.'

The land-grant railroad experiment in Argentina
1: The lead provided by the United States

What did America expect of a land-grant railroad? It was a recent introduction in the United States, and Argentina was the first country outside North America to adopt the idea. While the point is often made that by the 1860s, Argentina was comparatively late in entering the railway age, this had the advantage of enabling the achievements of a land-grant rail system to be well known. Though still new, the approach was no longer theory but successful practice by the time Argentina introduced it. Indeed, the land-grant railroad became a cornerstone of United States Western policy so quickly that some analysis of its methods in the 1850s and 1860s is essential at this stage if comparisons with Argentina are to be made, and contemporary expectations understood.

The American prototype The age of the land-grant railroad had begun in the United States in 1850 with the Illinois Central, one of the most successful railroads ever built, and a model for the crucial role Americans expected railroads to play in frontier development in the second half of the nineteenth century. Congress had been granting a broad right-of-way through public lands to selected highways and canals since the 1830s. As far as railroads were concerned, the principle of land-with-transport as the means of increasing land values and attracting settlers into the wilderness was first applied as the frontier approached the Mississippi. Beyond, water shortage and even greater distances would face the immigrant in the Great Plains and the Mountain West, where rivers and canals no longer had a major role to play in the national transport system. The railroad was to be the great carrier and colonizer of the western two-thirds of the United States.

Congress awarded the first railroad land grant to the States of Illinois, Mississippi and Alabama, allowing right-of-way through public lands, together with alternate square-mile sections (640 acres) on each side of the railroad for a distance of six miles, or up to fifteen miles if sections had already been taken up. The odd-numbered sections within six miles of the right-of-way were retained by the federal government, and were to be sold at a minimum of $2.50 per acre, i.e. double the standard minimum for federal land, thus ensuring that the government could receive as much from half the land as if no free land grant had been made. At this stage, the railroad was to be a major north–south axial line, running from the western end of the Illinois and Michigan Canal to the port of Mobile, Alabama, and was thus able to gain support from the rival sectional interests in Congress.

Illinois took the lead, however, turning over its federal land grant of some 2,595,000 acres in February 1851 to the newly chartered Illinois Central Railroad Co. In addition to raising the funds and building the railroad, the company was given responsibility for attracting immigrants to the State, selling the land, and thus increasing the amount of taxable property. It was to promote towns, and encourage agriculture and industry. As an immediate return on the land grant, the State of Illinois was to be paid 7 per cent of the gross revenue of the railroad, in lieu of other State taxes. Construction costs were estimated at the equivalent of £4,700–£5,690 per mile (more drainage and forest clearance would be required in the wetlands of southern Illinois), and included the use of British iron and American rolling stock. Work began in 1852, and the 705-mile railroad, the biggest single transport undertaking in the United States up to that time, was completed on schedule in 1856, linking Chicago, the Great Lakes, and the upper Mississippi country to the State's southern boundary at Cairo.

The Illinois Central had sent its ablest negotiators to London, where the bulk of the funding for such an ambitious project had to be secured. After a somewhat slow start, including rejection by Baring Brothers and Rothschild, British investment increased rapidly as favourable progress reports began to appear in *The Times* and *The Railway Times*, and the potential of the land grant in attracting permanent settlement and business to the line caught the public imagination. The first-ever public issue of American railroad bonds on the London Stock Exchange was that of the Illinois Central in June 1852, accompanied by detailed advertisements in all the leading newspapers and periodicals. Promotion and follow-up were so successful that by the 1860s, financial control of the Illinois Central Railroad had actually passed into foreign hands (mostly British and Dutch), with over three-quarters of the stock held by British investors.

Visitors published vivid accounts of the extraordinary efficiency of a land-grant railroad in achieving a swift transformation of the frontier. 'A railway for hundreds of miles through the wilderness,' said one of them excitedly, 'not to *accommodate* but to *create* traffic.' Another investigator, Captain Douglas Galton, travelling through Illinois in 1856, stressed the unrivalled advantages such a system would offer if it were to be applied to the development of British colonial possessions and other new territories:

> When the Illinois Central was first opened the country was nearly uninhabited; stations were placed at every 8 or 10 miles, round which villages and in some cases towns have sprung up, and fields of corn and herds of cattle are now to be seen on every side. ... Population is flocking

in, ... the rails are laid easily and cheaply, and their establishment is immediately followed by the settlement of the country.'[29]

The Illinois Central weathered the financial panic of 1857, suspending dividends in 1857 and 1858. Given the speed of its 705-mile construction, however (in itself, one of the railroad's most significant achievements), the line was sufficiently well established to benefit from the Civil War boom in farm production, and in the movement of troops and supplies.

(a) *Establishing priorities.* From the start, the financial history of the Illinois Central was inseparable from its land policies. Indeed, as one historian noted, 'the Illinois Central Railroad, in the first decade of its existence, was primarily a land company and secondarily a railroad company'.[30] The Illinois Central was the real pioneer, penetrating more undeveloped portions of the State than any other line. The task of disseminating information about this unknown region was given priority. Officials advertised ceaselessly, and when they continued to do so without cutbacks during the financial recession of 1857, British investors demanded to know why so much money was being 'wasted' in this way. The railroad's president, continually monitoring progress in the field from his purpose-built 'office' railroad car, was incensed at being forced by London to trim his advertising budget in 1858–59:

> I differ entirely from the view of the London committee and many of the shareholders, who have censured the administration of the Land Department as unnecessarily extravagant. [As a result], we are not advertising, have no outside agents, distribute very few pamphlets and sell very little land. ... Emigration is being diverted to other localities and we are lost sight of.[31]

Being 'lost sight of' was death in the cut-throat competition for immigrants now being waged by other railroads in Illinois, as well as by the other Midwestern States. Illinois Central officials complained that British investors, ever-anxious about dividends, had no understanding of frontier conditions, nor any idea of the amount of work involved in attracting settlers into one wilderness rather than another. The railroad's president, a vigorous New Englander, was not prepared to tolerate London's interference over the management of the company. He invited prominent British MPs, bondholders and shareholders to Chicago, arranged tours, attracted favourable publicity, and won support for his methods and for the future of the railroad. Although the controls of the European money-market could never be ignored, the president of the Illinois Central contrived to retain the initiative for the organization and running of the line, as well as for its land-grant policy. This became a characteristic separation of power. American railroads needed British investment and British iron; they did not need, and would not accept, British directives on how to build the line and run the business. By and large, British investors learned to live with it.

(*b*) *The importance of the speculator: opportunities and controls.* There were two classes of land purchasers in the region at this period – speculators and settlers. The variety to be found among the speculators, so often a pejorative term, was crucial to the diversification of the settlement pattern. The most numerous speculators were the settlers themselves, small farmers purchasing with a view to future expansion. Others ranged from local businessmen, bankers, editors, lawyers, and politicians, investing money in land on the side, to the indispensable professional speculator – individuals or corporations with enough capital to specialize in land sales and operate on a very large scale.

Speculators of this type must be judged not only on how much land they acquired, but, more significantly, on how much effort they made to introduce basic improvements and then resell quickly at reasonable rates. After 1850 in Illinois, professional speculators were competing for the first time with what the land-grant railroad could offer to prospective settlers. As a result, many professional speculators, operating outside but adjacent to the railroad land grant, were forced to be more flexible, becoming a dynamic element in regional colonization. They frequently began by buying up the quarter-section (160 acres) bounty lands, often in large blocks, from soldiers unwilling to go west and become farmers after discharge. To these blocks, and other extensive land purchases (made at minimum prices but on which taxes had immediately to be paid), professional speculators set out to attract prosperous, small-scale capitalists and skilled yeoman farmers, able and willing to pay more than the poorest settlers could afford.

It was the professional speculators, along with the railroad, who shouldered the task of advertising on a massive scale. They opened their own land agencies, employed travelling agents, and commissioned a steady flow of promotional literature – booklets, maps, prospectuses, and newspaper advertisements in the Eastern States and in Europe. Although abuses by the large-scale speculator occurred, they were not widespread here; the pressure of public opinion (and action) among the small settlers in a rapidly growing frontier region was a strong control on persistent malpractice. The absentee speculator in particular was universally disliked, and any Eastern capitalist who made no effort to improve and settle the land, preferring to pay taxes and await a rise in land values, was roundly condemned. Idle lands and absentee landlords were considered a restriction on individual local liberty, and an affront to the community. Even in the case of the regionally-based professional speculator, the record shows that where local hostility became too troublesome, the speculator sold off quickly, or transferred his lands to a local man, and moved on.[32]

(c) *The need to maintain momentum in settling the frontier.* A sense of urgency prevailed. While the large-scale speculators were left to pursue their own business, the Illinois Central Railroad blazed a trail of advertising and publicity in the Eastern States and Europe unmatched by any railroad or land company up to that time. The numbers of agents were increased at the Atlantic and Great Lakes gateway ports, and in Norway, Sweden and Germany. Successful farmers in Illinois who had originated in Scandinavia or Central Europe were encouraged to return on promotional trips. Free travel on the Illinois Central Railroad was offered to prospective purchasers, and to the whole family if the purchase was agreed. Canadian settlers were also a target for special promotion, much to the anger of immigration officials there. Extra inducements, such as the guaranteed purchase of farm produce for a fixed period at the highest available prices, coupled with a one-third discount on freight charges, were provided on any land slow to attract buyers, while special attention was paid to prosperous settlers contemplating a move out of State – Scandinavians, for example, thinking of shifting to Minnesota.

Extended credit, low interest rates, and small advance payments were widely available to settlers on the land grant, provided they agreed to make the stipulated improvements in a given time. At least one-tenth of the land purchased on credit was to be fenced and cultivated in the first year, and an additional tenth to be fenced and cultivated in each of the following four years, so that by the end of five years at least half the farm would be fenced and cultivated. No taxes were paid by settlers on the Illinois Central's land grant until final payment on the property had been made, and the title to the land had been secured. Given the overwhelming desire for farm ownership, most sales were completed within the ten-year period demanded by the State legislature, although some delinquents exploited the leniency of a company famous for its reluctance to evict, until an eventual forced change in company policy led to forfeiture and resale where abuses had occurred. Prices were normally $6 per acre and upwards, with much first-class farm land selling for $10–$12 per acre.

By 1855, the Illinois Central had begun a detailed survey and valuation of the whole of its land grant, with examiners required to assess, among other points, topography and soil quality, drainage, water supply, proximity to timber, prices charged for cutting posts and rails, the cost of breaking prairie soil and the availability of people to do it, livestock prices, distance from the railroad, and distances from the nearest farms, churches, schoolhouses, towns, villages, store, post office, sawmill and gristmill. Distances to county and township roads were also to be recorded, together with precise information, for example, as to whether or not bridges existed over streams that had to be crossed to reach the nearest railroad station.[33] Plans were prepared from the notes of the examiners so that the prospective purchaser could see at a glance the nature of the land in each section. Such detailed inventory by the land-grant railroad company was an important contribution to geographical knowledge and to the accelerated economic development of the region.

By the end of the 1860s, the Illinois Central had disposed of well over 2,000,000 acres of its land grant – more than 80 per cent of the total. Only a portion of the less fertile and poorly drained region in southern Illinois remained, triggering new company incentives and a fresh advertising campaign. Tracts of forty acres and upwards had been available from the start, while the opportunity to purchase a whole section, or more, had attracted many prosperous farmers and small capitalists. Large-scale farming in Illinois, however, employing labourers or tenants, was the exception, not the rule. Even the large farms did not usually exceed 4,000–6,000 acres, and although these were often important centres of innovation, the average size of the popular owner-operated farms in Illinois in the 1850s–1860s was about 150 acres.

(d) *Growing competition from the trans-Mississippi West.* Critics claimed that the railroad's land record was overpraised, and that only the incompetent could fail to sell land and attract permanent settlers to the fertile prairies of northern and central Illinois. But to those who insisted that the land each side of the Illinois Central Railroad virtually sold itself, the company was swift to point out the variety and vigour of the competition. Not only was there 'doorstep' competition from later land-grant railroads in Illinois, but also from those in Wisconsin, Minnesota, Iowa, and Missouri – all of whom borrowed freely in their advertising from the methods and promotional literature pioneered by the Illinois Central. Even prospective settlers attracted in the first place by the Illinois Central's offer were often poached by other States and other railroads at the gateway ports if rival agents were given half a chance.

The mobility of the frontier emphasized the need to seize the moment. Just as Ohio and Indiana in particular had lost settlers to Illinois in the 1860s, so Illinois watched 150,000 of its own people move on to States farther west in the same decade. Indeed, by the early 1870s, Illinois was regarded as a major source of emigrants by the new transcontinental railroads, which were now busily applying the high-pressure sales and advertising techniques learned from the Illinois Central to many who had only recently arrived in the Midwest. Nevertheless, the first land-grant railroad had already done its work with startling effect. Between 1850 and 1860, the population of the thirty-one counties served by the Illinois Central Railroad increased by 150 per cent, compared with a gain of 52 per cent elsewhere in Illinois. German and Scandinavian immigrants were the largest foreign element. The area under cultivation in the State had nearly trebled, and farm values increased nearly fivefold in the same decade.

So successful was the land-with-transport model in attracting business, the land-grant railroad companies soon came to regard each other as the most powerful competitors for new settlers, even after the introduction of the federal government's Homestead Act in 1862. This Act rounded out a diversified national land settlement policy by granting what were effectively free quarter-sections to citizens who had worked the land and lived on the 160-acre plot continuously for five years. Those settlers likely to move on again before the five-year period was up, and who wished to benefit from the work they had already put into the homestead, were able to purchase their quarter-section after six months' residence for $1.25 an acre. Although eighty-acre homesteads were permitted within the federal alternate-section holdings inside the railroad land grant, most government homestead land was outside the land-grant banding, and more than 15–20 miles from the railroad. Longer distances and higher transport costs to market were characteristic of many homestead tracts. Even so, the attraction of free land to poor settlers was a uniquely powerful inducement, and the existence of the Homestead Act encouraged particularly liberal down-payment and credit facilities by the land-grant railroads in certain areas.

With its checkerboard pattern of alternate sections, the land-grant zone had maintained a system of checks and balances between government and private interests, and allowed a variety of skills and initiatives to find scope for expansion within and adjacent to the railroad's growth corridor. The Illinois Central's successful land-grant experiment was important both in its scale and its timing. By attracting settlement quickly through the combined land-with-transport package, it emphasized the speed and effectiveness of the railroad in the development of the public domain, and fashioned a model in the humid Midwest that was immediately adapted to the development of the more arid lands in the trans-Mississippi West. In 1862, Congress made preparations for the first transcontinental railroad by granting the new Union Pacific Railroad and California's existing Central Pacific Railroad alternate sections in a ten-mile band on each side of their rights-of-way, and then doubled the width of the band and the consequent land-grant award in 1864.

From then on, Land Department officials at the Illinois Central received many requests from the growing number of trans-Mississippi railroads for assistance in organizing their own Land Departments, and for advice on the best methods of stimulating immigration. No other railroad in the world had been so widely advertised and become so well known in both Europe and the United States up to that time as the Illinois Central. The land-grant railroads were now to shoulder the main burden of colonizing a new Far West – not because no other agencies were at work, but because they attracted some of the most gifted and versatile talent in the business, and developed a programme of advertising and regional promotion on a scale unmatched by the Federal Government, or by individual State and Territorial immigration agencies.

The land-grant railroad experiment in Argentina
2: attempts to follow the lead of the United States

Between 1865 and 1870, while supervising the construction of the Central Argentine Railway, William Wheelwright also began promoting settlement on the land grant in the standard North American style. In Rosario, as luck would have it, he found just the person to help him.

William Perkins: 'an American booster for the "American" railroad' Born in Toronto in 1827, Perkins had spent much of his early life in Ohio before leaving Cincinnati to seek his fortune in California at the start of the Gold Rush. In 1849 he discovered the realities of frontier life at the Sonora mining camp east of Stockton, first as a prospector and then as a partner in an outfitting store – a lively, exhilarating experience, Perkins recorded in his journal, full of strangers, opportunity and enterprise. 'All that makes up the enjoyment of a bustling life has entered into mine: dangers, labors, and excitement of every kind, success in worldly affairs, good friends, a free spirit and a clear conscience.'[34] Sonora grew rapidly, attracting many American and German prospectors, as well as becoming a major centre for 'forty-niners' from Mexico, Peru and Chile, together with some from Argentina who had been living in exile in Chile during the Rosas era.

By 1852, however, Perkins was looking for fresh excitement. Sonora, capital of the new Tuolumne County, had become too dull and respectable for one who was still a frontiersman at heart. Perkins's Chilean and Argentine friends urged him to return with them to South America, where, particularly in Argentina, new opportunities were emerging following the defeat of Rosas. Convinced that the Far South was the land of the future, Perkins sailed to Chile, spent some time in Valparaiso and Concepción, married the sister of an Argentine friend, and eventually crossed the Andes to arrive in Rosario in 1860. He was immediately impressed with the potential of the region for American-style frontier development – particularly with the prospect of the land-grant railroad from Rosario to Córdoba, and the stimulating presence of William Wheelwright, whose energy and optimism revived Perkins's memories of the California pioneers. Perkins and Wheelwright became kindred spirits, meeting in Rosario at a propitious moment as the negotiations for South America's first land-grant railroad got under way.

William Perkins at once took on the role of regional booster. Like many frontier promoters in the United States, he began with the local newspaper, writing articles on the agricultural and commercial possibilities of the region, the importance of irrigation (using his knowledge of windmills and pumps in California), the future of the railroad, and the need for immigrants. He soon became joint editor of the Rosario newspaper *La Patria*, and promptly changed its name to *El Ferro-Carril*. In a country dominated by pastoral interests, Perkins was especially keen to encourage the introduction of experienced yeoman farmers of the type that had settled so successfully on the Illinois Central's land grant. In November 1863, at the invitation of the provincial governor, he toured the three pioneer agricultural colonies in Santa Fe province (La Esperanza, San Gerónimo and San Carlos), established between 1856 and 1859 under private concession with varying amounts of government assistance. Perkins published a series of detailed reports in *El Ferro-Carril*, before giving them wider publicity in booklet form in Spanish, English and German.[35] Some mistakes had been made. The main lesson learned, Perkins stressed, was the importance of a good start – competent farmers, well-chosen locations, basic infrastructure, and easy access to an expanding market. This was the first systematic attempt to document the successes and failures of the colonization projects, and in June 1864, Perkins was officially appointed local secretary of the new Commission for the Promotion of Immigration.

Perkins revelled in the new opportunities at Rosario, where he had now become a leading member of the business community. In addition to his newspaper work, Perkins resumed his old California trade as an outfitting merchant, broke new ground by opening a hotel close to the waterfront and the site of the new railroad station, and expanded further by becoming a partner in a general agency handling imports, exports, and real estate.[36] He continued to write his editorials with the same range and vigour that characterized hundreds of similar local newspapers in the American West, all boosting their own frontier development and clamouring to be heard by the outside world. With his constant emphasis on the importance of agriculture, Perkins discussed the potential for cotton cultivation in Argentina, tobacco cultivation in Santa Fe province, irrigation techniques, new farm machinery, and the value of agricultural expositions, as well as defence of the frontier, the trans-Andean railroad, public lands, new schools, and street paving – familiar fare to any Western promoter. The details might differ in southern South America but the message was the same.

In November 1864, Perkins launched his own newspaper in Rosario, *El Cosmopólita*. At the same time, he stepped up his writing for *The Standard* in Buenos Aires, published letters in *The Brazil & River*

Plate Mail, and, still as local secretary of the Commission for the Promotion of Immigration, carried on an extensive correspondence with enquirers in Europe, North America, Australia and New Zealand. Many of Perkins's letters were translated by Argentine immigration agents in Europe and published in German and French newspapers. In 1866, Perkins also sponsored and organized the establishment of a colony of North American farmers, mostly old acquaintances from California, in the north of Santa Fe province on the San Javier tributary of the Paraná.[37]

By the mid-1860s, therefore, as the construction of the Central Argentine Railway got under way, Perkins was the obvious choice to take charge of organizing the land grant and attracting settlers. Here was no vague, theoretical supporter of the land-grant principle. As his correspondence shows, Perkins had followed the progress of the Illinois Central Railroad, and was also well acquainted with the legislation in the US Congress between 1862 and 1864 on the new Western railroad land grants. He hurled North American facts and figures back at local Argentine landowners who 'pretend that the concession made to the Central Argentine Company is excessive and unprecedented, and that consequently they have a right to oppose it'. Perkins urged them to put the Central Argentine's land grant into perspective, and to take a more far-sighted view. Wheelwright reflected that he could not have hoped to find a better Land Superintendent, particularly one who also openly shared Wheelwright's own concern at the disastrous interruption to steady frontier expansion caused by the so-called 'defense of national honor' in the Paraguayan War.

Perkins left Rosario in 1868, making his way to Europe via North America, where he examined the latest developments on the land-grant railroads in the Midwest and paid a brief visit to his childhood home in Toronto. Then it was on to London, and discussions at the company headquarters in the City. Travelling through Europe, Perkins concentrated on recruiting experienced farmers, and by February 1870 he was back in Argentina, ready in March to escort the first group of twenty-five Swiss families by rail from Rosario to Roldán, where careful preparations had been made for this new contingent of land-grant railroad settlers. Wooden dwellings had been built; wells dug; food-stocks laid in; ploughs, harrows, seed and ox-teams were available, and wire fencing ready to hand. As Guillermo Wilcken observed in his subsequent report on Argentina's agricultural colonies, Perkins had been so practical and businesslike, the first settlers at Roldán were able to start work within an hour of their arrival.[38]

Lots were available for sale or rent in units of 20–40 *cuadras* (about 80–160 acres). Land could be purchased for the equivalent of £1 (US$5) per acre, with sales spread over five years after a small down-payment. Tenants were encouraged to switch from renting to purchase, especially during the first three years. Several of the procedures for moving and marketing produce in the early years were similar to those originally offered by the Illinois Central Railroad, although freight rates were higher. Interest rates on material supplied in advance (at cost price) were as high as 10 per cent. Perkins wanted farmers with capital who could pay off credit advances, plus interest, within 3–4 years. Long-term dependence was discouraged. Enterprising colonists were rewarded, however. Perkins waived repayment and interest on goods supplied in advance where successful colonists had, with his consent, used their profits on home and farm improvements, and on achieving greater productivity.

Perkins's agents in Europe collected groups of settlers and dispatched them from Le Havre, Marseilles and Genoa. Two more colonies were quickly established along the line at Carcarañá and Cañada de Gómez, but after that, efforts to attract more Swiss, French, German and English colonists met with little success, and the fourth colony, Tortugas, organized in 1871–72 some seventy miles from Rosario, was largely taken up by Italians from Lombardy and Piedmont.

Loss of support in London: the decision to separate railroad and colonization responsibilities on the Central Argentine In 1870 came a crucial parting of the ways. Shortly before the railway reached Córdoba, the Central Argentine transferred its land grant to a newly formed company, the Central Argentine Land Co., incorporated in London on 28 March 1870 with a capital of £130,000 divided into £1 shares.[39] On the face of it, the action was designed to improve administration and stimulate new investment without any fundamental division of interest. Most of the Central Argentine Railway directors were on the new board, and William Perkins continued as Land Superintendent in Rosario. Half the Land Company shares were transferred to the railway contractors (Brassey, Wythes & Wheelwright) in accordance with the original agreement that half the land grant should form part-payment for the contract price, and the directors confirmed their responsibility for colonization. But the separation of the finance and administration into two distinct companies was to reduce that responsibility, and completely undermine the rationale of a land-grant railroad. The new land company was not to be the indispensable land agency of an American land-grant railroad, working within the railroad's organization, and closely involved with its development. Although the stated purpose of the Central Argentine Land Co. was to attract new investment for colonization, the opportunity to combine railroad and settlement promotion into a single operation was deliberately abandoned. The Railway Co. was freed of the obligation to populate its 250-mile 'growth zone', and use land-grant revenue to boost railroad revenue as part of an integrated economic exercise in frontier development. Indeed, the Central Argentine Railway Co. retained the government's annual 7 per cent guarantee on investment until as late as 1884.

The Central Argentine Land Company was no more impressive as a dynamic force for change. Despite protestations to the contrary, neither the directors nor the shareholders were interested in financing a long-term programme to advertise the land and maintain a steady flow of settlers. Few knew anything at all about the region. Fewer still had any idea of the amount of work involved in attracting immigrants, or how the United States managed to make the complex exercise look so simple. For a while, William Perkins maintained support in London with his enthusiastic reports about Roldán (Bernstadt). There, a recent visitor had seen hundreds of Swiss colonists 'building, ditching, fencing, ploughing, and planting trees ... altogether, a cheerful aspect'. Perkins was highly praised – 'one of the most active and intelligent agents in the cause of emigration to the Argentine Republic'.

Cañada de Gómez had already become a major centre of agricultural innovation, its dynamic performance much admired by President Sarmiento on a visit to the colonies in February 1870.[40] Paul Krell, Wheelwright's son-in-law, had located his highly mechanized farm of 5,120 acres at this site, introducing steam ploughs, harvesters and threshing-machines. There were huge fields of alfalfa for Krell's own livestock, and for sale to other colonists. Cattle, sheep, pigs, horses and oxen were raised, as well as wheat, maize and fruit. At Cañada de Gómez Krell was in fact attracting a mosaic of smaller farmers to settle around him in standard land-grant style – some with 80-acre lots, others with more starting capital taking up to 320 acres, and one developing a 700-acre holding. By this time, Wheelwright and Perkins, who was thirty years younger, had become both colleagues and friends, each delighted with the transformation already achieved along the first few miles of the land-grant railroad. One of the last visits Wheelwright made before his death in 1873 was to the colonies along the Central Argentine Railway, still seeing them, and the land grant, as the key to the future of Argentina.

Wheelwright's death was a severe blow to Perkins, personally and professionally. Without Wheelwright's authority and long association with the history of the land grant, Perkins found little backing from the directors and hundreds of small shareholders for the business of colonization. Thomas Brassey, the most influential London-based supporter of the ideals of the company's land-grant railroad, was also dead; a sick man when the Land Company had been hived off in March 1870, Brassey died later that year. Land Company directors who were also members of the Central Argentine Railway board were well aware that the prosperous Buenos Ayres Great Southern Railway was not encumbered with any formal responsibilities for colonizing the land adjacent to its right-of-way, a point that could be emphasized by the Chairman and Deputy Chairman of the Great Southern who were now also directors of the Central Argentine Railway. Moreover, there were no Argentine government guarantees on the Land Company's dividend; no dividends were payable 'except out of the surplus receipts of the Company after paying or providing for all outlay and expenses'.

'Outlay and expenses' made gloomy reading for British shareholders – a depressing catalogue of agents' fees, assisted passages, surveys, infrastructure, and credit advances. The Land Company was not a charitable foundation, they reasoned; unsecured dividend meant small returns at best for at least the next few years. Establishing and assisting colonists over a period of time would be expensive; South America lacked the resources and technical know-how of the United States. British investors in Argentina wanted immediate and reliable returns, and were loath to accept what was often required of investors in the US at this period, namely, a willingness to hang on, and ride the rough with the smooth. William Perkins was obviously a hard worker, and progress reports on the first four colonies were encouraging; by 1872, they had between them attracted a population of 3,000. But when that same year Perkins requested the next major allocation of funds to establish new railroad settlements beyond Tortugas, his appeal fell on deaf ears.

With their insistence on an immediate return on investment, Land Company shareholders at once began to question Perkins's emphasis on agriculture, as well as the necessity of organizing colonization in such a rapid and formal manner. Surely colonists would come spontaneously in their own good time, and private speculators purchase concessions as a business venture at local level. It was noted that British merchants in Buenos Aires had already purchased portions of the land grant; in 1867, *The Brazil & River Plate Mail* listed twenty-two individuals who had done so, all of them leading representatives of business or railway interests in the Plate area, and none of them dedicated to promoting systematic small-scale agricultural colonization in the region.[41] More enthusiasm had been shown, both in Buenos Aires and London, in the traditional pursuits of the English colonists around Frayle Muerto (Bellville), where 'young men of good family ... have settled down with large herds of cattle and sheep, and are delighted with their prospects'.[42]

Shareholders' objections to financing colonization in Argentina were greatly strengthened by an adverse Parliamentary Report on the subject prepared by the British Chargé d'Affaires at Buenos Aires, H. G. MacDonell, and published in 1872.[43] Perkins could draw little comfort from the fact that in an otherwise totally negative document, MacDonell considered that 'the colonies on the Central Argentine Railway are the only ones deserving the notice of immigrants'. But the land-grant settlements were then damned with faint praise. The management was good but the initial outlay heavy. There was risk of drought, the problem of locusts, the danger of Indian attack, railway freight rates were too high – it was premature to judge the final outcome. Premature or not, however, it was MacDonell's 'duty to warn' that success was not simply a question of time and perseverance. The Santa Fe colonies of Esperanza and San Carlos, established in the 1850s, had 'undoubtedly made some progress, but, considering the time they have been in existence, will be no comparison with the remarkable advance to development of the British Colonies or of certain territories in the United States'. The Argentine Government was far too complacent about the country's 'natural advantages' for the immigrant, and MacDonell commended the evident growing reluctance of German, Scandinavian, and English settlers to choose the River Plate region – so politically restless, and so different in its customs, language, and religion. With the increasing imperial and United States competition for North European immigrants,

MacDonell's request that the Report be well publicized by the British Government was speedily granted, and its 'undisguised truths' cast a shadow over Argentina's prospects in general, and the Central Argentine's land-grant colonies in particular, as a popular field for Northern and Central European immigration.

Perkins reflected bitterly on the time lost in the 1860s, especially the crucial post-American Civil War period, when the United States launched its great drive for frontier expansion into the Far West while Argentina wasted time and effort in the war with Paraguay. The USA was an immensely powerful competitor for new immigrants under any circumstances, and its new railroad and homestead legislation in 1862 had given fresh impetus to westward migration in the late sixties. At this critical stage in Argentina, however, the image beyond Buenos Aires had been one of increasing instability. The Central's railroad construction and land-grant settlement had both been delayed, so that despite impressive initial results, given Perkins's limited manpower and resources, too little had been accomplished by the early seventies to win the day. Perkins's familiarity with the land-grant railroad model in the United States had confirmed his unshakable belief in its possibilities for Argentina, and he was devastated by the loss of support by the Central Argentine Land Co. William Wheelwright had been happy to leave the colonization work in Perkins's hands while he himself concentrated his final years on completing the Boca & Ensenada Railway. Now, the task for which Perkins had felt all his earlier life had been a preparation had been abandoned. In 1873, he resigned from the Land Company and at the early age of forty-six became semi-retired. Unlike the North American West, he reflected, remembering his California years, when one door closed on the Argentine frontier, another did not open to beckon him forward. Although he continued to act as Rosario correspondent for *The Standard*, and supplied occasional pieces on commerce and agriculture, Perkins became a shadow of his former self, an isolated American-style booster stranded by the ebb-tide. There was no second chance to develop the American land-grant railroad model, and to demonstrate its value in stabilizing settlement on the frontier by promoting farm ownership. Perkins died in Rosario in 1893.

United States assessments of the Central Argentine experiment as a model for future development

Abuse of the land-grant principle (1) Americans familiar with maps of their own land-grant railroads found the absence of the wide checkerboard pattern of alternate railroad and government landowner-ship along the Central Argentine a disconcerting feature. A *three*-mile land grant each side of the right-of-way was always narrow by North American standards, but even that had reflected the initial difficulties encountered by Wheelwright in 1862–63 in confirming the land-grant award. At one stage in the discussion, Argentina's Interior Minister Rawson had proposed an 'alternate lot' pattern of a different kind, whereby alternate slabs of land, each the full width of the land grant, would be ceded to the company.[44] This was rejected by Wheelwright. Not only did it halve the land grant, the proposal ran counter to arguments already put forward by Wheelwright and accepted by Rawson – that the rapid, systematic colonization of the land grant was indispensable to the increase of freight and passenger traffic, and that the sooner the Central Argentine Railway became profitable, the sooner the Government would be free of having to pay the 7 per cent guarantee. Private landowners and speculators lacked the desire to colonize the region, and could strangle the efforts of a land-grant railroad. Wheelwright prevailed.

The fact that Americans considered the land grant narrow, while Argentines agonized over the fact that it was to be made at all, underlined the contrasted social and political environments North and South. One practical, well publicized advantage of the United States public domain had been reflected in the pioneering Illinois Central Railroad land grant; wherever land within the *six*-mile band each side of the right-of-way was found to be already taken up, the company was immediately empowered to reach farther out for *another nine* miles to secure its allotted sections, i.e. up to fifteen miles from the railroad on both sides of the right-of-way. Not so in Argentina. When Wheelwright and the Central Argentine Railway met the problem of prior claims to ownership within the land grant (a frequent occurrence), the result was a protracted series of legal battles until the provincial governments of Córdoba and Santa Fe, still protesting that *all* the land along the railway was either provincial or private property, were forced by the National Government in 1866–67 to cede the land, and organize any necessary sales at its 'unimproved' value. As one visitor noted:

'The United States welcomes the railroad with open arms and generous facilities; in this part of South America [along the Central Argentine], people do not readily part with their land to assist the railway, however valuable its proximity is to them hereafter.'

The sharp division of ownership and lack of co-operation between the Central Argentine Land Co. and the provincial authorities could be sadly restrictive. While Perkins and the Swiss settlers at Bernstadt, for example, had laid out tree-lined plazas, built a school and a church, improved homes, warehouses, and the railroad station, and paid their taxes, the province of Santa Fe had declined to build a court-house or any other public building within the land grant.[45]

Abuse of the land-grant principle (2) Even more serious than the lack of checks and balances inherent in the checkerboard pattern of railroad and government holdings was the disastrous mismanagement of the combined land-with-rail economic package by the Central Argentine Railway Co. From an American viewpoint, this was a blow from which the 'New West' never recovered. It was not that Americans were ignorant of local constraints and unaware of the strong, traditional Hispanic attitudes to landownership; old property claims in the South-western United States inherited from the Spanish period were a characteristic feature of the regions acquired from Mexico in 1845 and 1848. It was simply that Argentina's first land-grant railroad had been a major opportunity for change – a bold break with the past and a model for the future.

If change was resisted, Argentina's land-grant railroad experiment was doomed. As E. H. Talbott of Chicago emphasized in 1880, railway companies must see to it that they retained direct control in the colonization of their land grants. 'Having wild land along their lines, railway companies must strain every nerve to secure its settlement. . . . Nothing could be more suicidal than for such railway companies to dispose of their land to a syndicate of speculators.'[46] London, operating in Argentina, took a different view. Following the separation of the Central Argentine Railway Co. and the Central Argentine Land Co. in 1870, both sets of shareholders aired new grievances. The Land Co. on the one hand soon forced the abandonment of planned colonization in favour of land speculation without strings. The Railway Co. on the other immediately began to grumble at the cost of track and station improvement, and were annoyed further by Argentine complaints that too few stations had been built along the line to Córdoba; the company had not kept faith with Wheelwright's plan to locate stations every 8–10 miles along the full stretch of the 247-mile trunk line. Yet the need to upgrade the facilities, and write up additional capital of £400,000 in order to do so, was not 'due to erroneous or unrealistic initial costing'[47] (the traditional British view), but to the unwillingness or inability to grasp the purpose of a land-grant railroad. Having turned over the land grant to another company in 1870 for a virtual giveaway price, the original gift of the land was conveniently forgotten. As one Central Argentine Railway share-holder observed plaintively in 1874, calmly forgetting that the land sales were supposed to finance improvements to the pioneer line: 'The investors had built the house but had nothing for the furniture.'[48]

The money for the 'furniture' was accumulating in the Central Argentine Land Co. Having abandoned its direct responsibility for colonization, the directors reported that the Land Co. was in a flourishing condition; the dividend for 1882 was 15 per cent, and there was a handsome reserve fund – all this at a time when the Railway Co. was still claiming its 7 per cent government guarantee.[49] In 1888, the Land Co. reported that it could have raised its dividend for 1887 from 22½ per cent to 40 per cent: 'At the present time we are labouring under a plethora of cash.' Political considerations advised caution in the payment and publicizing of such blatant profits. The directors still acknowledged that they had 'a moral obligation' to encourage settle-ment of the land grant but denied that there was any standing agreement with the Government to do so, once again ignoring the fact that the terms of the original concession were written in, word for word, to the 'Objects of the Company' at its incorporation in 1870.

The directors were now pressing for the purchase of extensive tracts of new land, claiming that the disposal of the Central Argentine land grant was virtually completed. Unless more land was acquired as a matter of urgency, 'we shall find we have accomplished our work, and that the 900,000 acres originally conceded to the company has been disposed of, and that every acre has been colonised and utilised, and then we shall be in the pitiable position of "having no work to do"'.[50] But the fact was that the Central Argentine Land Co. had sold only a little over *half* of the land grant; 385,000 acres were still on the books,[51] with no effort being made actively to promote sales and development, and find buyers for land slow to shift without special incentives. Railroad land agents in the United States were familiar enough with the need for fresh promotion and vigorous salesmanship in certain sections of their land grants. In Argentina, however, more land acquisition was the only solution sought to flagging sales. The new Santa Fe and Córdoba Great Southern Land Co., for example, had recently acquired some 4,340,000 acres in these two provinces; now was the time to join the increasingly profitable land boom. In January 1889, the Central Argentine Land Co. was quietly liquidated in London, and replaced by the new Argentine Land & Investment Co. Ltd. The spirit of the land-grant railroad had been buried years before.

Changing United States perceptions of Córdoba: the city becomes a 'dead end' rather than a growth point for future expansion

'The railway will infuse new and more vigorous blood into Córdoba,' wrote one well-travelled businessman in the late 1860s; 'when the line is completed, Córdoba will become another great nerve centre of progress.'[52] With the eventual arrival of the Central Argentine Railway at Córdoba in 1870, the United States had responded swiftly to new regional opportunities. The Commercial Agency in Rosario was immediately upgraded to Consulate level, and the first US Consulate established in Córdoba. There, it was assumed, 'the sound of the locomotive's whistle and the chatter of the telegraph wire' would quickly break the silence of the old, conservative city.

An Argentine National Exposition was organized at Córdoba in 1871, but the anticipated boom did not occur. Instead, in the early seventies, the US Consul reported a decline in Córdoba's business, and a marked reduction since 1870 in the number of Americans living there. At the end of 1874, he advised the State Department that it would be no great loss if the Consulate were to be abolished.[53] Washington was more optimistic, however, given its expectation that Córdoba held a key position in the forthcoming development of the Argentine West. Times were hard. The United States was also experiencing a depression in the mid-1870s. Prospects would improve. The Consulate was maintained, but successive reports remained negative, and continued to underline the contrasts between potential and actual performance.

Lack of commercial growth Despite the geographical advantages of the site, observed the Consul, Córdoba at the end of the 1870s was still not showing any signs of becoming a regional growth point: 'its commerce is of little importance, and is confined almost exclusively to supplying its own wants'. The railroad had arrived, but not the new population and new enterprise that Americans expected from a well managed land-grant line. There was no custom-house in Córdoba, and 'troops of carts and of mules' continued, with the railroad, to transport the only significant items of regional trade, i.e. hides and wool. 'The only manufacturing that is entitled to the name is tanning, including tanning goatskins called *cordobans*.' Sugar from Tucumán was now reaching the riverine cities by rail, but rice, tobacco, and cotton, all produced in the Córdoba region, were 'still looking for a market'. No attempt was being made to *create* and *expand* business in the region: 'There is not a single American merchant in this city, and only two English merchants, one a small grocer, the other a hardware house.'[54] These two were joined over the years by more foreign agents, particularly Italian and French, but even in the late 1890s, the US Consulate reported that in Córdoba 'a merchant would import one-twentieth or one-thirtieth as much as a similar one in Buenos Aires, which stock will then remain upon his hands for years before he is able to place it'.[55]

Lack of industrial growth The deadening hand of the government guarantee, in one form or another, continued to stifle enterprise and cushion incompetence in the American view, whatever Argentina's declared intentions might be not to subsidize poor business practice. In Córdoba, a shoemaking machine shop and a textile factory had already failed. 'These establishments always seek a subsidy, or exclusive privilege from the national or provincial governments, generally procure it, then linger on a few months and finally expire. The country may be said to consume everything and manufacture nothing.' Excessive tariffs were placed on imported goods on the pretext of protecting home manufactures, 'but since these do not exist, the tariffs are imposed solely for the purposes of revenue'.[56] The Vice-Consul had nothing more favourable to report on Córdoba's manufacturing performance in the 1880s: 'An immense establishment for the production of porcelain-wares was begun some years ago under a government guarantee of 7 per cent interest upon the capital invested, but it has not yet done anything towards earning the percentage for itself.'[57]

Lack of irrigation projects Córdoba, sited at the junction of the Humid and the Dry Pampas, was in an important transition zone, and American consular officials continued to be exasperated by the region's failure to create new agricultural markets by expanding irrigation. Small beginnings could be made; there was no need to think only in terms of grandiose schemes which were never started at all. Indeed, the State Department pressed the point, specifically requesting more information during the 1880s on the extent of irrigation in the Córdoba Consular District. The Vice-Consul struggled to oblige. In 1888, he noted that a reservoir had been constructed in the mountains [Sierras de Córdoba] to control flooding. 'And although none yet exists, an irrigation scheme is *about to be* inaugurated here.' Nothing more was reported on the matter. There was no interest in expanding agriculture; livestock dominated the economy. 'The price of camp land has more than tripled in the last ten years, and it is now generally wired in, and put under the charge of overseers and peones.'[58]

Loss of a uniform railroad gauge: Córdoba abandons the United States principle of 'one continuous line' The Central Argentine Railway had not been extended beyond Córdoba. As the US Minister in Buenos Aires emphasized in 1863 at the time of the original concession, the company was permitted to prolong the railway towards the Andes, but *without the land grant* and *without the guarantee*. Without these inducements, the Central Argentine decided to go no further. Nursing the 7 per cent guarantee, the Central made Córdoba its terminus, and left the government to boost the company's business by constructing two 'feeders' to the Central's trunk line – one from Villa Nueva to Villa Mercedes (via Río Cuarto), a 160-mile line which opened to traffic between 1873 and 1875, and increased revenue on the southern section of the Central Argentine – the second, a 340-mile line from Córdoba to Tucumán, completed in 1876. But while the state railway to Villa Mercedes (the first section of what became known as the *Andino*) adopted the existing 5'6" gauge, a narrow, metre-gauge line was selected for the extension to Tucumán. This break of gauge at Córdoba not only introduced additional delays and trans-shipment costs, it also represented a psychological break. Instead of marking a dynamic regional growth point on a forward-rolling frontier, as anticipated in the 1850s and 1860s, Córdoba was to become, in a sense, the end of the road. Once a staging-post on the long overland trail into Upper Peru, Córdoba would now be drawn ever more strongly towards the River Plate region, less to the North and West. The city was to be an 'edge-settlement', confirming the margin of the Humid Pampa as the effective limit of Argentina's economic interests and investment. Córdoba now stood at the gateway to narrow-gauge country; despite some later rail development to the north and east, a major part of the great Northwest had been relegated to permanent frontier status.

In the 1870s, therefore, on the important matter of gauge, there was growing divergence between Argentina and the United States. Americans noted that while the USA had moved decisively in the 1860s towards establishing a uniform gauge in preparation for national expansion into the West, Argentina had now done exactly the opposite. The early multiplicity of railroad gauges in the United States is sometimes forgotten. In 1860, the country's 30,600-mile rail network, virtually all of it still east of the Missouri–Mississippi River line, was operating on seven different gauges, and the Civil War was to expose the weaknesses of such a system in both the North and the South.[59] In 1862, President Lincoln stipulated that the great Union Pacific–Central Pacific Railroad should not only be built of American iron, but that it must use a standardized gauge throughout in order to operate as 'one continuous line'. In the 1820s, using imported English rolling-stock, the Baltimore & Ohio had followed George Stephenson's 4′8½″ gauge (made standard by Parliament in 1846), and the B&O was followed in turn by such key networks as the New York Central, the Pennsylvania, and the Illinois Central. Pressure from these four railroads to provide an interconnecting national system from the Atlantic seaboard to the Pacific, via the economic heartland of the Northeast and the Midwest, resulted in the decision by Congress in 1863 that the Far West's new transcontinental railroad should adopt the 4′8½″ standard gauge.

Not that narrow-gauge railroads had no part to play in the development of the American West. While the Consulate in Córdoba was reporting the construction of the metre-gauge railway to Tucumán, and a *decauville* line to the lime and marble quarries in the Sierras de Córdoba, narrow-gauge railroads were also being introduced into the American West. Unknown in the United States before 1870, the first 3′ narrow-gauge network for passenger and freight traffic was built in Colorado, and narrow-gauge also became popular in Utah and Nevada in the 1870s. But mineral lines aside, narrow-gauge in the American West (like the assortment of gauges in the Old South) was converted to standard-gauge during the 1880s, as isolated frontier regions threw off the restrictions of discrete circulation and hitched themselves to the Eastern markets. At the same time, a uniform railroad gauge was considered vital to the promotion of faster inter-regional circulation *within* the West, a key factor in persuading more Easterners and Europeans to visit, settle, and invest there. Argentina had tied selected centres to the coastal ports, but was doing nothing beyond the margins of the Humid Pampa to promote new inter-regional circulation. Indeed, throughout Argentina's rail network, it was easier to make radial journeys into Buenos Aires and out again than to attempt shorter, cross-country connections. Americans in particular were critical of the fact that variations in Argentina's railroad gauge quickly became permanent, not temporary features of the so-called 'national' network. This was totally inconsistent with the changes and adjustments necessary in a maturing railroad system. The choice of narrow-gauge for the Córdoba–Tucumán railway was in any case considered to have been a major error; it had saved relatively little in construction costs, since most engineers in the United States agreed that the case for significant cost-cutting when building narrow-gauge was valid only in mountainous terrain. The long-term disadvantages were severe.

The United States downgraded its Consulate at Córdoba in 1906, and Rosario subsequently had no difficulty in handling the meagre reports. The anticipated growth rate at Córdoba had not occurred. There was little commercial activity, still no American businesses, and only six American residents. In addition to the lost opportunities associated with the land-grant railroad, stagnation reflected local conservatism compounded by government apathy to any concerted national development programme for the arid and semi-arid lands. Such a programme would be burdensome, and irrelevant to the animal products and grain export economy based on the Humid Pampa. Apart from rail connection to the Cuyo fruit and wine-producing area to supply the *porteño* market, and the need for a military presence in the Chilean borderland from time to time, the majority of Argentines saw no other reason to mount a sustained, co-ordinated development strategy for the West or the South.

This is not to ignore the government legislation of 1908 (Law #5559) which called for the construction of five 'Development Railways', three of them in Patagonia, nor that of 1909 (Law #6546) which was intended to promote irrigation projects in the interior, and authorized the Government to negotiate with the railway companies to undertake the work on behalf of the State.[60] Little came of this new legislation, however. Railway construction in Patagonia was to be slow and half-hearted, part of it abandoned well short of the projected destinations. Work on the irrigation schemes was also limited, and largely delayed until the 1920s when existing irrigated acreage was extended in the Cuyo region, and more new land was brought into cultivation in the Negro Valley.

Thus, sixty years after Wheelwright and others had emphasized the importance of Córdoba as a growth point for new national development in the railroad age, Miguel Cárcano was still having to make exactly the same point in his classic study, *Evolución Histórica del régimen de la Tierra Pública*, first published in 1917. Córdoba, city and province, with its rich agricultural and industrial potential, should become the pivot between the prosperous Littoral and the sluggish Interior, funnelling the business demands of the one into the inert circulation system of the other. Ironically, by 1917, Cárcano was also regretting Argentina's failure to adopt the land-grant railroad policy as a major device for national development. The government had avoided following words with action, and lost a golden opportunity by neglecting to place direct responsibility on the railroads for the systematic colonization, at a fixed price, of land grants bordering their lines.[61]

In the 1920s, however, it was the Americans who most consistently deplored the railroads' feeble efforts to promote colonization, and the strength of the opposition in the Argentine Congress towards making them do so. In 1927, the US Chargé d'Affaires reported the creation of a new 'Argentine Railway Colonization Consortium', noting that representatives of the BA& Pacific, Great Southern, Central Argentine, Entre Rios, and other railway companies had met the President to formulate 'a general plan of colonization to be carried out by the railways themselves without direct financial assistance from the Argentine authorities'.[62] There was nothing further to report. Despite the long-term advantages of such a scheme to the companies and the country, the Minister observed two years later, when it came to taking on the job of colonization along their lines, the English-owned railways were 'all interest but no action'.

The wider implications:
Argentina fails to exploit its key location
in the Southern Cone

Argentina's future railway strategy was apparent by the end of the 1870s – railways would conserve, not innovate. Despite the new economic growth sustained by the enlarged rail network in the ensuing decades, the country's transport revolution introduced no comparable change to traditional social attitudes and practices. The result was that:

1 The railways assumed no direct, wide-ranging responsibility for attracting immigrants to Argentina, nor for encouraging small-scale landownership in the rural areas.
2 Notwithstanding the expanded agricultural production at Tucumán and Mendoza, the railways created no major new growth zones outside the Littoral, no counterbalance to the vastly increased power and influence of Buenos Aires and the Humid Pampa which the railways themselves helped to consolidate.
3 The railways promoted no significant new development of the dry lands, and created no 'New West' in Argentina.
4 The railways acquired no significant international role on the subcontinent, and promoted no new transcontinental growth in the Southland.

Argentina never implemented, or even clarified, a national railway policy beyond that of the need to service a narrowly-based export economy and keep foreign investment flowing into the pastoral and agricultural heartland of the Humid Pampa, less than one-tenth of the total national area. While the point is often made that the railways destroyed the old regional markets of the interior, that in itself was not crucial. Many of these colonial regional markets, though long on tradition, had remained backward and become increasingly isolated in the early nineteenth century. What really mattered was that in destroying the old markets, railways failed to create new ones in the interior. Earlier transcontinental trade routes with Chile and Peru declined; in the second half of the nineteenth century, the two most important products of the North and West – sugar from Tucumán and wines from Mendoza – were to be firmly tied to the domestic market of Buenos Aires.

The failure of the land-grant railroad model in the Southland continued to be regarded by American observers as one of Argentina's

major self-inflicted wounds. After the award made to the Central
Argentine Railway, only five other lines ever received land grants in a
country which, by 1914, boasted the greatest railway mileage in the
New World after the United States and Canada. In the late 1880s, land
grants had been made to the Santa Fe and Córdoba Great Southern
Railway, and also included in railway concessions made to Carlos
Casado in Santa Fe province, and to the Chubut Co. in Patagonia.
None matched the style or the aims of the pioneering Central
Argentine Railway's land grant. After the brief but remarkably
successful efforts of William Perkins, the net effect of the land-grant
railroad in Argentina was not to promote homesteads and owner–
occupation but to sell large blocks of land at inflated prices. As a result,
there was virtually no diversity of scale among the land speculators
other than large or very large operation; small-to-medium speculators
comprising small capitalists and yeoman farmers did not follow the
railroads across the Pampa.

In the United States, seventy-nine land-grant railroads were
authorized after 1850, twenty-one of which were direct beneficiaries of
Congress. The awards involved a total of some 200,000,000 acres, a
figure later reduced to around 158,000,000 acres following forfeitures
resulting from failure to comply with legal requirements. Of this, title
to more than 108,000,000 acres had been confirmed by 1907 – over 68
per cent of the total. The Illinois Central's pioneering land grant had
been 2,595,000 acres. Although not every railroad in the American
West was to receive a land grant, and among those which did, some
land remained unsold, the great primary penetration railroads
employed the land-with-transport principle on a huge scale and with
remarkable results: the Santa Fe (Atlantic & Pacific) system received
17,000,000 acres, the Union Pacific 20,000,000 acres, the Southern
Pacific (Central Pacific) system 24,000,000 acres, and the Northern
Pacific a record 44,000,000 acres.

Not that the land-grant railroad was problem-free or a panacea for
all ills. Abuses occurred, and lines were extended so quickly into
undeveloped sections of the West that not all could generate enough
traffic to survive. Overbuilding, railroad speculation and watered stock
were nothing new to the United States. Nevertheless, concluded
economists Cleveland and Powell in 1909,

> it must be said that land grants did contribute very largely toward the rapid
> upbuilding of the West, and that far-reaching political and economic

changes have been brought about in consequence. . . . It is also certain that a large part of the success of the Homestead Act has been due to the preliminary opening of unsettled areas by railroads constructed under stimulus of grants of land.[63]

The 1870s: the beginning of the end of the 'new' Argentina No understanding of the United States subsequent critical appraisal of Argentine railroad achievement can be grasped without due attention to America's own Western experience. At the end of the 1870s, Argentina's railway mileage was still limited – a mere 1,380 miles in 1879, with state-owned lines a substantial proportion of the total. In this crucially formative period, it was unfortunate that Argentina did not expropriate the Central Argentine Railway (as it threatened to do) and pursue the goals of a land-grant railroad with the help of experienced North Americans recruited for the purpose, together with administrators from the successful provincially-owned *Oeste* in Buenos Aires. The Argentine Government was already a major shareholder in the Central Argentine. It is often claimed, though not convincingly, that British investment would have ceased, or at least declined catastrophically, in railways that were not British-owned, British-managed, and protected for the most part by the fixed-income guarantees. Yet a strong case can be made for the complete abandonment of the system of government-guaranteed dividend by the end of the 1870s, with the requirement that railways become sufficiently profitable to attract private and public investors independently.

There were at least five matters of policy identified by Americans in future years that Argentina would have done well to find the will and the courage to enforce in the 1880s, having phased out the government guarantee, and embarked on a programme of national development in practice as well as in theory:

1 Insistence that railways give urgent and sustained attention to the creation of new freight and passenger traffic on all routes.
2 Greater use (though not exclusive use) of the land-grant railroad model, organized by those who knew how to operate the system successfully and who believed in its objectives.
3 A requirement that new railway construction in the Humid Pampa always be matched by some approved form of new construction on the frontier.
4 Greater determination to maintain a balance between state-owned and foreign-owned railways (though Americans disliked both

these types of ownership), but not one that produced the subsequent geographical split with the major foreign companies concentrated on the Humid Pampa, and the state-owned lines consigned to the remote frontier zones.

5 The adoption of a uniform standard (4'8½") gauge, with conversion of the relatively limited amount of track built on broad-gauge and narrow-gauge to the standard-gauge already introduced in Entre Rios. With the total length of track in Argentina still less than 1,500 miles at the end of the 1870s, the great expansion of a uniform network between 1880 and 1914 would have pioneered uninterrupted long-distance rail transport, both within Argentina and throughout the Southern Cone.

Some failures would undoubtedly have occurred, but not as many as it was convenient to assume if new business had been vigorously promoted. The strengths and weaknesses of the United States development model were already sufficiently apparent in the American West for Argentina to be able to pick and choose what could best be applied in the Southland.

Argentina needed to start taking risks at the end of the seventies. It did not do so. There were wars of words, and wars with Indians on the adjacent frontier regions, but genuine risk-taking was nowhere in evidence. So far as the railways were concerned, apart from the willingness to be persuaded that a government-guaranteed dividend of around 6–7 per cent was still essential to the uninterrupted flow of foreign loans for network expansion, there was strong opposition by many politically powerful groups to expropriation, not only of the Central Argentine, but to the whole principle of government involvement in running railways and public utilities. The Argentine elite lacked the desire, even when they could find the resources, to take over the railways. Yet at the end of the seventies, the skeletal rail network was well balanced, and strategically placed to form the foundation of internal regional development and controlled expansion beyond the Humid Pampa into the north, west, and south of Argentina, once the Indian threat had been removed.

The philosophy of building railroads quickly and cheaply into undeveloped territory, and promoting new business and new industry by a carefully integrated policy of land sales and settlement was never adopted. If the reasoning behind the US-style handling of the railroad as a developmental device was ever understood, it was never followed.

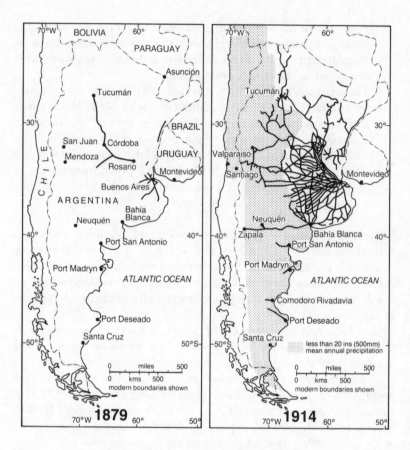

Figure 3 Argentina's railway network, 1879 and 1914

The lethargy and mismanagement of the Central Argentine Railway in the 1870s and 1880s helped to emphasize the image of 'shoddy' initial construction which had plagued the line from the beginning, and which petulant shareholders were only too ready to confirm as the source of all their troubles. The Buenos Ayres Great Southern was widely regarded in both Argentina and London as prosperous and efficient – a model of sound policies and good management in a frontier environment.

Yet no American would have recognized the Great Southern as a pioneering railroad, built to open and develop new lands. It played safe. It extended its lines slowly through what was potentially some of the most productive land in the New World, and then mainly to established settlements in the Humid Pampa where substantial volumes of traffic could be reliably predicted in advance. It did not see itself as an aggressive creator of new business; minimizing risk was of paramount concern. Financial safeguards in one form or another were demanded for new construction. Estimates of freight traffic were invariably modest, an inevitable consequence of the failure to give top priority to the creation and support of new business in new territory. As a result, shareholders' income was safeguarded primarily by high freight rates. The Great Southern's rates were having a crippling effect on traffic, one commentator noted in the mid-1880s: 'Ordinary rates are all but prohibitive as regards agricultural produce, as may be judged by the *offer* of traffic to the company if they could quote special rates.'

Unlike railroads in the United States and Canada, those in Argentina were slow to introduce new techniques for the storage and shipment of grain. They were also extremely reluctant to provide additional wagons at harvest time. Lack of adequate rolling stock at peak periods was a perennial complaint by Argentina against British companies. Although some of the state railways were also unsatisfactory in this respect, the British companies were felt to have the resources to enlarge their wagon fleets, and to double or treble their traffic if they did so. Predictably, the Great Southern and Central Argentine, among others, argued that the provision of more rolling stock merely resulted in cars lying idle for the rest of the year. United States railroad companies in similar situations looked for other business. They also took an early lead, unlike the railway companies in Argentina, in building grain elevators at local railroad stations, in disseminating information and raising standards among local farmers, and in promoting new techniques for cleaning, classification, and bulk storage. 'The marketing of wheat is conducted on the most wasteful methods', reported an American Midwestern observer in Argentina in 1899–1900, completely taken aback by the congestion at the ports, the exposed piles of sacked wheat left beside the railroad tracks, and the lack of adequate barns and storage elevators – in sum, the primitive arrangements still tolerated by one of the world's leading wheat exporters.[64] One of the most striking impressions to be gained from a study of the annual reports by the major British railway companies in Argentina over the years is the lack of any serious interest in providing technical and agricultural extension services for farmers until the 1920s. What was offered then, in scattered, fitful efforts to improve productivity, and to increase and diversify traffic after half a century of neglect by the railway companies, was too little and too late.

1880s–1920s In the 1880s, the railways' role in transporting Argentina's arable and livestock products direct to the ports and the international market gave strong regional identity and cohesion to the Humid Pampa. It also confirmed the measured, cautious style of the Great Southern, given to following, not initiating, demand, and content to make sound, steady profits in which reliability of dividend was the deciding factor. Higher profits could be made in banking, and in certain urban utilities and import–export houses, but the security of British railway investments in Argentina held a special attraction for the shareholders. British company policy preferred to convert increased profits into increased dividends. In the United States, provided railroads paid a steady 6 per cent or so in real terms, there was general expectation that profits would be ploughed back to finance improvements and new business expansion. Indeed, in the mid-1880s, following a burst of construction across the West, US railroads were estimated to be earning no more than 5 per cent on the total investment.[65]

In 1889, in a further move away from state ownership, the provincial government in Buenos Aires sold the *Oeste* railway to a newly created British company, the Buenos Ayres Western Railway. By 1890, state lines represented only 10 per cent of the total railroad investment capital. Under French and Argentine management, the *Oeste's* original six-mile line, opened in 1857, had expanded to nearly 730 miles, and become one of the most successful and competitively run railways in Argentina. It was a constant reminder that efficient railway operation was not a British prerogative. But whatever the ideological arguments or financial needs of the government in selling the *Oeste*, competition with the Great Southern had been the *Oeste's* undoing. The new London-based syndicate worked in close co-operation with the Great Southern, several of whose directors were on the board of the Buenos Ayres Western. The *Oeste's* plans (in 1887–89) to construct more than 900 miles of new line in Buenos Aires province were reshaped to provide clear, uncompeting zones of operation for the Great Southern and the Western.

This comparatively early zoning of territory was in marked contrast to the United States Western experience. Although early monopolies were not unknown – California's Central/Southern Pacific was a case in point – American railroad companies fought each other to penetrate rival areas, and often succeeded in doing so in the pioneering phase before amalgamation and corporate control. In Buenos Aires Province and the western lands, the elimination of competition was a feature of the pioneering phase itself. This was consistent with general British policy, which held to the view that new lines should be built by established railway companies. Competition was considered undesirable since it encouraged rate-cutting, which led to a deterioration of standards. Americans noted the frequency with which the British complained of 'unfair competition'. 'We call it "wholesome rivalry",' commented one US railroad economist; 'limitation of competition would seem to be opening the way for British railways to go to sleep with impunity.'[66]

By the late 1880s, however, the Great Southern, the Western, the Central Argentine, and the Buenos Ayres & Pacific – the 'Big Four' among the British-owned railway companies – had all secured their own catchment areas, while confirming the Humid Pampa as *the* sphere of safe, lucrative operation. With or without the government guarantee, the perception of railways as virtually automatic revenue producers was enhanced by the fact that none of the successful 'Big Four' companies was a genuine risk-taker. With the exception of the interest shown by the BA & Pacific in tapping the already well-established wine and fruit trade of the Mendoza region, none of the 'Big Four' had ventured beyond the most agriculturally and pastorally productive regions of Argentina located within 300–400 miles of Buenos Aires. By the late eighties and nineties, the Buenos Aires region itself was also generating soaring passenger revenues, as well as considerable freight traffic in response to demand for urban and port improvement. One way or another, it all added up to 'a paradise for the railroads', observed an American visitor. It was like 'spinning across a billiard table, where rails could be laid with wonderful rapidity and at very little cost'.

The general euphoria about railways led to the 'mania' of the late eighties, when between 1886 and 1890, the national and provincial governments between them awarded railway concessions for over 11,000 miles of new lines, most of them secured with an annual guarantee of 5 or 6 per cent. Few had ever been surveyed, and the majority were never intended to become operational. Scarcely anyone inside or outside the Argentine saw them as anything more than a device to attract foreign investors by means of the guaranteed dividend: 'Most of these concessions were given to English syndicates, with directories in London, and out of sight of their obligations here', wrote US Minister Hanna in 1888, in a highly critical report. 'They have given more attention to the collection of their coupons, than to the careful and enterprising operations of their investments.'[67] As J. H. Williams noted in a later analysis, not only had general inflation at this period blinded the government to the serious liabilities incurred in granting subsidies to lines which were likely to prove unprofitable, but 'the eagerness of British investors to absorb Argentine securities of all kinds was a strong inducement to promoters to obtain guaranteed concessions wherever possible'.[68] Two of the major criticisms traditionally levelled by Americans against guaranteed dividends as a method of promoting railroad construction in Argentina were summarized by J. S. Duncan: (1) The amount required from the government for topping-up dividends was unknown in advance and therefore difficult to budget for; (2) the railroad company, knowing its income was certain, had insufficient incentive to increase gross revenue or to decrease operating expenses. It was not difficult to arrange the accounting so that excess revenue, which was supposed to be repaid, did not occur at all.[69]

The guarantee system was not abolished until 1907, and then with such generous benefits in low taxation and import exemptions that the railways accepted the change with alacrity, and a second 'railway mania' was triggered between 1907 and 1914. While it is fair to say that the need to secure a reasonable return on investment was an entirely proper requirement on the part of the British-owned railway companies in Argentina, the method of achieving it encouraged a blend of caution and complacency in business management at a time when a much broader and more aggressive view of the country's needs was required. This was not the perception in London, however, nor in many of the most influential sectors of the River Plate community. The Great Southern's early abandonment of the guarantee had merely reflected the existing activity and rich potential of the Buenos Aires market and the Humid Pampa. Given the freedom from taxation at this time, and the government subsidy for new construction, the Southern's decision to free itself from the 7 per cent guarantee earned the company an accolade of outstanding efficiency and dynamic performance which it did not deserve. Nevertheless, the solid, dependable Great Southern became the style-setter in a generally receptive environment, although the Southern's elaborate construction and high working expenses evoked strong criticism from time to time even among English railway engineers, let alone among Americans.[70]

'Major expansion' by the Great Southern normally referred to extensions solely within the Humid Pampa. In 1895, as an isolated exception, the company responded to pressure from the central government to build a line across northern Patagonia from Bahía Blanca to Neuquén, via the middle Negro Valley, to facilitate troop movements to the Chilean border. The track took nearly four years to complete, by which time the immediate danger of war with Chile had passed. The Southern, however, had been given generous inducements, including a government grant of more than £150,000 towards building costs, right-of-way and other land, and a fifty-year exemption from import duties on all equipment used in the construction and subsequent operation of the line. As part of the agreement, the company was also given incentives to construct additional wharves and warehouses at Bahía Blanca. At the inauguration ceremony in 1899, President Roca praised the directors of the Great Southern for not having spared money, time, or effort in the building of the railway.[71] Turning the compliment around, however, it was a pity that the Southern had not *saved* money, time, and effort on the line, and been required to invest all three in a linked programme of pioneer regional development. There was no attempt at the time to couple this military-inspired penetration of the Dry Pampa fringe with new business promotion, significant new settlement, or systematic expansion of irrigation along the Negro Valley. Even so, both the Argentine Government and particularly the Great Southern were satisfied with what they had won from the deal.

Continued failure to provide adequate railroad infrastructure in the 'New West' North Americans who became familiar with the Southland continued to criticize the discrepancy between word and deed in Argentina's own assessments of its national development. They noted President Luis Sáenz Peña's announcement that, by the early nineties, the country's railways 'had brought civilization and progress even to the remote frontier regions', and failed to see any evidence for such a statement in the South, or in most of the West.[72] In 1907, they noted Emilio Mitre's defence of low railway taxation – 3 per cent of net income after a 60 per cent deduction for working expenses, sweetened still more by a new forty-year period of duty-free import for railway construction and operating materials – on the ground that Argentine railways were still 'in the cradle, in their infancy'.[73] But Argentine railways were not in the cradle; Argentina had been in the railway age for more than half a century. By 1907, there were 13,750 miles of railway, and by 1914, the second 'mania' of construction had pushed Argentina's total to almost 21,000 miles. The overwhelming impression among informed North American observers, however, was that this dramatic boom in construction had been concentrated in the existing 'no-risk' areas; for the most part, the powerful British companies in particular had stayed firmly within the old, well-trodden ways, servicing a lucrative but narrowly-based grain, meat and wool export economy still virtually confined to the Humid Pampa. Moreover, 'the permission given by Argentina ... to cripple the lines of communication within its borders by building railroads to different gauges is an economic blunder which has cost them more than any revolution'.[74] Given Argentina's climatic advantages compared with Canada, Australia, or parts of the trans-Mississippi West, given its seaboard location, fertility, level terrain, and population potential, the verdict was that the so-called 'United States of South America' was performing in a backward and short-sighted manner – in a most unAmerican manner too for a newly developing state with an enormous agenda.[75]

North Americans were not impressed by the fact that a prominent British railway journal of the 1880s had called the Buenos Ayres Great Southern 'one of the three finest lines in the world'. The dramatic railroad expansion in the American West during the 1880s (which had more than doubled the region's mileage in a single decade) had given a fresh edge to the merits of American-style railroad construction in the development of new territories – merits that Argentina had first heard argued by William Wheelwright and Allan Campbell in the 1850s–1860s. In one of the classic studies of American railroad engineering in the second half of the nineteenth century, A. M. Wellington again emphasized the appropriateness of American-style railroads in the opening of new lands. Though by no means uncritical of some United States lines, he saw nothing to commend in the expensive self-indulgence of so much railroad construction elsewhere:

> It is the complacent fashion of foreign critics to assume that American railways cost less because they are of inferior construction, ... but it is entirely possible to build both a *good* railway and a *cheap* one. In railways generally, both in design and construction, an enormous expenditure is incurred for purposes which are wholly unnecessary, and subserve no useful end. ...
>
> 'Rough Country' is a purely relative term. To the tyro, the rolling hillocks of Ohio, Michigan and New Jersey are rough. The same man, with a little experience in really rough country, will take the worst the Rocky Mountains or the Andes can offer with equanimity. ... No country in which most of the surface has a layer of soil over it deserves the name of rough. It needs but a little study and care to get several lines of reasonable cost through it.[76]

Wellington underlined the railroad's prime responsibility to create and sustain new economic growth on the frontier – to work quickly, and continue to add one type of enterprise to another as new ideas, new skills, and new investment increased land values and consolidated settlement. The railroad company had more to do 'than put up its buildings, and station a man at the receipt of customs. The railway company is like any one else with something to sell ... *its business is the selling of transportation*, and it is of vital importance to railways to make the largest possible sales of their wares.' Railroads were in the drumming business, and 'the object of the drumming business is *to get all the business possible*'.[77]

This emphasis on *business creation* on the frontier, so fundamental to the policies of America's Western railroads and so lacking in the pronouncements and performance of British railway companies in Argentina (except on the few occasions when they were coerced into action), meant that Americans anticipated, and generally made allowances for small gains and slow growth in marginal areas. Reviewing the great surge in railroad construction in the United States in the early 1880s, which included the expansion of new transcontinental railroads in the West, Hadley observed in 1885:

In the three years 1880–1882 we built 29,000 miles of railroads, an addition of thirty-four per cent to the railroad mileage of the country. Not more than one-third of these were justified by existing business. Another third, perhaps, were likely to be profitable at some future date, or at any rate to be of real service to the community; but not now.

Yet, Hadley continued, this was where the advantage of America's rapid, economical style of construction came into its own. There was nothing to be said in favour of railroads that found it 'easier to spend their surpluses in extra ornament or extra salaries, than in reducing rates'.[78]

The voice of the American West became more authoritative as, by the late nineteenth century, it became the voice of experience. If the railroads did not do their own pioneering in the wilderness, nothing and nobody else could do so on the scale required. The US railroad engineer, E. B. Dorsey, was more disturbed by what English-style railways, equipped with traditional English rolling-stock, were leaving undone in new lands than he was impressed by their expensive engineering. England's inability 'to rush the railroad through' and start work immediately on creating traffic, however modest, was a constant irritant to American railroad men who observed 'this serious deficiency' at first hand. With comparative evidence now before them, South American railway specialists were beginning to agree. In the early nineties, J. J. Castro concluded that Argentina would have done better 'to adopt *the American plan of railway construction and lay down the greatest number of kilometers with the smallest capital possible. . . .* Improvement is made as the traffic grows.'[79]

The need for a greater sense of urgency in Argentina was again made forcibly by the American engineer Bailey Willis, who in 1911–13 was employed by the Argentine Government to undertake railway survey work in Northern Patagonia. Willis brought a lifetime's experience to the task, both as a senior member of the US Geological Survey, and as an engineer and surveyor assigned to work in the early eighties on what was then America's most northerly transcontinental railroad, the Northern Pacific. In some of the most difficult mountain terrain in the Northwest, Willis had been involved in selecting routeways, evaluating resources tributary to the line, and estimating potential freight traffic. Later, he was a strong supporter of the campaign to create, in 1899, the Mount Rainier National Park.

The prospect of helping to promote new frontier development in

Argentina made a strong appeal to Bailey Willis. A 400-mile, broad-gauge government railroad was to be built from Port San Antonio on the Atlantic coast to Lake Nahuel Huapí in the Andean Cordillera, and after three years, British-trained Argentine engineers had surveyed the first 125 miles across the relatively easy terrain west of the port. Willis was asked to assist in locating the railroad through the canyonlands beyond, sticking closely to the existing specification. 'It was a question of getting grades and curves demanded by standard construction on European lines,' the American noted with some impatience. 'Had we adhered to such requirements in the West we never would have crossed the Rockies.' Willis and his team surveyed several routes, recommending economy. 'However, orders came from the Director General de Ferrocarriles in Buenos Aires to follow the more difficult line.' The Yankee complied: 'We designed a corkscrew with a tunnel.'[80]

In his official report to the Argentine Government in 1914, Willis regretted that European standards of engineering practice, which required 'a thoroughly permanent character' from the start, ruled out temporary construction and rapid progress. 'This policy differs from that of many North American railroads projected in similar undeveloped regions, where the practice is to push the construction forward as rapidly and as cheaply as possible, with a view to securing traffic and obtaining some return upon the investment at the earliest possible date.' If that policy had been followed in this case, Willis emphasized, there was every likelihood that the San Antonio Railroad could have been completed to Lake Nahuel Huapí by 1913.[81] (As it was, the line remained less than one-quarter completed by that date, and did not reach Bariloche until 1934.) Time lost by using the British approach delayed the start of co-ordinated regional development, and left the project vulnerable over a longer period to fluctuating world money markets, and to domestic changes of policy and diverted funds. Argentina took such a limited view of its national territory, Willis noted, and even in the twentieth century still exaggerated distances in a quite extraordinary manner. 'Even in Buenos Aires, people speak of Patagonia as far away, ... yet Lago Nahuel Huapí, the principal feature of the future national park in the Andes, is no farther from the metropolis of South America than ... Denver from Chicago.'[82]

Following United States practice, Willis and his team had also reported on the development potential of the region tributary to the new railroad, surveying and mapping branch lines and a new route into Chile, new zones of improved pasture and irrigated agriculture, and a

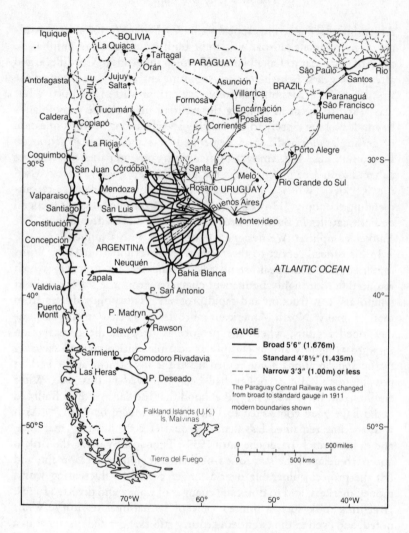

Figure 4 Railway gauge diversity in southern South America, 1920

major new site for a hydroelectric power station and manufacturing centre. Back in Buenos Aires in 1914, however, Willis soon discovered that the Great Southern Railway was strongly opposed to these initiatives, including greater expansion of the State railways in Patagonia. Further regional development, if any, would be sponsored and controlled by the Great Southern's own line to Neuquén which, between 1910 and 1913, had been extended west for another 116 miles to Zapala after the company had seen government plans for the three new 'Development Railways' to be built in Patagonia. The Great Southern's general manager, 'a blunt English businessman', invited Willis to call on him and explain his proposals. 'As I rose to go,' Willis recalled, 'the Manager remarked: "No doubt your work is of much value. But you will understand that it is not to the interest of the Ferrocarril Sud that the National Railways should be extended." I understood. I felt the weight of the British lion's paw.'[83]

The problem of the first transcontinental railway

> A railroad not put through to its ultimate destination is largely a worthless affair. Instead of reaching a seaport or an important terminal it simply runs up a tree.[84]

In July 1872, the US Chargé d'Affaires Dexter Clapp was pleased to report the official celebration in Buenos Aires to mark the completion by J&M Clark of the first telegraph link between Argentina and Chile: 'This is the forerunner of a Railroad over the same route.' The transcontinental vision would become reality. President Sarmiento had called a national holiday, messages were exchanged with Santiago, and the principal guest of honour, William Wheelwright, was warmly praised for his early pioneering enterprise in developing South America's telegraphs, steamships, and railroads.

More ominous was the separate but simultaneous report by Robert Crawford, chief engineer on the Transandine Railway Survey expedition of 1871–72. As he passed through Buenos Aires en route to the Cordillera, Crawford found that already 'the original popularity of the Transandine scheme [among the national and provincial governments] was decidedly on the wane'.[85] A proposal to extend the *Oeste* to Santiago and Valparaiso via the Planchón Pass had been presented to Congress in September 1867, and soon one of the company's locomotives running to the end-of-track settlement of Chivilcoy, 100 miles beyond Buenos Aires, was proudly carrying the name *Voi a Chili*.[86] By October 1867, the US Minister reported keen interest in the project, and growing rivalry between Buenos Aires and Rosario for control of the western routeway, noting that Rosario was pressing for a branch line to Chile to be constructed from the Central Argentine Railway at Villa Nueva in order to forestall the *Oeste's* ambitions. By the early seventies, however, neither the *Oeste* nor the Central Argentine and its feeders was displaying any interest in extending beyond the Andean foothill zone. In the eighties, the same could be said of the *Oeste's* successor, the Buenos Ayres Western, and even of the so-called Buenos Ayres & Pacific Railway, which was registered in London in 1882 with the 7 per cent government guarantee, but which effectively confined its far western interests to the three Cuyo wine, fruit, and alfalfa-producing provinces of Mendoza, San Juan and San Luis. Shareholders were assured 'that the Company would have nothing to do with the work of piercing the Andes'.[87]

The old oasis settlement of Mendoza had eventually been reached by the government's *Andino* railway in 1885, more than thirty years after Lieutenant MacRae, USN had first encountered Mendoza's optimism about the early construction of the line. A special celebratory excursion marked the official opening of the *Andino* in Mendoza and San Juan, and US Minister Thomas O. Osborn found the whole journey to the foothills one of his happiest and most memorable experiences in Argentina. Nothing had reminded him so vividly of a railroad trip across the American West. 'The road is equipped with American cars and locomotives, and it was with peculiar national pride that I witnessed most of the party, for the first time, introduced to the magnificent Pullman Sleepers – seven in number made in the United States, and which did us such good service on our journey.'[88] Much of the barren land through which they had travelled could be made productive if irrigated; the government was talking seriously now about the 'Transcontinental Railway' to Santiago and Valparaiso – all told, Osborn felt he had good reason to be positive about the future of the region.

Responsibility for the construction of Argentina's portion of the transandean railway had been passed to the Buenos Ayres & Valparaiso Transandine Railway Co., registered in London in 1886, and charged with the completion of a 111-mile, metre-gauge line from Mendoza to the Chilean boundary via the Uspallata Pass. Alternative passes through the Andes had been discarded in favour of the traditional colonial routeway, despite its unsuitability in terms of elevation and severe snow accumulation. The track climbed steeply from a height of 2,375 feet at Mendoza to 10,471 feet at Summit Tunnel. Exposure and sharp gradients were even more of a problem on the Chilean side; in all, six sections of rack-rail were required. The first fifty-seven miles out of Mendoza were opened in 1891, but funds became increasingly hard to attract in the nineties, and work was not fully resumed in both Chile and Argentina until 1904. Through-traffic by rail began only in April 1910 with completion of the two-mile tunnel at the international boundary, beneath the Uspallata Pass.

Meanwhile, the Buenos Ayres & Pacific Railway had established a controlling interest in the Argentine foothill zone in 1907 by taking over the rapidly expanding broad-gauge network in the Cuyo provinces owned by a rival British company, the Argentine Great Western, and also by agreeing to manage the Argentine Transandine Railway (formerly known as the Buenos Ayres & Valparaiso Transandine Railway), then nearing completion. In 1909, following an approach from the Argentine Government, the Buenos Ayres & Pacific consolidated its control of the Cuyo traffic by acquiring the portion of the *Andino* railway west of Río Cuarto.

All this emphasis on network consolidation east of the Andes merely confirmed the North American view that the Southland's first transcontinental railroad had 'run up a tree'. From the start, the Transandine Railway was unsatisfactory both as a *transandean* and as a *transcontinental* connection. Apart from the lack of uniform gauge and administration, insufficient snowsheds and snowploughs often resulted in annual closure in May or June for up to six months at a time, even longer in bad years. Americans in particular drew attention to the fact that any earlier intention to make the line a going concern had been undermined by the failure to cope at the outset with the snow problem. They recalled that the variable patterns of snow accumulation in the Andes had even influenced Wheelwright's plans for locating the first transcontinental railway back in the 1850s. On a journey through South America in April 1889, US Special Commissioner J. C. Walker was instructed to report to the State Department on the progress being made on the transcontinental railroad. He followed the various segments of the route from Santiago to Buenos Aires, and recorded discussions with engineers near the Uspallata Pass where *over five miles* of tunnel were being planned. Walker was optimistic about the future value of the railroad; the journey had reminded him of the

American West.[89] American travellers were later to be less impressed by the comparison – 'The Central Pacific Railroad built over 40 miles of snowshed in the 1860s in the Sierra Nevada for the first trans-continental railroad,' complained one, kicking his heels during an interrupted journey; 'Crossing the Andes is not a greater railroad undertaking than crossing the Rockies.' What's more, he added, '*There should be one gauge from ocean to ocean.*' Another passenger, having endured a series of delays on the Argentine side, could only numbly record his astonishment

> that a closer agreement has not been arrived at with the Chilian State Railway, which takes up the journey from Los Andes to Santiago and Valparaiso. … It is just a little irritating on a somewhat belated arrival at Los Andes, after the completion of seven-eighths of the journey, to find that the train which should have effected the last lap has already left.[90]

Lack of funds had forced the engineers to push the rails higher and reduce the tunnelling while ignoring American advice to increase snowshed provision in wood or stone. Rock falls, mud flows, and flooding also damaged track and bridges with such monotonous frequency that the company balance-sheet became a nightmare. The route soon became little more than a minor tourist attraction, with passengers accepting mule, horse, or stagecoach transport through the mountains, wherever sections of the track were closed, as part of an Andean adventure. Before long, such excitements had been abandoned in favour of motor transport, supplemented in the 1930s by the PANAGRA air service, while the Argentine and Chilean governments set up interminable working parties to investigate, without much enthusiasm, how continuous rail communication might be restored. Apart from the delays due to weather conditions and variations in gauge, travellers who were accustomed to smooth long-distance through-traffic in Europe and North America complained of lack of co-ordination on the Transandine. Despite some effort to integrate the service after 1923, the feeling persisted that South America's transcontinental line had been cobbled together from a Chilean system and an Argentine system, with nothing but trouble in between.

Freight traffic remained negligible – mostly Argentine flour, together with small quantities of timber, miscellaneous foodstuffs and domestic items. Freight was always second to passenger traffic as the Transandine's source of revenue, averaging less than 38,000 tons annually between

1910 and 1932, and less than half that figure by 1934 when heavy financial losses, coupled with severe snowfall and flooding, led to prolonged closure. Passenger traffic offered little to cushion the disastrous freight record. The peak years for passenger movement were the two opening years – 346,612 passengers in 1910, and 351,962 in 1911. After that, the novelty factor began to wear off, there was little railway company promotion, and fewer than 18,000 through-passengers were recorded in 1920. By the early thirties, annual first- and second-class passenger traffic had slumped to around 16,000.[91]

While the Transandine Railway reports made gloomy reading, its managing company, the Buenos Ayres & Pacific Railway, welcomed the growth of the Cuyo wine and fruit traffic along its own section of line in the early years of the twentieth century. Even before the delayed completion and dismal performance of the Transandine Railway (as well as tariff barriers) had reduced the commercial potential of new trade with Chile, the effect of terminating Argentina's broad-gauge system at the foot of the Andes had proved decisive. The completion of the rail link in 1885 had turned Mendoza and San Juan firmly to the east, and by establishing unified control of formerly three separate railway companies in 1907, the BA & Pacific had greatly strengthened the influence and authority of Buenos Aires in the foothill zone. Cuyo wines, fruit, vegetables, and even livestock now found their market around the River Plate as the railway narrowed the physical frontier of separation between the Cordillera and the Littoral formerly created by the Dry Pampa. Transandean trade between the 'edge-settlements' of Argentina and the Pacific slope which had survived from colonial times to the pre-railroad age declined almost to extinction. The international boundary between Chile and Argentina had become more divisive, more consciously Andean; paradoxically, the Transandine Railway served to separate rather than join, and to confirm the increasingly theoretical nature of the link between the two states. Military, political, and commercial considerations demanded fast rail transport to selected points on the Argentine western border-land, not on the Pacific. Argentina was content, like the Buenos Ayres & Pacific Railway, to popularize the company's regular abbreviation – 'the Pacific' – but at the same time to confine whatever interests they both claimed to have in that Ocean to the eastern foothills of the Andes.

The initiatives for transcontinental rail linkage belonged to Argentina, given the contrasted size of the two countries, and the greater range and thrust of railway construction and investment on the eastern side. Although it has been argued that the main objective of the Buenos Ayres & Pacific Railway's policy remained the consolidation of its hold upon the trunk route to Chile,[92] there is no real evidence that this was the case. The elimination of rail competition *to* and *within* the central Argentine foothill zone was always crucial to the company, and efforts were made to stimulate trade and diversify production in the Cuyo provinces in the 1920s. But there were no sustained initiatives by the Buenos Ayres & Pacific to capitalize on the through-route to Chile, or, as a matter of policy, to boost freight and passenger traffic on the international line. In 1882, the company had simply acquired the 360-mile Mercedes-Villa Mercedes portion of what, in the heady days of the early 1870s, had been a contract awarded to John Clark to build Argentina's share of the transcontinental railway in two sections: one from Buenos Aires to Mendoza–San Juan, the second a westward transandean continuation to the Chilean border, to link with the line to Valparaiso. The plains section had always been regarded as the profit-maker – in construction as well as traffic. Indeed, when the US Minister in Santiago first saw the proposed construction costs on the Argentine side in 1874, he informed Washington that from his own experience in the railroad business, the line across the Pampas could be built at *less than half* the estimates agreed to by the Argentine Government, and backed by the 7 per cent guarantee.[93] Aside from a few early general statements by the Buenos Ayres & Pacific about the possibilities of expanding trade with Chile (chiefly in live cattle), the physical and political problems of working the international line soon reinforced the company's traditional view that the mountain railway into Chile was a tiresome distraction from its main regional concerns. In 1923, the Buenos Ayres & Pacific rid itself of the 1907 agreement to manage the Argentine Transandine Railway Co., and was extremely reluctant to mount a rescue operation in the 1930s.

Even Chile and Argentina never seemed to know why they were building the Transandine Railway. It became a symbolic, apparently unavoidable exercise which neither state, despite, or because of, their mutual distrust of each other, appeared willing to be the first to abandon. The idea had been initially attractive; optimism about a transcontinental railway between Chile and Argentina is a striking feature of the literature in the late 1860s and early 1870s. Of course, William Wheelwright's personality and influence were still strong at this time, but there was plenty of evidence in the writings of both

British and American travellers and officials that they were confident the work would go ahead, whichever route was finally selected. One remarkable reflection of the mood is found in the frequency with which maps of the whole of the Southern Cone from the Pacific to the Atlantic coasts were included in books and pamphlets of this period, maps on which trails and proposed railways were marked, and a sense of long-distance movement and linked interior development in both Chile and Argentina clearly conveyed. Such maps became virtually non-existent by the late seventies. After that, the preoccupation with 'national' area and 'national' rail nets determined the cartographers' frameworks, and nowhere was this loss of the continental perspective more damaging than in the Southland.

New proposals from the West Coast with the opening of the Panama Canal The United States had soon dropped the image of its own first transcontinental railroad as 'the passage to India'. The opening of the Suez Canal in 1869, just six months after the completion of the Pacific Railroad, removed the possibility at that time of the United States diverting much of the Oriental trade away from the traditional routes in the Old World. The result was that even greater attention was given to the role of transcontinental railroads in the United States and Canada as agents of national cohesion and internal development. With this in mind, L. E. Elliott of New York emphasized that South America should not allow the opening of the Panama Canal (in 1914) to diminish the pressing importance of building more coast-to-coast railways in the Southern Cone: 'No one with knowledge of the internal needs of South America doubts the necessity for strengthened transcontinental links.'[94]

One may sympathize with the opinion of many South Americans, Argentines particularly in this case, that North Americans under-estimated the importance of international boundaries. North Americans, it was argued, forever tiresomely praising the virtues of transcontinental railroads, would do better to absorb the fact that the states in the Southern Cone did not stretch 'From Sea to Shining Sea'. Chile, however, took the initiative. Spurred on by the building of the Panama Canal, as well as by the construction of the Arica–La Paz Railway up to Bolivia in 1906–13, and the extension of the Antofagasta & Bolivia Railway to La Paz in 1917, Chile gave urgent attention to the exploration of new transandean routes into Argentina, particularly those to the south of the Uspallata line, where passes through the

Cordillera were much lower. 'The Uspallata Pass is one of the worst of the Andean "gateways"', reported an American engineer visiting Chile in 1913. The reason for its selection could only have been an unwillingness to break with tradition; there was nothing to commend it as the route for the trail-blazing transcontinental railroad. During the early years of the twentieth century, a further eighteen Andean passes were explored or re-examined with a view to railway construction. From among these, by 1914, Chile had made preliminary surveys, and given wide publicity to fifteen possible railway routes through the Andes into Argentina, three of which were specifically linked to Argentine lines, either proposed or under construction:

1 *The Mejillones/Antofagasta–Salta Transcontinental* was to be the most northerly line, although the final choice of the Socompa Pass (12,657 feet) was delayed until 1923.

2 *The Talcahuano/Concepción–Bahía Blanca Transcontinental* was to link the Buenos Ayres Great Southern line at Neuquén and Zapala to a branch of the Chilean Central (Longitudinal) State Railway run from Curacautín. It would use the Pino Hachado Pass (6,100 feet), need no rack sections, and be on continuous broad-gauge throughout.

3 *The Valdivia–San Antonio Transcontinental* was to link with the Argentine State Railway being extended from Port San Antonio across Northern Patagonia to Lake Nahuel Huapí. Bailey Willis had surveyed a practical railroad pass into Chile (El Cajón Negro, 4,459 feet) as part of his development programme for the region, prepared in 1911–13. This line was also to be on continuous broad-gauge and rack-free, joining the Chilean Central State Railway just north of Osorno.

It would be difficult to exaggerate the enthusiasm for these proposals shown by many Chilean officials at this time. American and European travellers also praised them as a welcome step forward – indeed, reference to the plans for the new lines became a regular feature of books and articles published on southern South America between 1910 and the early 1920s. For the first time in fifty years, maps showing future transcontinental rail routes across the Southern Cone, linking Chile and Argentina, became commonplace.

In London in 1917, the Chilean Minister Agustín Edwards, attending a lecture at the Royal Geographical Society, discussed the new opportunities now available to his country as a result of the completion

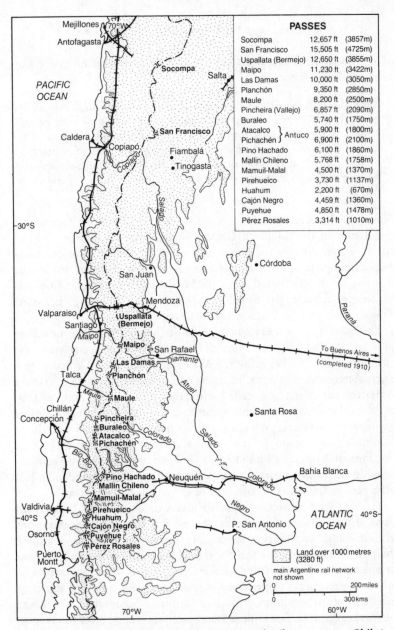

PASSES

Pass		
Socompa	12,657 ft	(3857m)
San Francisco	15,505 ft	(4725m)
Uspallata (Bermejo)	12,650 ft	(3855m)
Maipo	11,230 ft	(3422m)
Las Damas	10,000 ft	(3050m)
Planchón	9,350 ft	(2850m)
Maule	8,200 ft	(2500m)
Pincheira (Vallejo)	6,857 ft	(2090m)
Buraleo	5,740 ft	(1750m)
Atacalco	5,900 ft	(1800m)
Pichachén	6,900 ft	(2100m)
Pino Hachado	6,100 ft	(1860m)
Mallin Chileno	5,768 ft	(1758m)
Mamuil-Malal	4,500 ft	(1370m)
Pirehueico	3,730 ft	(1137m)
Huahum	2,200 ft	(670m)
Cajón Negro	4,459 ft	(1360m)
Puyehue	4,850 ft	(1478m)
Pérez Rosales	3,314 ft	(1010m)

Atacalco } Pichachén } Antuco

Land over 1000 metres (3280 ft)

main Argentine rail network not shown

0   200 miles
0   300 kms

To Buenos Aires →
(completed 1910)

Figure 5 Andean routeways and transcontinental railway surveys, Chile/ Argentina, 1900–14. Feasibility studies for new transandean rail connection at this time were sponsored mainly by Chile, and concentrated on the lower passes of the southern Andes.

101

of the Panama Canal, and the proposed development of new transcontinental railways:

> With the opening of the Panama Canal it is only natural that all the
> products of Western Argentina should find their way to the sea through
> Chile. At the beginning, raw material on its way to the markets of the
> United States and Europe; afterwards, in the course of a very few years, the
> abundant raw material from the Argentine Republic will be transformed in
> Chile into more valuable products, using our iron, ... coal, ... and water-
> power.[95]

Not surprisingly, Chilean interest in a new 'reverse' continental
circulation in the Southern Cone sounded warning bells in Buenos
Aires. While North American scholars in Argentina were currently
emphasizing the potential importance of new railroad expansion
westward and southward from Bahía Blanca,[96] Argentina itself was
becoming increasingly hostile to the idea of boosting any new
Transandean–Pacific Coast–Panama Canal connection.

The hostility was temporarily set aside, however, in the immediate
post-war period as a new wave of American investors arrived in the
Southern Cone. In 1919, the US Minister in Buenos Aires reported a
dramatic revival of interest in transcontinental railroads after visiting
American capitalists had made it clear that such projects were vital to
the Southland's regional development, and would be among the most
popular in attracting American investment: 'In order to facilitate
commercial expansion, ... it is essential that the southern and northern
portions of Argentina be linked to Chile by transandine rail connection.' In such an atmosphere, Buenos Aires had been persuaded to dust
off a few of the plans on file, and to show some enthusiasm.[97]

The image of underdevelopment was now dominating US perceptions of the Southern Cone. Aside from a few scattered concentrations
of economic activity (far fewer, and much more widely scattered
than Americans new to the Southland had been expecting), it was
astonishing to discover, one of them reported in 1923, the extent to
which the resources in the interior provinces were still lying dormant
for lack of proper transportation facilities. Some took the point
further, suggesting that United States interests should offer to invest in
the surveying and construction of the most difficult sections of new
transcontinental railroads across the Cordillera in Chile and Argentina,
with an optional arrangement to run the lines once completed. With an
eye on more favourable opportunities for market penetration on

the West Coast, there was clear support for Chilean initiatives in proposing new transcontinental links, since Americans both in Chile and Argentina continued to dismiss the existing Transandine Railway as nothing more than an expensive showpiece, capable of handling only seasonal passenger traffic, light freight, and express packages. The real work-horse transcontinental railroads would be built to the north and the south.

A northern line had been earmarked as a priority as long ago as the 1850s by William Wheelwright, whose name and transcontinental transport strategy were now frequently recalled by American commentators in the 1920s. The growth of the Atacama nitrate industry had subsequently shifted the Chilean end of the proposed transcontinental rail route northward from Wheelwright's original terminus at Caldera–Copiapó to the larger port of Antofagasta, but the railroad's significance as a *transcontinental*, not merely as a *transandean*, line was still fundamental to Americans' perception of its purpose. An Antofagasta–Salta railroad would not only bring livestock and agricultural produce from the Argentine Pampas to the West Coast market, it would also open up rich mining country on both sides of the Andes, and encourage new irrigated agriculture and commercial activity in a moribund interior. The failure of Chile and Argentina to develop a mining frontier straddling the Southern Cone was always regarded as a major limiting factor when compared with the North American experience. And though the nitrate industry was declining in the 1920s, the varied mineral resources of this broad expanse of the Cordilleran mountain-and-foothill zone were still virtually untapped. A rail link between Antofagasta and Salta would also introduce an element of regional competition with the powerful British-owned and operated Antofagasta (Chili) and Bolivia Railway Co., which in 1908 had absorbed rival American railroad interests on the Bolivian altiplano, and by the 1920s exercised monopoly control over the bulk of Bolivia's mineral export trade.[98] Americans welcomed the enthusiasm shown by the citizens of Antofagasta and Salta in the proposed rail link between them, reporting the creation in 1920 of vigorous lobby groups in both towns to promote the 'Pacific Railroad'.

In the early 1920s, therefore, American observers perceived a reawakening of interest in transcontinental rail links across the Southern Cone, links that would foster long overdue internal regional development, and at the same time offer opportunities for American investment and commerce. Chile at least was abandoning the 'Chinese Wall' image of the Andes; influential sections of the press now emphasized Chile's potential as a 'continental carrier' between the Atlantic and the Pacific trade. Under the Alessandri administration, reported the US Minister in Santiago, Chile was showing more interest in new transandean railroads than at any time since the Balmaceda era.[99] But the euphoria was not to last. Before long, American officials were recording growing opposition to the Antofagasta–Salta line in both Chile and Argentina. The powerful landowning class in central Chile, supplying foodstuffs to the northern nitrate centres, were blocking any attempt to open that lucrative market to the Pampas suppliers. In Atacama, the trade in live cattle trailed over the Andes from Salta was all that Chilean agriculturalists were prepared to tolerate from Argentina. 'They ignore the fact that they are unable to supply all the needs of the nitrate areas', complained the American Consul in Antofagasta, who reported the huge coastwise import of agricultural products into northern Chile from Peru and Ecuador. As a result, Pacific shipping interests were also opposed to any reduction in their trade. That was the trouble, the Consul observed wearily; there was no atmosphere of business creation, no willingness to make the promotion of increased traffic on *all* routes a central theme of regional development. But hostility to a Salta–Antofagasta rail link was also growing in Argentina, where railway and other dominant interest groups in Buenos Aires were opposed to 'the deflection of agricultural products from the northern districts westward into Chile'.[100]

Ironically, the only major railway construction in the Americas that was stimulated by the opening of the Panama Canal was in Florida. Determined to link Key West to the United States rail network and tap new trade in Cuba and the Caribbean, entrepreneur Henry Flagler completed his spectacular 156-mile railroad through the Everglades and the Florida Keys, from the existing railhead in Miami, in 1912.

In Argentina, however, tightened money markets and trade depression in the late 1920s reinforced the country's unwillingness to promote transcontinental rail linkage in the Southland, which, it was reasoned, would advance the interests only of Chile and the United States, to the detriment of those of Buenos Aires. A flow of studies from the USA analysed the scope of the new American commercial offensive in the continent as a whole in the early twentieth century; the popularity of such titles as 'From Panama to Patagonia' confirmed

Argentina's worst fears, and strengthened its resolve to foster the Atlantic rather than the Pacific connection. In the twenties and thirties, no gaps were closed, no 'last spike' celebrations held, no new transcontinental railroads crossed the Andes.

With Chile and Argentina looking in opposite directions more determinedly than ever, the isolation of the Southern Cone was emphasized rather than modified by the opening of the Panama Canal. Given Argentina's size and pivotal location, the country's antipathy to economic development and integration of the Southland as a whole, spearheaded by transcontinental railroads and colonization, marked the end of a particular style of growth and opportunity in the Far South so far as many Northerners were concerned. In the words of one American writing in the 1920s, and well acquainted with the American West and with Argentina:

The rail network stops somewhat abruptly at the western border of the Pampa. Beyond are a few threads of space-traversing lines ... there is no continuous development of new western lands that will continue in the future as it has gone on in the past. Rather it is a chapter in Argentine development that is now closed.[101]

Notes

1 J. B. Alberdi, *The Life and Industrial Labors of William Wheelwright in South America*, Boston, 1877, pp. 24–5.
2 W. Wheelwright, 'Proposed railway route across the Andes, from Caldera in Chile to Rosario on the Paraná, via Córdova', *Journal of the Royal Geographical Society*, XXXI, 1861, pp. 154–62. (Read to the Society 23 Jan. 1860.)
3 Quoted by Alberdi, *Life and Industrial Labors*, pp. 133–4.
4 D. Stevenson, *Sketch of the Civil Engineering of North America*, London, 1838, pp. 192–3, 195.
5 *Ibid.*, pp. 258–9.
6 *Journal of the Franklin Institute of the State of Pennsylvania*, VI, 1830, pp. 178–93.
7 E. Hungerford, *The Story of the Baltimore and Ohio Railroad, 1827–1927*, New York, 1928, I, pp. 62–3.
8 E. W. Watkin, *A trip to the United States and Canada*, London, 1852, pp. 122, 124.
9 'Railway-engineering in the United States', *The Atlantic Monthly*, II, 1858, pp. 644–5.

10 Stevenson, *Sketch of the Civil Engineering*, pp. 253–4.

11 Capt. D. Galton, RE, *Report to the Lords of the Committee of Privy Council for Trade and Foreign Plantations, on the Railways of the United States*, presented to both Houses of Parliament by Command of Her Majesty, London, 1857, p. 4.

12 Watkin, *A trip*, pp. 120–1; Galton, *Report*, p. 11.

13 Watkin, *A trip*, p. 121.

14 J. B. Alberdi, *Bases y Puntos de partida para la organización política de la República Argentina*, Buenos Aires, 1852, pp. 42–4.

15 Allan Campbell, *Report to His Excellency Dr. Don Santiago Derqui, Minister of the Interior, on the Survey of the Paraná and Córdova Railway, with estimates, maps, plans, and profiles*, Rosario, Argentine Confederation, 30 Nov.1855, pp. 20, 29–33, 36–44, and *passim*.

16 T. C. Clarke, 'The building of a railway', in *The Railways of America: their construction, development, management, and appliances*, London and New York, 1890, p. 10.

17 R. C. Kirk to US Secretary of State, Buenos Aires, 30 March 1863, *Diplomatic Despatches from U.S. Ministers to Argentina, General Records of the Dept. of State, Record Group 59*, Washington, D.C.

18 J. Fair, *Some Notes on my earlier connection with the Buenos Ayres Great Southern Railway*, Bournemouth, 1899, p. 9.

19 W. Hadfield, *Brazil and the River Plate in 1868*, London, 1869, pp. 146–8; and *Brazil and the River Plate, 1870–76*, Sutton, Surrey and London, 1877, p. 226.

20 Hadfield, *Brazil ... 1868*, p. 146; *The Times*, 6 Feb. 1869, 17 Feb. 1869, 20 Nov. 1869, 27 May 1870.

21 Fair, *Some Notes*, Appendix.

22 W. Wheelwright to T. Brassey, London, 4 April 1864. (Correspondence in A. Helps, *Life and Labours of Mr. Brassey, 1805–1870*, London, 1872, p. 369.)

23 Public Record Office, *BT 31/14352/1049*.

24 Hadfield, *Brazil ... 1868*, pp. 115, 120.

25 *Ibid.*, pp. 122, 265.

26 W. Wheelwright to R. C. Kirk, Buenos Aires, 13 May 1866, enclosed in *Diplomatic Despatches from U.S. Ministers to Argentina, General Records of the Dept. of State, Record Group 59*, Washington, D.C.

27 W. Wheelwright to US Secretary of State, Rosario, 5 Mar. 1868; Buenos Aires, 8 July 1868; *Despatches from U.S. Consuls in Rosario, Argentina, General Records of the Dept. of State, Record Group 59*, Washington, D.C.

28 R. A. Seymour, *Pioneering in the Pampas*, London, 1869, Preface, pp. 74–5, 131–2, 153–5.

29 Galton, *Report*, pp. 6–7, 3.

30 P. W. Gates, *The Illinois Central Railroad and its Colonization Work*, Cambridge, Mass., 1934, p. 149.

31 Quoted by Gates, *ibid.*, p. 182.

32 *Ibid.*, p. 114.

33 From *A Circular of Instructions to Examiners of Illinois Central Railroad Lands*, Chicago, 12 Feb. 1855; see Gates, pp. 167–8.

34 W. Perkins, *Three Years in California, 1849–52 (The Journal of William Perkins, life at Sonora, 1849–52*, ed., with Introduction, by D. L. Morgan and J. R. Scobie, Berkeley, California, 1964). Written in English, the *Journal* was translated into Spanish by Perkins's daughter, and first published in Buenos Aires in 1937.

35 W. Perkins, *The Colonies of Santa Fe; their origin, progress, and present condition, with general observations on emigration to the Argentine Republic*, Rosario de Santa Fe, 1864.

36 Perkins, *Journal*, pp. 50–1. See also Perkins's personal collection, *Artículos varios* (Archives, Biblioteca Argentina, Rosario). Also J. J. Gschwind, *Guillermo Perkins, su contribución al progreso económico argentino*, Rosario, 1936.

37 *The Brazil & River Plate Mail*, 7 Jan. 1867; *The Standard*, 8 and 14 June 1867. See also G. Wilcken, *Las Colonias. Informe sobre el estado actual de las Colonias Agrícolas de la República Argentina, presentado a la Comisión Central de Inmigración por el Inspector Nacional de ellas, 1872*, Buenos Aires, 1873, pp. 133–6.

38 Wilcken, *Las Colonias*, p. 148.

39 Public Record Office, *BT31/1528/4827*.

40 Hadfield, *Brazil … 1870–76*, p. 102 (Visit made Sept. 1870); *Brazil … 1868*, p. 242. Pres. D. F. Sarmiento to Major F. Ignacio Rickard, Buenos Aires, 12 Feb. 1870, see F. I. Rickard, *The Mineral and Other Resources of the Argentine Republic (La Plata) in 1869*, London, 1870, pp. 271–6.

41 *The Brazil and River Plate Mail*, 6 April 1867, p. 13.

42 *Ibid.*, p. 8.

43 H. G. MacDonell, 'Remarks on the River Plate Republics as a field for British emigration', *Parliamentary Papers*, LXX, 1872, pp. 1–47.

44 R. Scalabrini Ortiz, *Historia de los Ferrocarriles Argentinos*, Buenos Aires, 1940, pp. 91–2. The author is critical of later land speculation, but fails to note that the separation of railway and land interests on the Central Argentine in 1870 was not part of Wheelwright's original plan.

45 Wilcken, *Las Colonias*, p. 155.

46 E. H. Talbott, *Railway Land Grants in the United States; their History, Economy, and Influence upon the Development and Prosperity of the Country*, Chicago, 1880, p. 9.

47 C. M. Lewis, *British Railways in Argentina, 1857–1914*, London, 1983, p. 40.

48 *The Brazil and River Plate Mail*, 8 Aug. 1874, p. 10.

49 *Herapath's Railway and Commercial Journal*, 9 June 1883, p. 698.
50 *South American Journal*, 9 June 1888, pp. 337–8.
51 *Ibid.* p. 326.
52 W. Latham, *The States of the River Plate: their Industries and Commerce*, London, 2nd edn 1868, p. 339.
53 B. W. Green to US 2nd Asst. Sec. of State, Córdoba, 2 Dec. 1874, *Despatches from U.S. Consuls in Córdoba, Argentina, General Records of the Dept. of State, Record Group 59*, Washington, D.C.
54 B. W. Green to US Sec. of State, Córdoba, 1 Nov. 1877, *ibid.*
55 J. M. Thome to US Asst. Sec. of State, Córdoba, 2 Aug. 1897, *ibid.*
56 B. W. Green to US Sec. of State, Córdoba, 1 Nov. 1877; 3 Mar. 1879; *ibid.*
57 J. M. Thome to US Asst. Sec. of State, Córdoba, 30 June 1888, *ibid.*
58 *Ibid.* See also critical comments by the Buenos Aires Consul, after touring Córdoba, on the province's failure to develop its potential for irrigated agriculture (E. L. Baker to US Sec. of State, Buenos Aires, 23 Jan. 1883, *Despatches from U.S. Consuls in Buenos Aires, Argentina, General Records of the Dept. of State, Record Group 59*, Washington, D.C.).
59 G. R. Taylor and I. D. Neu, *The American Railroad Network, 1861–1890*, Cambridge, Mass., 1956, pp. 6, 14. The seven gauges were 6′0″; 5′6″; 5′4″; 5′0″; 4′10″; 4′9¼″; and 4′8½″.
60 Law # 5559 (28 Aug. 1908): '*Development of the national territories*'. A wide range of public works projects included railways from Port San Antonio to Lake Nahuel Huapí, from Comodoro Rivadavia, and from Port Deseado, with branch lines.

Law # 6546 (28 Sept. 1909): '*Irrigation in the zone served by the national railways*'. Authorization included:
1 Studies for the exploitation of the rivers Negro, Limay, Neuquén, Segundo, Tercero, Quinto, Seco, Río de la Sauces, Mendoza, Atuel, Diamante, Tunuyán, Salado (Santiago del Estero and San Luis), Colorado, and Dulce.
2 Feasibility studies for irrigation projects in the provinces of San Luis, San Juan, La Rioja, Catamarca, Tucumán, Salta, and Jujuy.
3 Railway companies to receive government 'Irrigation Bonds' at 5 per cent interest for the cost of the construction work, and duty-free import of the necessary materials.
4 Government expropriation of land where necessary to extend irrigation; once completed, the irrigation works to be transferred to the respective provincial authorities.
5 Money from the sale of the *Andino* railway to be used to help finance irrigation.

61 M. A. Cárcano, *Evolución histórica del régimen de la tierra pública, 1810–1916*, Buenos Aires, 1917, 2nd edn 1925, 3d edn 1972, pp. 233, 146.
62 P. L. Cable to US Sec. of State, Buenos Aires, 29 Mar. 1927, 'Economic

Matters (Colonization)' in *Records of the Department of State relating to the Internal Affairs of Argentina, Record Group 59*, Washington, D.C.

63 F. A. Cleveland and F. W. Powell, *Railroad Promotion and Capitalization in the United States*, New York, 1909, pp. 250–1, 255.

64 F. G. Carpenter, *South America: Social, Industrial, and Political*, Akron, Ohio, 1900; New York and Chicago, 1901, pp. 343–4.

65 A. T. Hadley, *Railroad Transportation*, New York, 1885, p. 101.

66 W. Z. Ripley, *Railroads: Finance and Oganization*, New York, 1915, pp. 473, 599.

67 B. W. Hanna to US Sec. of State, Buenos Aires, 29 July 1888, *Diplomatic Despatches from U.S. Ministers in Argentina, General Records of the Dept. of State, Record Group 59*, Washington, D.C.

68 J. H. Williams, *Argentine International Trade under Inconvertible Paper Money, 1880–1900*, Cambridge, Mass., 1920, p. 88.

69 J. S. Duncan, 'British Railways in Argentina', *Political Science Quarterly*, LII, 1937, pp. 566, 578.

70 In 1885, the Great Southern was criticized for allowing £61 10s out of every £100 earned to be spent on working expenses: 'In this country [Britain] the average is only about £52, and Argentine railways are supposed to be easier to work. The Central Argentine spends only £40 out of every £100 earned. The Great Southern's working expenses were only £50 out of every £100 earned in 1875. Why it should mount to £61.10sh. in ten years is evidently more than the Board themselves can explain.' *Herapath's*, 17 Oct. 1885, p. 1076.

71 W. Rögind, *Historia del Ferrocarril del Sud, 1861–1936*, Buenos Aires, 1937, pp. 194, 196, 207.

72 Pres. Luis Sáenz Peña, Annual Message to Congress, May 1894, in H. Mabragaña, *Los Mensajes*, Buenos Aires, 1910, V, p. 163.

73 Emilio Mitre, *Diario de Sesiones*, Cámera de Diputados, Buenos Aires, 5 Aug. 1907, p. 682.

74 W. S. Barclay, 'The First Transandine Railway', *Geographical Journal*, XXXVI, 1910, p. 560.

75 Typical of several such assessments by North Americans at this time is that contained in a confidential report by W. P. Lord to US Sec. of State, Buenos Aires, 3 Oct. 1900, *Diplomatic Despatches from U.S. Ministers to Argentina, General Records of the Dept. of State, Record Group 59*, Washington, D.C.

76 A. M. Wellington, *The Economic Theory of the Location of Railways*, New York, 1877, pp. xxi, 188–9; 1887 edn, p. 840.

77 *Ibid.*, pp. 52–3, 193.

78 Hadley, *Railroad Transportation*, pp. 52, 126.

79 J. J. Castro, *Treatise on the South American Railways and the Great International Lines*, Montevideo, 1893, pp. 146, 588.

80 B. Willis, *A Yanqui in Patagonia*, Stanford, Cal., 1947, pp. 61, 62.

81 B. Willis, *Northern Patagonia. Report for the Ministry of Public Works, Argentina*, New York, I, p. 39.
82 *Ibid.*, p. 25.
83 Willis, *A Yanqui*, pp. 142–3.
84 Ripley, *Railroads*, p. 48.
85 R. Crawford, *Across the Pampas and the Andes*, London, 1884, p. vi.
86 T. J. Hutchinson, *The Paraná; with incidents of the Paraguayan War, and South American recollections, from 1861 to 1868*, London, 1868, pp. 111–12.
87 Chairman's statement, AGM, *The Times*, 29 April 1886.
88 T. O. Osborn to US Sec. of State, Buenos Aires, 20 April 1885, *Diplomatic Despatches from U.S. Ministers to Argentina, General Records of the Dept. of State, Record Group 59*, Washington, D.C.
89 J. G. Walker to US Sec. of State, Buenos Aires, 24 April, 1889, *ibid.*
90 W. H. Koebel, *Modern Chile*, London, 1913, p. 215.
91 US Dept. of Commerce, *The Railways of Argentina*, Latin American Transportation Survey, Railway Section, prepared by E. R. Johnson, Washington, D.C., 1943, pp. 180–1. See also *Annual Reports*, The Buenos Ayres Pacific Railway Co. Ltd, 1906–36; The Argentine Transandine Railway Co. Ltd, 1911–30; The Chilian Transandine Railway Co. Ltd, *passim*.
92 Lewis, *British Railways*, p. 168.
93 C. A. Logan to US Sec. of State, Santiago de Chile, 4 Jan. 1874, *Diplomatic Despatches from U.S. Ministers to Chile, General Records of the Dept. of State, Record Group 59*, Washington, D.C.
94 L. E. Elliott, *Chile: Today and Tomorrow*, New York, 1922, pp. 252–3.
95 *Geographical Journal*, XLIX, 1917, p. 278. Edited discussion on 'The Geography of South American Railways'.
96 For example, P. E. James, 'Geographic factors in the development of transportation in South America', *Economic Geography*, I, 1925, p. 260.
97 F. J. Stimson to US Sec. of State, Buenos Aires, 12 May 1919, 'Communication and Transportation (Railway)' in *Records of the Department of State relating to the Internal Affairs of Argentina, Record Group 59*, Washington, D.C.
98 Fifer, *Bolivia*, pp. 247–8, 191.
99 W. M. Collier to US Sec. of State, Santiago, 27 Nov. 1923; 15 Apr. 1924, 'Communication and Transportation (Railway)' in *Records of the Department of State relating to the Internal Affairs of Chile, Record Group 59*, Washington, D.C.
100 G. D. Hopper to State Department, Antofagasta, 16 Nov. 1925; 21 Nov. 1928, *ibid.* A 560-mile metre-gauge railway was opened between Antofagasta and Salta in 1948, but failed at this late stage to stimulate sufficient growth to pay its way. The line was closed as an international route in 1980. In the event, the railway never introduced new regional

challenge to the interests of the Antofagasta (Chili) and Bolivia Railway Co., since a line already owned by the company became the first section of the route out of Antofagasta, and the company later operated the whole of the Chilean section on behalf of the government.

101 M. Jefferson, *Peopling the Argentine Pampa*, American Geographical Society Research Series, No. 16, New York, 1926, p. 162.

3

The lack of 'Western-style' developers in the Southern Cone
– settlers, boosters, traders, and tourists

Settlers

> There is something of home to the American in this view from the high railroad bridge over the Malleco; it is the end of old Chile, the Chile of the sunny stretches, of dusty roads and old Creole life. ... Here begins the rainy, woodsy country. ... We have entered the *Frontera*.

In 1918, the American Geographical Society commissioned a series of field studies by Mark Jefferson to assess the progress of European colonization in temperate South America. Between 1921 and 1926, Jefferson published his findings on Chile, Argentina, and southern Brazil in a series of memoirs and papers that formed the first general survey in English on the achievements and potential of rural colonization south of Capricorn.[1]

The impact of German colonization in southern Chile Jefferson had first visited Chile in 1886. Now he found that parts of southern Chile displayed some of the most remarkable results of early German agricultural colonization to be found anywhere in the New World. During the late nineteenth century, American commentators had noted that while Argentina inevitably held the railroad initiatives in the Southern Cone (for good or ill), Chile was more likely to be the pace-setter in expanding the region's settlement frontier. There was little doubt that the impetus for the economic development of the cool, dry lands in the central interior would come from Chile, as farmers and pastoralists moved across into Patagonia, where Argentina was apparently incapable of attracting immigrants in sufficient numbers. As late as the 1920s, the Mendoza region and Cuyo oases were still the only part of the foothill zone, indeed, as American and other travellers were often astonished to find, *the only part of the entire interior of Argentina* that had managed to attract any significant European immigration. And even round Mendoza, the US Consul-General in Buenos Aires observed, much of the land remained idle and awaiting development, probably by farmers from Chile. Farther south, the passes were lower, the transandean movement easier. Moreover, the south of Chile had been an early focus of successful agricultural settlement.

American perceptions of Chile as a dynamic, forward-looking state had been influenced both by the introduction of steam navigation along the Pacific Coast in 1840, and by new legislation to encourage colonization in 1845. The two developments were linked. The Chilean Constitution of 1833 declared that its territory extended 'from the desert of Atacama to Cape Horn' and after the defeat of the Peru-Bolivia Confederation in 1839, Chile began to inject a visible Chilean presence north and south of the central heartland, prompted by the discovery of rich new guano deposits on the Atacama coast, and, in the far south, by the fact that Wheelwright's first two ships (delivered from Liverpool to Valparaiso in 1840) had steamed through the Strait of Magellan, rather than having to follow the traditional sailing-ship route around the Horn. In 1843, a Chilean expedition took possession of the Strait and established Fort Bulnes, followed in 1849 by the creation of Punta Arenas. In 1846, the first German colonists arrived at Valdivia. Chile, it was noted, was thus adopting the North American practice of backing claims to territory not by words but by actual settlement and land use, a policy pursued elsewhere in South America only by Brazil.

By the early 1850s, Lieutenant James Gilliss, USN had already identified the successful introduction of German immigrants at Valdivia as a pioneering venture of great future significance to the Southland: 'hardy, industrious, frugal' colonists whose impact was reinforced by the arrival of more German settlers at Lake Llanquihue in 1852, and by the founding of Puerto Montt a year later. The new Chilean colonization law had provided for family farms of up to 25 *cuadras* (about 100 acres), initial assistance with tools, seeds, food-stuffs, and transport, tax exemption for twenty years, and the automatic award of Chilean citizenship by act of settlement. A resourceful young Berliner, Bernhard Philippi, ably supported by a group of German merchants in Valparaiso, had taken the lead in recruiting

German colonists to south Chile. Earlier, he had explored the region as a collector for the Berlin Natural History Museum, and in 1843 had accompanied the Chilean naval expedition to claim the Strait of Magellan. Americans approved the practical approach to immigration favoured by Philippi and others like Kindermann, Frick, and Pérez Rosales – a strong Chilean supporter of German colonization who had just returned to the Southland from the California goldrush. All these agents emphasized the importance of ceaseless promotion through personal contacts, articles, pamphlets, advertisements, and colonists' letters. Some of the promotional material was redesigned after a tour of the American Midwest had provided a glimpse of the variety of methods being employed there with such outstanding success. Whether destined for North or South America, German immigrants went to better themselves economically, but Chile also appealed to those hoping to maintain a strong German cultural identity overseas for longer than appeared possible in the United States: 'a frontier without Yankees' that would avoid the need to be assimilated into an alien 'American' society.[2] For although German immigrants to the United States, like others, usually set out with the intention of recreating in more favourable surroundings their essentially European-style communities, the sheer weight of numbers, greater mobility and opportunity, and the pervasive spirit of change (as well as official discouragement of schemes for exclusive national settlement of permanent ethnic or religious enclaves as a long-term goal) all resulted in a high degree of assimilation.

Between 1846 and 1866, some 3,500 German immigrants settled in the provinces of Valdivia and Llanquihue. Despite the isolation, dense forest, high rainfall, and poor early harvests under back-breaking conditions, the newcomers' skill, versatility and persistence saw them through. Here were North European immigrants, assisted by local Chiloteans, American visitors reported, cutting out a new frontier in a potentially rich resource area far from the old Chilean core. They were well placed to become part of the future growth zone that would spread south from Talcahuano and Concepción, and also ideally situated to develop transandean trade links with Argentina. Most of the immigrants had come from west of the Elbe, and included farmers, tradesmen, and artisans, many of them with some capital of their own. Peasant farmers usually had another skill, or another trade, so that the Valdivia region in particular became an important centre of innovation, and from the start was characterized by a remarkable range of both agricultural and manufacturing activities. Tanneries, brickworks, saw-mills, flour mills, soap, shoe, and furniture factories, breweries, distilleries, and shipbuilding quickly made their appearance. Farm products included oats, barley, rye and wheat, potatoes, butter, hams, lard, pork, lamb, fruit, cider, wool, honey, beeswax, and lumber – much of it sent north to the main Chilean markets, or exported to other West Coast ports, and to Europe. In 1870, the Chilean government established a regular steamship service on Lake Llanquihue, and another 400 or so German immigrants arrived in the province soon after.

The American Minister in Santiago, making a regional tour in the mid-eighties of 'the much talked of settlements in southern Chile', found a landscape around Valdivia that reminded him of the upper Hudson Valley and Lake George – a pleasing prospect of cultivated fields, herds of cattle, solidly built villages, tree-lined squares, and country stores. Farther south at Puerto Montt, the community of some 3,000 had just completed an iron pier, and laid out a fine promenade along the waterfront. Travelling inland over a corduroy road for ten miles through dense forest and old clearings, Roberts reported considerable signs of prosperity as he approached Lake Llanquihue: 'nicely cultivated farms with rail fences, free from weeds, and comfort-able farm houses. ... At the lake we found a good country hotel, and a better table than could be found at many a city hotel with great pretensions.'[3] Returning to Valparaiso from Puerto Montt via Corral (Valdivia) and other ports of call, his steamer laden with farm and factory products from the predominantly German colonies, the American Minister reflected on the potential of a region most Chileans regarded as uninhabitable. Enterprise, thrift, and perseverance were being applied. How refreshing it had been to see the range and productivity of the North European family farms instead of the sprawling inertia of the *hacienda*.

Not least among the achievements of the German immigrants in the Valdivia-Osorno-Lake Llanquihue-Puerto Montt region had been the very small numbers of immigrants involved in creating these pioneer communities. The total German emigration to Chile between 1846 and 1914 was only about 11,000, and of these, no more than around 5,600 are estimated to have settled in southern Chile. Indeed, in the Southland as a whole, many more German immigrants were attracted to Brazil and the River Plate region.[4] The bulk of German immigrants of course went to the United States. In the nineteenth and early twentieth centuries, nearly six million Germans emigrated to America, over 90 per cent of the total German migration, and together with Austrians, German-Swiss, and Russian-Germans, the largest single 'national' group entering the United States. German immigrants had in fact been the prime target for railroad and other agents in the Midwest and northern Great Plains ever since the 1850s. By comparison, therefore, the German emigration to Chile was a mere trickle even in the boom years, but the relatively high proportion that went to southern Chile was crucial. They established a dynamic society which at the same time possessed exceptional permanence and stability, maintaining a remarkable balance of rural and urban skills. As Mark Jefferson observed: 'These were great accomplishments, so significant and important to Chile, indeed, that it is hard to realize how slight a thing numerically the German element was and is.'[5]

To some extent, however, the German settlements in Valdivia and Llanquihue provinces became victims of their own success. Not only were agents in Germany recruiting more Protestants than the Chilean authorities were prepared to tolerate, the government also became anxious about excessive German influence and identity in the region. In opening the *Frontera* to more mixed European colonization in 1882–89, Germany was no longer the major source. A mere 1,110 Germans, one-sixth of the total, were distributed among twelve of the colonies established, and the preponderance of Spanish and Italian immigrants that was to characterize subsequent decades now became apparent. Many of the new arrivals were also poorer, more footloose, inexperienced in farming techniques, and much more ready to give up farming altogether and look for work in town. By the end of the 1890s, some fifteen years after the founding of the oldest *Frontera* colonies, about half of the families who had been settled there had abandoned their farms. This applied to colonists of all nationalities, although Germans and Swiss were less likely to go. There was a significant failure in the *Frontera* to establish a stable rural economy based on the family farm, as in the German settlements in Valdivia and Llanquihue; before long, much of the land was publicly auctioned and consolidated into large estates at the expense of the Chilean and foreign colonists, the Chilean squatter, and the Indian.[6] There were more colonists introduced into the *Frontera* than farther south, Jefferson concluded after studying the region, but the results had not been so striking.

One of the most noticeable features of United States assessments of the German settlements in southern Chile is a dismissal of the 'permanently Teutonic' threat that isolated communities of 'German hearts and German hands' was said to pose to Chilean society. US Minister Roberts, for example, had reported in the 1880s that 'While the German colonists are highly appreciated, the fault found by the Chilians with the Valdivia Colony is that it continues German in sentiment, language, and national feeling, rather than Chilian. I am inclined to think, however, that this is more in appearance than reality.' By 1900, American Minister H. L. Wilson, amid praise for the remarkable progress made in the provinces of Valdivia and Llanquihue, was already deploring the serious decline in German colonization, and the increasingly feeble support in general for any national immigration policy:

> The problem of peopling Chile, although recognized in the program of all political parties, has never received approval of the nation as a whole. The efforts of the government and of the few small groups of enterprising men, have been impotent of late years in the face of national indifference and pronounced antagonism to the influx of foreigners in great numbers.
>
> The only colonists who have made a pronounced and visible impression upon Chile, are those of German nationality. ... The German, of all the foreigners resident in Chile, has to be reckoned with as a positive force, ... [whose] influence is felt in almost every avenue of Chilean life. ... It is fair to say that the influence of the German in this country, while furnishing some cause for apprehension, has nevertheless been healthy in its effects and generally for the benefit of the Chilean people.[7]

Jefferson too, in the aftermath of the First World War, gave particular attention to the 'widespread notion that southern Chile was thoroughly Germanized': 'a myth' in his opinion, which failed to separate the important early German influence on the social and economic development of the region from the evolving German-Chilean society of subsequent decades. No one disputed the impressive contribution to life and landscape made by the small numbers of German immigrants; 'they had given value to worthless southern lands'. The majority of the population, however, even in the 'German' towns, was Chilean, and Jefferson, like other Americans, was neither surprised nor dismayed by the vitality of the German ethnic identity as shown in the region's cultural institutions, and in the widespread bilingualism.[8] This was a far cry from 'pure German states beyond the seas'.

A similar point was made by Jefferson with reference to many of the old German colonies in Southern Brazil. In Rio Grande do Sul, for example, the *industrial structure* was essentially German, the *people* on the other hand were not Germans but Brazilians.[9] By the turn of the century there were 200,000 German-Brazilians in Rio Grande do Sul alone, well distributed on family farms specializing in rye, potatoes, maize, cattle and hogs, and in small manufacturing towns and cities. 'By 1909 there was scarcely a large estate left in the zone of the European settlements' reported Preston James: 'Although the dominant theme of the region is Brazilian, it is a new kind of Brazil.' Italian and other pioneers shared in this development, but the Germans had expanded more widely. In assessing the distinguishing character-istics of the Brazilian Southland, James concluded, 'there can be no doubt regarding the great contribution made by the German pioneers, who, as in southern Chile, led the way into the forests'.[10]

The early momentum of German colonization in southern Chile, however, was lost by the mid–1870s. The restrictions imposed by the Chilean Government in order to produce a pattern of more mixed European colonization in the *Frontera* in the 1880s merely emphasized the greater economic, social, and religious opportunities available in the United States. This was particularly true of the American West, where, for example, the vigorous promotion of German, Dutch and Scandinavian immigration by the Northern Pacific Railroad and its organizer Henry Villard (born Heinrich Hilgard in Bavaria) pioneered the transformation of the northern lake region, wheatland, rangeland, and timber country stretching from Minnesota to Oregon and Puget Sound. Many among the later waves of German immigrants to the western United States, mostly poor tenants or labourers from east of the Elbe, had been attracted by the provisions of the Homestead Act. Chile, by contrast, was now considered to have no more land suitable for the average colonist. There were no new waves of German pioneers to push out the forest frontier, expand markets, and promote the development of strong economic exchanges between Chile and Argentina. Such possibilities were noted by Anderson Smith in 1899 when he explored the Valdivia River by steamer, and broke his journey to take refreshment at a comfortable German farmhouse at Cuyinhue:

> Bunches of ostrich-feathers and an armadillo in the sitting-room pointed to the other side of the Great Cordillera, and we found that a close connection existed between the two sides here. In summer, with a good horse, the owner could cross to his lands on the other side – Argentina – in two days, by a good pass. ... There seems a considerable and lucrative business at

present with Argentina here, for the cattle of our friend were sent there, to be brought back in three or four years, when properly grown and fattened. Much wool also crosses from Argentina.

It had been an unexpected reminder of the transandean trade, Smith reported, 'a distant shake-hands with its traffic route', and a vision of the potential for the exchange of products between the two states.[11]

Charles Akers had been similarly impressed in the 1890s by the energy and enterprise of the German colonists in southern Chile, and had confidently predicted the spread of German and German–Chilean farmers, foresters, and livestock-owners from the Osorno region into the Nahuel Huapí area of Argentina, and beyond, as soon as transport links were improved. The Osorno lands were already nearly fully occupied, Akers reported after touring the region, and an outlet was being sought for the surplus population:

> Well laid out farms looked smiling and prosperous, and signs of German industry were visible everywhere ... stout pole and rail fences ... patches of timber in bold relief against the fields of wheat ... homesteads substantially constructed. ... The country, in fact, looked thoroughly populated, and contrasted strangely with the vast areas of land in Patagonia I had so recently passed over ... habits of thrift and economy have arisen to an extent that is absolutely foreign to Argentina.[12]

In 1911–13, the American engineer Bailey Willis again stressed the vital importance of linking Patagonia to the German colonization zone in southern Chile, and was determined to find the practical means of doing so. Working both in Chile and Argentina, his Andean surveys had located a suitable pass north-west of Lake Nahuel Huapí for the proposed transcontinental railroad to Valdivia. 'As I rode the Cordillera I pondered the conditions, ... and the quality of immigrants to occupy the promised land. My mind turned to the Czechoslovaks, foresters and industrialists. ... I thought of Osorno and its thriving Teutonic pioneers.' The skill of the German pioneers in developing southern Chile's rainforest frontier had already impressed him on an earlier rail journey from Santiago to Puerto Montt. Familiar with similar environments in the Pacific Northwest, Willis was not surprised, merely well satisfied, by the solid achievement he found in the Valdivia–Osorno–Llanquihue region:

> Virgin forests, a rich, volcanic soil and abundant rainfall support a dense

growth of shrubs and fine trees, the like of which is not often seen outside of the tropics. Overhead all is green, even the tree trunks; underfoot among strong twisting roots all is morass and boghole. But cleared and drained it is a marvelously fertile land. Those who are bringing it into cultivation are Germans, colonists of the second generation.[13]

Instead of boosting immigration to Chile, however, national indifference had turned to outright discouragement by the turn of the century. The failure of the official Chiloé colonization project in 1895–97 merely confirmed the misgivings of those already hostile to the colonization principle, although what the venture really revealed was the poor site location in one of Chile's wettest rain forest regions, and the dire inexperience of most of the colonists. They had been recruited by government agents in Paris, and were largely made up of impoverished city-dwellers of mixed nationality.

Chile had indeed become 'the offspring of isolation'. Despite the fact, as one American economic geographer observed in the late 1920s, that 'a great deal of Chile's fertile land is still lying idle – only a third of the available farm land is used profitably for agriculture',[14] the whole of temperate Chile had effectively been written off by the end of the 1880s as a genuine growth zone for North European agricultural colonization. German immigration had slowed too soon to exert significant pressure on the land beyond the traditional confines of Chile and encourage a substantial eastward flow of German and German–Chilean settlers into Argentina. Although in Chile Palacios argued that one of the effects of foreign colonization in the *Frontera* had been the displacement of native Chilean peons over the Andes into Argentina, and Argentines professed themselves to be disturbed by the large numbers of Chilean and other foreigners farming and herding in Patagonia,[15] Americans were not impressed by the statistics. The fact that the Argentine Census (1914) recorded between 46 and 67 per cent of the population in the southern territories of Patagonia as 'foreigners' was not surprising when the total population was so small. But since southern Argentina had been in the 'pioneer age' for more than half a century, why were so many of these 'foreigners' still 'foreign'? Americans asked, begging a wider question.

American fieldworkers were among the first to note that the eastward movement of German agricultural immigrants from southern Chile had withered before its potential for stimulating further settlement and new regional markets had been realized – 'The comparative ease of negotiating the passes ... played an important part in the early peopling of many districts [of Argentine Patagonia] by Chilean Germans from the southern lands of Middle Chile', – observed C. F. Jones,[16] but there had been little follow-on – no sustained application of German knowledge, energy and persistence as in Northern Europe, to ditch and drain, improve and irrigate, and convert more of the bogs, sand dunes, and morainic deposits of Patagonia into fertile fields of rye, barley and potatoes.

In the extreme south, pioneer German and later settlers in the Ultima Esperanza district of Magallanes, under licence from the Chilean authorities at Punta Arenas, had been sufficiently numerous to justify the award of disputed territory in this region to Chile under the British Arbitration of 1902.[17] After the discovery in the late 1870s of the high quality of the sheep pasture in southern Patagonia, and the generally favourable climatic conditions both for meat production and for fine textured wools, Scots, English, Germans, Chileans and others had been attracted into the far south. Local mineral exploitation, including soft coal, gold and copper, diversified the economy. By 1914, Punta Arenas had a cosmopolitan population of some 20,000, where Germans and German–Chileans controlled 23.5 per cent of the total commercial capital, and Serbo-Croatians an additional 21.5 per cent. Strong reaction, however, was now developing against foreign economic control of the Magallanes region. Chilean nationalists were convinced that the almost complete foreign monopoly of landowner-ship in Magallanes, and of commerce in Punta Arenas, damaged Chile's economic progress and possibly threatened Chilean sovereignty over the region.[18] Americans, however, noted that such anxieties, real or assumed, were more characteristic of distant Central Chilean opinion than that of Magallanes itself, and waited to see what practical improvements would result from the discouragement of foreign colonists and locally-based enterprise, while control over much of Magallanes was officially passed to the largest Chilean-controlled interest in the territory, the Sociedad Explotadora de Tierra del Fuego.

American doubts proved well justified. An interminable wrangle developed after 1914 between the sheep estancia interests, led by the Sociedad Explotadora (and strongly supported as a matter of principle in Congress by the great landowning lobby of Central Chile), and those more concerned to increase Chilean population in the region by land-subdivision and renewed colonization. The achievement of some measure of subdivision was a feature of the 1930s, and subsequent policy continued to emphasize the economic, social, and political advantages that followed the promotion of a denser distribution of population in the Chilean Far South.[19]

As early as 1874, the US Consul in Buenos Aires had advised the State Department that he proposed in future to include information about Patagonia in his reports, for Patagonia was 'not the sterile country of our school geographies; with a little Anglo-Saxon or Teutonic enterprise, it might stare a bright future in the face. ... The rivers and fertile valleys of Patagonia, ... in my opinion, have great agricultural and commercial possibilities.'[20]

But a major expansion of German immigrants from centres on the Pacific and Atlantic coasts into the plains and plateaux of the interior never took place, and remained a dream in the minds largely of a few mid-nineteenth-century German intellectuals. Johann Wappäus was one of the strongest advocates of temperate South America, rather than the United States, as a field for 'national' agricultural colonization. He stressed the powerful cultural and economic impact of large numbers of Germans:

> settled in well organized colonies amongst any other people than the Americans (because of their prodigious power of assimilation) ...
>
> It appears to me not improbable that if it were possible to direct the present stream of our emigrants towards the temperate lands of South America, ... their descendants in the coastal lands of southern Chile would join hands with those at the mouth of the Rio de la Plata.[21]

German immigration to Argentina, however, remained relatively limited until after the First World War; in 1920, it was still less than 2 per cent of the total number of overseas immigrants who had entered the country since 1857, a total dominated by Italians (about 47 per cent) and Spaniards (about 32 per cent).[22] In the early 1920s, more German immigrants began to arrive – over 30,000 in 1921–24 – but by the end of the decade, the American Consul General in Buenos Aires reported a deteriorating situation. More than fifty years after the US Consul had first recommended the advantages of introducing 'Teutonic enterprise' into Argentina, it was revealed that the country was actually *losing* German colonists at the end of the 1920s:

> German immigrants, who came to the Argentine in fair numbers after the war, are apparently particularly dissatisfied and many of them state that

they find conditions if not worse, certainly not better, than where they came from ...

They have explained the difficulty they find in securing land, their inability to make savings, and have emphasized the high cost of living. Their letters to the villagers at home have been despondent and discouraging rather than hopeful.

Large numbers are therefore returning to Germany or trying to go to the United States or other countries. This is particularly significant for the German is usually the most pertinacious of immigrants. He seldom gives up, and the fact that many Germans who have been in the Argentine for three or four years are trying to get out of the country is perhaps one of the most discouraging features of the immigration situation from an economic point of view in the Argentine.[23]

The failure of Welsh colonization in Patagonia Argentina's interest in encouraging the first Welsh settlement in Patagonia in the mid–1860s had much in common with Chile's strong support for the first German colonization in the Valdivia and Llanquihue region twenty years before. Both represented the desire to introduce and expand new frontier zones far to the south of existing national core areas, a desire intensified in the 1870s–1890s in Argentina by recurring Chilean claims to all or part of Patagonia.

An advance party of 150 Welsh settlers arrived in Chubut in 1865, armed with a government contract and a range of incentives to bring 300 to 500 families from Wales to Patagonia each year for the next decade. The determination to resist assimilation, and to preserve the Welsh language and culture in an isolated portion of the New World, had some parallels with the earlier German initiatives, but in the event, the limited numbers and virtual total lack of farming experience and capital among the Welsh colonists severely restricted the role they had been expected to play as regional developers. 'Welsh dreamers down in the Chubut', was the laconic comment of the American Minister in Buenos Aires in 1899, underlining the general conclusion among United States observers in the Southland that the ability of German colonists to demonstrate their cultural identity in a practical way, through market innovation and strong economic development, was not matched by the Welsh.

Americans with experience of their own West were particularly critical in their perception of how little had been achieved by the Welsh colonists, whether in the lower Chubut Valley around Puerto Madryn, Trelew, and Rawson, or in the offshoot settlement of 16 October

(Esquel) established in 1885 in the upper valley, some 350 miles to the west. The first forty-three-mile section of the narrow-gauge Chubut Central Railway, opened in 1889, barely needed eight trips a year to carry the entire valley's agricultural output, and since virtually no one travelled anywhere, a visitor reported, passenger traffic could be written off. Passengers in fact contributed only 4 per cent of the revenue, while freight rates remained high. Bailey Willis investigated some of the Welsh settlements during his railway and regional survey work in Patagonia in 1911–13, and condemned much of what he found. Even at Esquel, Willis considered that the settlers, now in the third generation, had had ample time to be raising more crops for the domestic market, and breeding cattle and sheep for sale in Chile:

> Time for farmers and frontiersmen, you would think, to put the forests to the saw, to build good houses, to establish a village center, store, and church, to build bridges and improve the cart tracks into roads; men to form a well-knit, prosperous community, with 6,000 acres to the family, and to become an asset to the nation. That is what might have been, but it is not what has evolved.

About half-a-dozen in and around Esquel 'lived like decent farmers in cleanliness and reasonable comfort. The great majority lived in low, thatched cabins built of bamboo and mud, with smoke, dirt, and close quarters within, and the offal of slaughtered sheep at the doorstep. ... As for community ties, there is no evidence that any man knows his neighbor.'[24]

The steady stream of Welsh immigrants to the Chubut Valley had never materialized. The Welsh population was still only about 2,000 at the end of the eighties, and in the nineties an increasingly exasperated Argentine government began to encourage colonies of Italians to settle in the Chubut. Welsh struggles and Welsh nationalism in the Patagonian wilderness had attracted some interest in Britain, but by the end of the century, objective Argentine observers acknowledged the failure of the Chubut experiment as a vigorous North European settlement frontier. British visitors who studied the Welsh colonies without undue sentiment or bias frequently confirmed this view. In 1903–04, as leader of the official British survey party demarcating a section of the Chile–Argentine boundary, Colonel Holdich had reviewed the history of Welsh colonization in the Chubut, and spent some time at the 16 October (Esquel) settlement. Since he stayed at the most comfortable and prosperous of the farmhouses, Holdich was not made so aware of the primitive farming practices and the widespread domestic squalor that Bailey Willis deplored. Even so, Holdich noted the legacy of prolonged isolation, and the traditional unwillingness among the Chubut Welsh 'to spread themselves sufficiently far for the purpose of exploring the most likely districts for development. ... They have remained in the same place. ... All Patagonia was open to them – better country lay south on the Atlantic coast, at Santa Cruz, at Gallegos, and in the Magellan territory. ... They had their opportunity and they let it slip.' Holdich also observed a failure to adapt and to innovate. Having received a generous grant from the Argentine Government to get back on their feet after the floods of 1899 and 1902, the Chubut Valley colonists devoted the entire sum to repairing their old system of irrigation, instead of improving it and introducing new methods of flood control. 'They had no engineer among themselves, ... and declined to undertake a somewhat extensive piece of work [that] involved the use of "new-fangled" machinery of which they disapproved.'[25]

About 500 Welsh colonists left Argentina at the beginning of the twentieth century, most of them bound eventually for Canada. While British commentators would sometimes praise the Welsh effort, pleased apparently that the colonies had survived at all, American observers were generally critical of the failure of the Chubut Welsh over a forty-year period to make a more significant contribution to the economy of central Patagonia. It was a lost opportunity in a key location to promote greater regional development in the Southern Cone. Those Westerners who studied the Chubut at first hand found the environmental problems to have been exaggerated, and looked instead for more pioneer-minded settlement, more irrigated agriculture, more back linkages to the Pampas, and the creation of new forward linkages into the valleys of southern Patagonia, and into Chile.

The economic potential of Patagonia Along with regional and transcontinental railroad construction, Americans with experience in their own West continued to emphasize Patagonia's need for a more rounded economy, rather than the virtually exclusive reliance on pastoral activity. Such emphasis is found, for example, in the detailed scientific reports produced by the Princeton University expeditions to Patagonia in 1896–99. The members were all well prepared for the local conditions, wrote the leader, having 'tented it for many years on the windswept plains of Wyoming, Montana, and the Dakotas'.[26] The results of the surveys concluded that Patagonia had the potential to make a substantial contribution to Argentina's development, enlarging its national territorial consciousness and moderating the country's obsession with the Humid Pampa.

Patagonia possessed timber, mineral, and fisheries resources that had scarcely been touched; as for the agricultural possibilities, the investigators were surprised to find them so totally neglected at such a late stage in Argentina's 'modernization' period. Topography, hydrology, climate, soil, and vegetation studies revealed much greater regional variety than was commonly supposed. In Southern Patagonia, for example, the valleys of the Chico, Gallegos, and Coy (Coyle, Coig) rivers in Santa Cruz could all be irrigated without difficulty, and much more intensively developed. The Chico Valley, over 200 miles long and 5 miles wide, with its sheltering bluffs and warm, fertile soils, offered every advantage, Hatcher reported:

> There is little doubt that wheat, oats and rye, as well as alfalfa and all the hardier grasses, would thrive well, yet it remains practically unoccupied. *I do not hesitate to say that if such a valley existed anywhere within the present limits of the United States, displaying the same or similar conditions, every acre of it would, within a period of five years, be occupied by prosperous farmers and that it would, within a period of ten years, support a population of not less than fifty thousand persons, with prosperous towns connected with the coast by an efficient railway and telegraph service.*[27]

Attention was also drawn to the sub-Andean depression, and to the numerous valleys which extended westward from the edge of Patagonian plateau to penetrate not only the secondary but also the main range of the Andes before draining into the Pacific. While this lack of correlation between the line of highest peaks and the continental watershed was the reason for the difficulty in interpreting the terms of the boundary treaty (1881) between Chile and Argentina, the internal regional variety, and the possibilities for easy east-west interchange and new rail connection made this mountain junction zone a fascinating field area for the Princeton investigating teams: 'The country along and within the foothills of the Andes is in many respects the most interesting region in Patagonia, whether considered geographically or geologically.'[28]

The same emphasis on regional diversity and varied resources characterized the report on the surveys of Northern Patagonia led by

Bailey Willis in 1911–13 which culminated in the most detailed collection of scientific data, field observation, resource mapping, and potential land-use analysis that had ever been produced on the region.[29] On reading the full report in 1915, Isaiah Bowman, Director of the American Geographical Society, praised 'the clear-cut, authoritative interpretations. ... A comparable piece of work does not exist for any other part of South America.' Willis was in fact applying the same approach to this portion of the Southern Cone that other US army and railroad engineers, and members of the US Geological Survey, had been perfecting in the American West since the 1850s.

In addition to the transcontinental railroad survey between Port San Antonio and Lake Nahuel Huapí, Willis's team of American and Argentine scientists assembled a detailed inventory of soil types, vegetation, drainage, and potential productivity north–south along the Andean piedmont zone at the forest–grassland junction. Special attention was given to identifying areas between latitudes 39°40'S and 43°40'S suited to irrigated agriculture, dry farming, improved grazing, and commercial forestry. Careful plotting of the distribution of sheltered tracts would reveal more scope for intensive agricultural and pastoral development than was generally assumed. Above all, wrote Willis, hydroelectric power is the region's greatest asset, with the huge natural storage system provided by the lakes superior to that of the Puget Sound catchment area. So far as the study zone was concerned, there was an estimated energy potential of 6,824,000 metric horse-power, surpassing even that of Niagara.[30] On a glacial outwash plain at the eastern end of Lake Nahuel Huapí, completely screened by a large terminal moraine from the small town of Bariloche and the new National Park to the west, Willis surveyed the site of a proposed new industrial city. It was planned for 40,000, and would act as a service centre for a regional population of 100,000. Abundant hydro-electric power would support important new chemical and fertiliser manufacturing, as well as pulp and paper mills.

Location on the transcontinental railroad to Valdivia was a vital element in an integrated economic development for the region, Willis stressed, while the availability of cheap power and the possibility of a combined programme of exploitation and conservation of the forestry resources of the Southland was already attracting the attention of timber specialists from America's Pacific Northwest at the turn of the century. Far too much of the forest was dismissed as too inaccessible, too old, or too sodden to be of any use, Americans noted; however agreeable to Oregon and California, the temperate south of South America should not still be purchasing virtually all its softwood timber from the United States. The problems were evident but not insurmountable: at appropriate locations, 'means can be found gradually to replace these old overripe Andean forests with cultivated stands of useful lumber varieties', Willis reported. The results of occasional special investigations by North Americans in selected areas of south Chile and Argentina in the 1920s confirmed this assessment.

Dismissing the United States as a source of immigrants to the Southland Experienced American observers were unanimous that new settlers for the Temperate South of South America should not come from the United States. Opposition was initially based on the lack of protection, subsequently on the lack of opportunity. Fear of competition for European immigrants, or of a drain on America's own population, was not the issue. What counted was that the only future for the majority of immigrants to the Southland was 'as a worker for others, with no betterment on his own horizon', and official discouragement on the part of the United States to those of its citizens considering the move stemmed from the burden that destitute or disillusioned American colonists became to US consular and diplomatic personnel.

A small number of North American colonies had been established in South America by groups of defeated Confederates after the Civil War. One such example was Villa Americana, founded in 1867 some seventy miles from São Paulo. Visiting Yankees dismissed it as unAmerican, 'a bit of the slave-owning Southern Confederacy set down in Brazil', and certainly no evidence that a 'New West' was being created south of Capricorn. More interest was shown in the California Colony of Argentina, the first 'Western-style' pioneer American community in the Southern Cone. Founded by William Perkins in 1866 in north Santa Fe (see page 63), the core settlement of former 'forty-niners' had done remarkably well, receiving more families from California and the Southern States in 1867, as well as English and Welsh colonists moving north from the Rosario area. The Americans had all been experienced farmers, bringing with them capital and farm machinery. Brick homesteads had been completed, livestock fattened, maize, fruit and vegetable harvests gathered, and Indian attacks repulsed. As the colonists spread, however, Indian attacks grew worse, and the Argentine Government's failure to provide any protection for frontier settlement was widely condemned. American colonists were no strangers to Indian attack, but they expected support from army patrols, and evidence that a government which spoke of the need to attract immigrants to the interior took its responsibilities seriously.

In 1869, and again in 1871, the senior American colonists wrote to President Sarmiento on behalf of all, saying that they would 'willingly lay aside the plough and take up the rifle for six or even twelve months to assist the Government in putting down the Indians', if the Government would support their families while they did so, and recompense their time.[31] There was no response, and by 1873 many of the colonists had decided to cut their losses and return to the United States. Before long, as rebels in Santa Fe province ravaged the remaining homesteads, the last settlers packed their bags and prepared to make a fresh start in Texas. In July 1877, the American Minister in Buenos Aires informed the State Department that the California Colony was now abandoned.[32]

Prospects were little better along the Central Argentine Railway, particularly in the wilder sections of Córdoba province once army detachments had been withdrawn during the Paraguayan War. Again, Americans were disturbed not so much by 'routine' Indian raids, with the inevitable loss of livestock and some lives, as by the government's total neglect of the problem. When settlement of the Central Argentine's land-grant colonies began in 1869–70, American citizens found they compared unfavourably with their own New West, where opportunities under the Homestead Act were now available, and new land-grant railroads were open and hungry for business. The Union Pacific Railroad, for example, was now selling its enormous land grant in Nebraska and Kansas at $2.50 to $10 per acre, with a 10 per cent discount for cash, and low-interest credit. Only two North American families settled on the Central Argentine's land grant.

As the lack of protection from Indian or rebel attacks gave way in time to the more lasting problem of lack of opportunity, American officials were quick to pounce on any colonization scheme in the Southland involving US citizens. In a confidential despatch to the State Department in 1873, the American Minister in Santiago, C. A. Logan, reported the Chilean Government's plans to recruit 500 colonists from the United States. The number desired was small at the time, Logan cautioned, but he felt his Government had a duty to discourage, and prevent if possible, emigration to Chile from the US:

Whatever may be said of the advancement of Chile in the feale [perception] of civilization, in wealth, refinement, intelligence and general freedom, I have no hesitation in making the statement, that it is no country for an American to come to for settlement.

My observation leads me to the belief that practically, there are but two classes of people in Chile – the gentleman and the *peon* – the former an aristocrat, and the latter – well, if not a slave in the full political sense of the word, at least so in a social sense.'[33]

The Minister had himself been one of the early Kansas pioneers, and stressed that while a few resourceful American businessmen had made successful careers in Chile over the years, larger-scale American immigration should be avoided.

Similar comments were forwarded to Washington from Ministers in Argentina, Uruguay and Paraguay, where US officials were all involved at some stage in coping with the consequences of over-optimism in the northern press about the opportunities for American immigrant farmers in the Far South. 'Misapprehensions, mistakes, and exaggerations', wrote one US Consul, the result of distant ignorance or of superficial observations by a handful of American visitors on whirlwind tours. Northerners were conscious enough of the need for their own boosters in the American West, but the political and economic environment in the Southland was not that of the United States – boosterism backfired south of Capricorn. The Minister in Buenos Aires, for example, was angered by a glowing report on the opportunities for American 'homesteaders' in Argentina that had appeared in a recent issue of *Harper's New Monthly Magazine*:

Already a number of worthy, poor young men, some with wife and children left to follow – young men of scanty means, allured by this picture of prosperity, have left better opportunities in the United States than they will find here, and overwhelmed with bitter disappointment, have called at the Legation seeking the means of return to their homes.[34]

Neglecting the role of citizenship in the Southland: Argentina seen as the epitome of the problem Quite apart from discouraging even a trickle of immigrant American farmers and artisans into the Southland, US observers in the 1870s and 1880s were already commenting adversely on Argentina's inability to attract immigrants from Northern Europe. In theory, Argentina stressed the need for such settlers; in practice, Argentina grossly underestimated the size of the task.

Americans became increasingly conscious of the gap between

Argentina's professed admiration for the United States rapid westward expansion, and Buenos Aires' failure to adopt the methods America employed to achieve it. If Argentina really wanted to attract skilled immigrants from Northern and Central Europe to balance those from Italy and Spain, it would have to work hard and persistently to persuade them to come, and demonstrate clearly the economic advantages of becoming permanent citizens.

With the introduction of the Homestead Act in 1862, the United States had made US citizenship a central issue in the government's contribution to the task of peopling the West. It was 'An Act to secure Homesteads to Actual Settlers on the Public Domain', and offered ownership of a quarter-section of land (160 acres) at the end of five years for no more than the registration fee, provided settlement and cultivation requirements had been fulfilled (see above, page 59). This offer of virtually free land was made to the head of a family, twenty-one years or over, *who was already an American citizen or who intended to become a citizen* and was therefore prepared to swear at the time of naturalization to support the Constitution of the United States, and renounce all former foreign allegiance. Additions and extensions to the 1862 Homestead Act were made as the settlement frontier advanced west, by trial and error, into the arid and semi-arid lands. The Timber Culture Act (1873) and the Desert Land Act (1877) were two such examples. Abuses, failures or takeovers, where they occurred, were as much the result of a slow, often painful adjustment to the harsh physical realities of parts of the West, as to uncontrolled land speculation at the expense of the small farmer. Between 1862 and 1900, 80 million acres were registered; by the end of the 1930s, some 250 million acres had been distributed under the Homestead Act and its successive amendments.

In the second half of the nineteenth century, it is estimated that the railroads, land companies, and States or Territories receiving federal land grants for educational purposes under the Morrill Act of 1862 together sold at least five or six times as much land as was distributed under the Homestead Act. But the crucial adoption by the United States of a national policy of 'free land' in the 1860s, just as the organized opening of the trans-Mississippi West was about to begin, meant that the empty lands themselves became a major resource, with the possibility of landownership safeguarded by guaranteed title, and available to the poor. Why is it, asked one American investigating southern South America in the 1920s, that the great tides of European immigration have shunned, relatively speaking, the *temperate* Latin lands? Was it the greater freedom of trade elsewhere? Greater freedom of religion? Better public schools? All of these were influential: 'But the greatest drawing-card ever dangled before the eyes of a population beginning to press upon subsistence was that parcel of 160 acres of land which Uncle Sam during the nineteenth century presented to every European peasant with backbone enough to go after it. A homestead for the homeless. Land for the landless.'[35] Americans were already openly critical of the Southland's land policies (most often observed first-hand in Argentina), not least of the continuing acceptance of farm tenancy as the norm, the short leases, rising rents, and lack of systematic land survey. Worst of all was the side-stepping, maladministration and corruption that nullified 'the impeccably drafted mountain of official legislation lying in dust-covered heaps in the Ministry of Agriculture in Buenos Aires', as one observer put it, which had falsely promised land distribution, with secure title, to thousands of small farmers. Americans were similarly dismayed by the evident rootlessness of much of the population – hovels in place of homesteads, high levels of out-migration, and an apparent lack of permanent personal commitment to the land.

The widespread indifference, or opposition, among immigrants to the Southern Cone to taking up citizenship contrasted with the political and economic incentives to do so in the United States. One US Minister in Buenos Aires in the 1880s saw major weaknesses in a system that allowed an individual 'to live nearly a lifetime in one country, and claim citizenship and protection from another, without risk or responsibility in either'. Americans had always set a high value on US citizenship, balancing the need to encourage immigration (of free white aliens) with the dangers of making naturalization too easy. Citizenship was a privilege, James Madison had stressed, and Madison's words at the time of the founding of the United States were frequently quoted:

> It is no doubt very desirable that we should hold out as many inducements as possible for the worthy part of mankind to come and settle amongst us, and throw their fortunes into a common lot with ours. But why is this desirable? Not merely to swell the catalogue of people. No, sir; it is to increase the wealth and strength of the community.[36]

Exactly, observed US Consul Baker in so many words, as he set out what he perceived to be Argentina's fundamental problem a century later. There were no *inducements* for the overwhelming majority of immigrants to put down roots, become Argentine citizens, and strengthen the national community:

> European emigration, *in search of new homes*, does not seem to take kindly to the Argentine Republic. Notwithstanding its ambition to divide with the United States the honor of being an asylum for the toiling millions of the Old World who are striving to better their conditions, ... the great bulk of the exodus still finds its way to the shores of North America.
>
> It is very evident, that with the counter-attractions which the great Western plains of the United States hold out to the people, the Argentine Republic must offer special inducements.

Not only was Argentina's land policy fundamentally flawed, even its colonization procedures were too paternalistic:

> If the Argentine Government would offer its public lands for sale in small subdivisions, *and leave the selection of the locality to the immigrant himself instead of settling him on a particular spot without any option on his part*, there would be far more hope.
>
> An anomalous fact is that, as a rule, the immigrant to the Argentine Republic never becomes naturalized, and hence takes no part in politics or in the government of the nation.
>
> No matter what length of time they may live here, they decline to become 'citizens', but to the last retain their old nationality, – in this respect differing entirely from those who emigrate from Europe to the United States.[37]

Many preferred to remain free of local politics and local obligations, and to enjoy the extra protection provided by their own diplomatic and consular officials. In 1914, only 2.25 per cent of the total male foreign-born population in Argentina were naturalized; reflecting this fact, the European immigrant was generally referred to as an *extranjero* (foreigner) rather than an *inmigrante*.[38] Keeping one foot firmly in the Old World was helped by the cheap round-trip transatlantic fares, noted one American in Buenos Aires in 1911, studying the movements of seasonal Italian workers: 'Steamships carry them back to Italy for about what it would cost an American laborer to travel from Chicago to New York, second class.'

The word 'immigrant' in the United States officially meant one who was intending to stay. As the US Minister in Santiago informed the State Department in the mid–1920s, 'the term "immigrant" is simply not used in Chile and Argentina in the sense that we employ it in the United States'. American officials in Buenos Aires made the same point: 'Argentina still has a form of immigration designated "golondrina" immigration,' the US Consul General reported in 1929, in a wide-ranging discussion of the problem, 'a very considerable number of Italians and Spaniards who come to the Argentine every year for the harvest season *and have no thought of establishing themselves in the country*.' When this, and other out-migration patterns were analysed, the sixty-year span between 1870 and 1929 revealed disturbing trends. Even discounting the net losses during the 1914–18 period, over half the annual returns since 1870 showed emigration to be as high as 40 per cent of the immigration figure, while for thirteen of those years it was over 60 per cent, and was currently on the increase. Not only was Argentina's total population a mere ten million or so, with 'the greater part of the country still very sparsely populated', the high turnover of seasonal workers, 'part-time Argentines', was extremely discouraging. 'Definite settlers, not temporary sojourners, are required.'

Although most American analysts agreed with Mark Jefferson that 'seasonal workers had greatly assisted the Argentine people to make their harvests without burdening the labor market in the slack season', none disputed the fact that by the late 1920s the economy should have been geared to retaining and employing the bulk of these seasonal workers on a more permanent basis. Americans increasingly drew attention to the emigration statistics in discussions on the future agricultural and industrial prospects of Argentina, since the inability or unwillingness to reduce the scale of out-migration at this late stage in the country's development revealed serious internal weakness. Not that immigrants to the United States never returned to Europe. Some did so, and then went again to the USA; others returned home for good. 'While there has always been a fair outward movement of emigrants from the United States returning to their native country having acquired a competence,' noted Messersmith, 'this exodus always bore only a small relation to the number of immigrants arriving. In the Argentine, emigration has always been particularly large.'[39]

Before 1907, the US Government, unlike Argentina, kept statistics only of those who were rejected or deported, although the Immigration Commissioners had not completely ignored the question of the scale of voluntary emigration. In 1892, they published the results of an enquiry into *'Whether there is any considerable emigration from European countries of adult males unaccompanied by families with the purpose of returning to Europe after a limited period, and whether there is any considerable return movement of Europeans who have once settled in the United States; with the causes, if such movements exist.'* A Liverpool agent reported a seasonal movement of artisans, for example, fifty masons and bricklayers who went regularly to Boston in the spring and returned in the autumn. He booked 'a great many men' to Boston, Brooklyn, and Cleveland in this manner, and similar activity was reported by the agent in Glasgow. The reason was the high wages in the USA, and low rates for the Atlantic passage, 'so that men could pay their passage both ways and still earn more than they could by remaining at home'. At Marseilles, enquiries revealed a return movement 'of very small proportions', including German merchants who had spent a few years in the United States 'presumably for the purpose of learning American methods of doing business'.[40]

In 1875, the US Minister had informed the State Department of President Avellaneda's intention 'to open up a fresh stream of hardy Northern European immigrants by providing them with passages to Buenos Aires at the same cost as they would pay to the United States'. Yet neither the Argentine Government nor the people appeared alive to the fact that attracting skilled immigrants was a business, and an aggressive, competitive one at that. 'They think because a certain number of Basques and Italians come out spontaneously,' wrote another observer, 'that a portion of the surplus population of Northern Europe will migrate to their shores. But in fact, the census of the Argentine Republic is ridiculously small.'

No one disputed that in peopling its trans-Mississippi West, the United States had the advantage of 'denser masses at the back to feed the necessary full stream of immigration and impel the more adventurous forward', but at the same time, the United States had a huge territory, much greater isolation from the Atlantic sea-board, and, over extensive areas, a much more hostile geographical environment awaiting settlement in the second half of the nineteenth century than did Argentina. Argentina's resources were more limited, it was true, but the task was straightforward, given a grasp of essentials and the requisite political will. At no time did the United States perceive Argentina's size as a problem; it was not even regarded as a particularly large state – the 'vast distances' of which the country spoke so frequently were dismissed as being more mental than physical.

Boosters and traders

Boosters for railroads, new towns and new business in the United States, exploring the possibilities of expanding their activities beyond the American West into South America in the nineteenth and early twentieth centuries, found little encouragement in the Southern Cone.

The most persistent complaint made by US officials and travelling businessmen was their inability to compete on equal terms with British, French and German commercial interests when these all had the advantage of direct subsidized steamship services from Europe to Uruguay, Argentina and Chile. Most irritating of all was the perception of the River Plate region as a commercial backwater so far as many in the USA were concerned. Trade in Brazil's tropical produce, and other business, maintained direct steamship service between New York and Rio, but delays of six months were not unusual in moving merchandise and correspondence on to Buenos Aires. If only we could expedite mail, small packages, and samples on a reliable basis, the US Consul grumbled, we could build the circulation of American periodicals and trade papers whose advertisements and products would be so well suited to local needs.[41] The new US Minister to Argentina was appalled to discover, soon after his arrival in the mid-1870s, that there were *eleven* direct steamship lines from Buenos Aires to Europe, *none* to or from the United States; 'even foodstuffs and cotton goods of *American* origin are coming here re-exported as English products'. The point was again reinforced by the American Minister in Montevideo in the late 1880s; it was a waste of time to send any mail to him direct, Bacon informed the State Department in a terse memo. Just endorse all communications 'via England': 'they come with more regularity and dispatch'.[42]

The news from Chile was no better. 'You cannot find an American publication of any kind in a store, or club, in Santiago. ... All, or nearly all, they learn about us is filtered through English channels', observed the Minister. British, French and German steamship lines were being modernized and enlarged: 'while the flag of the Great Republic can only be seen on a few old whalers, from Panama to the Straits of Magellan. What a sad commentary upon our enterprise! We spend millions annually for internal improvements but not a dollar to enable us to contend for the vast commerce of South and Central America.'[43] The United States was indeed preoccupied and fully stretched with its 'internal improvements', both in consolidating development in the industrialized Northeast and in speeding frontier expansion across the West. Trade with Argentina had declined since the early 1870s, and the effect of the United States Wool and Woolens Act of 1867, raising the import duties on unwashed wool (Argentina's principal export to the USA), had soured commercial relations between them. Nevertheless, the purchasing power of the River Plate area, Europe's dominance of the market, and the growing pressure by United States manufacturers for new outlets, revived American interest in the region.

In Buenos Aires itself, requests for greater US involvement in Argentina's development were orchestrated by Consul Edward L. Baker, a tireless promoter whose skills and energy kept him in post through successive US administrations from 1874 until his death in 1897. A Harvard law graduate who subsequently spent many years as a newspaper editor in Illinois, Baker brought to Argentina much of the practical drive and enthusiasm that helped to build the American West. He reorganized and streamlined the work of the American Consulate, and then proceeded for more than twenty years to send a series of Consular Reports on the resources and economic potential of the Argentine that were regarded as models of their kind by the State Department. Baker was not an undiscriminating booster. He became progressively more critical of Argentina's extravagance and ostentation, its resistance to change, its neglect of genuine homesteading and of attracting North European immigrants, its ignorance of Patagonia, its complacency about the future. There was no doubting the possibilities, however; reports and statistics on agriculture, livestock, irrigation potential, forestry, mining, manufacturing, transport, trade, tariffs, labour, and immigration were well received in Washington as being 'complete, valuable, and free of "padding"'. It was the practice in the United States to distribute well-informed Consular Reports to the press, and to a variety of trade journals. As a result, they became part of the public domain, encouraging discussion and follow-up by businessmen and other interested parties.

Baker did not attempt to hide the difficulties Americans would encounter in penetrating a market so dominated by Europe: 'The trade of the country can only be secured by a steady pressure, by making an inroad here, by effecting a breach in the old wall there.' 'Whatever we accomplish,' Baker added, in returning to the theme, 'will have to be accomplished gradually – and in the face of bitter opposition and many discouragements.' Even so, the United States was right in its growing determination that the River Plate should become a prospective market for American manufactures.[44]

A new Western-style promoter now appeared on the scene – William Eleroy Curtis. Once Congress was convinced of the need for more information on Latin America, President Arthur, under the Act of 7 July 1884, appointed a three-man commission to go to South America 'to ascertain and report upon the best modes of securing more intimate international and commercial relations between the United States and the several countries of Central and South America'. Although employed originally only as Secretary to the Commission, Curtis later became a full member, describing himself as a Special Agent of the State Department, and taking a leading role in the organizing and carrying through of the investigation. In his earlier years, Curtis had seemed destined to remain one of that resourceful and indispensable army of boosters that helped to publicize the trans-Mississippi West. Born in Akron, he left Ohio after working his way through college, travelled west to explore parts of Texas, accompanied the Custer expedition to the Black Hills in Dakota Territory in 1874, and then, after more Western adventures, consolidated his work as a newspaper reporter in Chicago. There, he wrote the first of a series of snappy accounts of his travels in Colorado, Utah, and along the Old Santa Fe Trail – 'Bright and Breezy Little Books by William E. Curtis'. Making his mark as a lively, innovative journalist, he became managing editor of a Chicago daily, but soon decided to spread his wings, towards the East now rather than the West. In 1883, Curtis was appointed Washington correspondent for a group of Midwestern papers, with a roving commission to pursue any promising lead. At this very moment, Curtis caught the mood of growing interest in South America, and seized his opportunity. He was to be closely associated with the Pan American movement for the rest of his life.

Aside from his contribution to the Commission Reports submitted to Congress in 1885,[45] Curtis produced two major publications of his own based on the 1884–85 expedition. The first of these, *The Capitals of Spanish America*, was the impressive 700-page volume published in New York by Harper's in 1888 – a popular and highly successful work copiously illustrated in the style that distinguished many of Harper's publications on the American West at this period. Indeed, no publication on South America of this type, and on such a comprehensive scale, had ever been produced before for the United States market. It was a *tour de force*, fast, exuberant, and accurate in much of its description. Critics in Buenos Aires, however, complained, as they had done ever since the brief visit by two of the Special Commissioners in 1885, that Curtis had spent too little time there in the first place to write with any authority. Some pointed out that he had spent only a few hours in the city, while others conceded that, in all, about three days had been devoted to Argentina. Either way, the visit had drawn criticism for its brevity and hence, for its political insensitivity. *Porteños* were not mollified by the fact that an additional working week scheduled for Argentina had been lost because of delayed arrival in the River Plate following storms at sea, a point subsequent critics also chose to ignore. Rio de Janeiro, by contrast, remained unperturbed that as a result of these delays, the Commissioners had no time to visit Brazil at all! *Porteños* felt insulted; the Commissioners had even spent longer in Chile than in Argentina.

Commissioners Curtis and Thacher had not of course relied solely for information on hurried personal meetings in Buenos Aires; they had also drawn on correspondence, on written answers to question-naires sent out separately to American merchants in the River Plate region, and on Edward Baker's Consular Reports, although inevitably the Commissioners lacked the more measured view of Argentina that Baker acquired over the years. Generally optimistic about the progress already made, Curtis took too much at face value, assuming, for example, in the mid–1880s that Argentina's existing 'Homestead' regulations would in time produce a landscape containing many prosperous small farmers, as in the United States. Commenting on sections of *The Capitals of Spanish America*, and on popular magazine articles derived from it, the English press in Buenos Aires wrote some cutting pieces at Curtis's expense, although, they hastened to add, he had got some things right about Argentina: 'We do not wish to underrate the prosperity, promise or glory of this country. All Mr. Curtis says of it in his general remarks and inferences is correct, and its future is not overdrawn, but when it comes to details, ... then Mr. Curtis becomes wild and unreliable.' The erstwhile booster of the American West took all this in his stride, and moved swiftly on to a book aimed specifically at the US business community.

Curtis's second major publication based on the work of the Special

Commission was published in Washington in 1889 as *Trade and Transportation between the United States and Spanish America*. Some 350 pages in length, it was intended to identify the main obstacles to America's trade expansion southwards, emphasize the most promising markets, and reach a wider readership than the weightier Congressional Reports of 1885–86 could do. Attention was firmly drawn to the Southland: 'In the countries south of the Tropic of Capricorn, those of the temperate zone of South America, the foreign commerce is increasing with amazing rapidity.'[46] Britain had tripled her exports to Argentina between 1880 and 1885, and then almost doubled the 1885 figure by 1888. The lack of American agents, American banks, American credit, and American steamships was hammered home; if the American Minister had been shocked by *eleven* European steamship lines operating into Buenos Aires in the mid–1870s, Curtis reported that by the mid–1880s, the number had risen to *seventeen* different European companies controlling *twenty-three* different lines. And still not one steamship company bearing the flag of the United States. Even American sailing vessels were a tiny fraction of the total. The idea at this time of completing a railroad link southwards from the United States through Central and South America ('The Three Americas Railway') was based on the desire to challenge the dominance of European steamship transport.

Curtis was equally clear that American-style boosting should be softened in the Southland. While it was still the most direct and effective way to get the 'South American' message across to businessmen and manufacturers in the United States, once they set forth, particularly into the Southern Cone, they would have to adapt to a totally different style of operation. 'Mere "drummers", or soliciting agents, are nearly a total failure in either gaining or holding trade in these countries', he emphasized. 'Drumming' was best demonstrated by the Germans – quietly, persistently, and in Spanish. As a fellow-American informed the business community, after studying the nature of the competition in the late nineteenth century:

> Today, the Germans are the best traders in South America. ... There is no end, moreover, to the small German enterprises. They are by far the most active exploiters with regard to opening commercial houses in new centres. ... I have yet to find a city which the German drummers do not visit. These drummers usually speak Portuguese or Spanish. They have spent years in South America, and know the people and trade thoroughly. They take things easily and are content with small profits. They give from six to nine

months credit, and ask for no payment until after receipt of the goods.[47]

Curtis marshalled support of this kind in *Trade and Transportation*. With a range of statistics, detailed analysis of actual and potential openings for American commodities and manufactures, plus comparative studies of rival European business methods in South America, Curtis packaged his findings under bold sub-headings: MISTAKES OF AMERICAN MERCHANTS; WHY WE ARE SO FAR BEHIND; HOW TRADE MAY BE SECURED.

As yet, however, the United States government was not prepared to follow Europe's example and subsidize steamship companies south of Capricorn. The Argentine government had long ago offered a subsidy to attract an American line (originally with the strong support of Sarmiento), but there were no takers in the United States without additional topping up by the US authorities. Merchants and ministers in the Southern Cone continued to argue the case for improved transport services and additional consular posts. 'We do not seem to try, or to care to try to beat the English and the Germans', wrote one frustrated trade official to the State Department from Santiago in 1902. But the United States was prepared to wait a little longer. In a general report by the Consular Bureau at the turn of the century, the important contribution of a few key consular officials was recognized. Nevertheless, given the strength of the European competition, one hard fact remained: 'Our experience has been that Consular Agents in South America do very little to increase our exports.'

Tourists

> It occurred to me that, instead of making the conventional tourist trip purely by sea round South America, ... I would come north through the middle of the continent.
>
> (Theodore Roosevelt, 1914)[48]

The very small numbers of tourists to South America had no cause to break with centuries of travel tradition in the subcontinent – they skirted the coasts and called at the ports. The Temperate South was no exception. Unlike the experience of the trans-Mississippi West, no 'tourist frontier' rolled overland across southern South America in the nineteenth and early twentieth centuries.

With the opening of the United States first transcontinental railroad in 1869, the tourist industry had immediately become a vital element in the development of the American West, boosting passenger traffic and encouraging the affluent middle class from the Eastern States and from Europe to visit and invest in the region. Indeed, the West was one of the first underdeveloped regions in the world to use tourism as a deliberate strategy for economic growth. Western America's tourist industry expanded rapidly as more transcontinental railroads were built and connected, penetrating the wilderness, and exploiting the West's immense scenic and climatic resources with the help of railroad agents, hoteliers, tour operators, guidebook publishers, advertisers, artists, and illustrators. Even before the end of the nineteenth century, the business of travel had diversified enormously in the United States, with cheaper fares and extra facilities attracting thousands of new tourists, health-seekers, and service industries into the West to form part of its developing regional economy.[49] The West had given the world a new word –*transcontinental*, and to many Americans a new awareness of themselves and their country: 'There is no such knowledge of the nation as comes of traveling it, of seeing eye to eye its vast extent', wrote one New England editor after his first trans-continental journey in 1869. His readers were urged to make the trip and see some of the varied landscapes and resources contained within the United States, since along with a feast of other impressions, they would gain 'a new idea of what it is to be an American citizen'.[50]

By contrast, few Argentines or Chileans showed any desire to explore their own country. Lack of transport was not the real problem, Americans decided; there was little mobility even within the Humid Pampa or central Chile. Despite fierce national pride, there was paradoxically no curiosity to travel, no interest, even among those who could afford it, in discovering the diversity of scenery and resources on their own frontiers as part of a new 'national' experience. In Argentina, one New Yorker noted that it was only the foreigners who got down from the train at unscheduled stops to explore the surroundings, however novel or scenic these might be. As for Buenos Aires, *porteños* lived in a world of their own; in 1914, a traveller had been astonished to find: 'It may be safely said that in Buenos Ayres one will meet as many people of native birth who have visited Europe as have been to Rosario, and most certainly far more who have made the overseas trip than have faced the thousand miles railway journey to Tucumán.'[51] North Americans were themselves no strangers to the attractions of a

European tour, but the passionate, not to say obsessive, Europeanizing of the Southern Cone had serious dangers in the opinion of many American commentators; it was perceived as encouraging too many Argentines and Chileans to turn their backs on their own land – mainly with indifference, at worst with distaste.

Lack of initiative among the British railway companies British railways in Argentina made little attempt to promote tourist travel, either by making the journey itself an enjoyable experience, or by stimulating hotel development outside Buenos Aires and creating new tourist resorts. By the turn of the century, the capital's beach resort of Mar del Plata, with its casino and range of sporting activities, had become a fashionable offshoot of city life, in much the same way as Pocitos and later Punta del Este near Montevideo, and Viña del Mar near Valparaiso also serviced their metropolitan regions. But this was not what Americans were looking for when they arrived in increasing numbers in the early 1900s to assess what the Argentine railways had done to pioneer the tourist industry. Next to nothing, they discovered.

As late as 1914, three of the 'Big Four' British-owned railway companies had each only recently decided to sponsor one hotel away from the immediate coast zone. The Central Argentine Railway ran the Sierras Hotel in the Alta Gracia Hills near Córdoba, an overnight journey from Buenos Aires; in 1912–13, the first direct rail link between Córdoba and the hill resort was opened. By 1914, the Great Southern Railway had located the Sierra de la Ventana Hotel in the south of Buenos Aires Province, pressured into such a move by mounting criticism of their neglect for nearly thirty years of a major beauty spot on the line to Bahía Blanca. 'It is difficult to understand the absence of any pleasure or health resort in the Sierra de la Ventana', wrote one traveller in 1910; here was a dramatically isolated hill region thrusting through the level pampa, and adjacent to the railway, yet still 'an empty canvas' to the tourist. Why had there not been hotel and spa development? 'Lovers of nature and of the picturesque need not fear this advent. There is room in the range for a dozen such to enter without effecting any appreciable mark on the landscape.'[52] Away to the west, the Buenos Ayres & Pacific Railway had taken over the small Puente del Inca hotel and spa in the Province of Mendoza, at the entrance to the Uspallata Pass. Not surprisingly, Americans dismissed assertions by the British railway managements that all that was necessary had been done; on the contrary, the railroads' failure to create a domestic tourist industry was yet another lost opportunity for regional development. With fewer resources, the state-owned, narrow-gauge railway (Central Norte Argentino), running north from Córdoba, had already shown more initiative in promoting tourist traffic by opening a health and pleasure resort in the Córdoba hills, and announcing plans in 1913 to build more hotels at intervals along their line. But the state railways made little headway at this time in developing the tourist industry, while in the Andes, the tracks still had far to go to reach the embryonic Nahuel Huapí National Park.

Restricted ticketing arrangements by the British railway companies also came in for heavy criticism by Americans, and increasingly by Argentines anxious to attract 'foreign globe-trotters'. Although each railway company had its own period-ticket, all steadfastly refused to adopt the 'Circular Ticket' which would have allowed tourists and others to travel over different company lines. In the United States, Thomas Cook and his son, later with the enthusiastic support of George Pullman, had personally negotiated 'through' and 'circular' tickets with the American railroad companies after the Civil War, and with their co-operation, had successfully pioneered both escorted and independent rail travel using the simplified ticketing system – in the Eastern States in the late 1860s, and across the American West in 1872–76. Fifty years later, the Thomas Cook & Son agency in Argentina, now one of the major railway countries of the world, was still struggling against fierce resistance by the 'Big Four' networks to introduce the type of flexibility and sense of business creation in the travel industry that Americans were long accustomed to.

Thomas Cook's agency in Buenos Aires, opened in 1912, was almost exclusively concerned with booking steamship passages to Europe, and with European, Egyptian, and Far Eastern tours. Closer to home, 'Cook's Personally Conducted South American Tour' was based on the Royal Mail Steam Packet Co. or the Pacific Steam Navigation Co. service, and normally called at twelve South American ports. A side-trip from Buenos Aires to the Iguazú Falls or the Paraguay Missions could be arranged on request, and a journey on the Transandine Railway substituted for the journey through the Strait of Magellan. While the majority of Americans took 'the transcontinental railroad', snow conditions permitting, many British passengers preferred the all-sea journey as being 'more scenic and more comfortable'. Seasonal closure of all or part of the Transandine Railway in the Northern Hemisphere's summer months was always a major disadvantage to promoters who had hoped to make the line a kingpin of the Southland's tourist industry. This railroad never laid a firm foundation for the travel business on which automobile transport could rapidly build and diversify. Rail, road, and air traffic volumes all remained small. In the 1920s, when efforts to create a new tourist industry in the Southern Cone began elsewhere to show results, the Transandine Railway went into permanent decline.[53] *Cook's South American Traveller's Gazette* (*La Revista de Viajes*), a monthly which began publication in Buenos Aires in 1912, only ever contained isolated references to the Transandine Railway. Among the wealth of information on Europe and the Old World, the magazine included short general essays on the South American states which could do nothing to disguise the fact that tourist facilities were minimal. Even in the 1930s, the range of choice had changed little since 1912. Readers in Argentina and Chile always found more advertisements for tours of the American West than for tours of the Southern Cone. Characteristically, Argentina's British railway companies never advertised their hotels in the *Gazette*.

After the opening of the Panama Canal, the Boston-based travel company of Raymond & Whitcomb (which in the 1880s had followed Cook's example by introducing tours to California and the American West), began to promote a 'Round South America Cruise'. Rail excursions to Mexico City had been available for years as one of the many side-trips on the California tour, but in 1918, the company launched 'The Raymond & Whitcomb Exceptional Tour to South America', and urged 'Go now – it's about to change and develop!' The Panama Canal itself immediately became a tourist attraction, but American promoters had to concentrate on making the long haul around the coast of South America less tedious – faster ships, first-class on-board facilities, more varied ports-of-call, new and well organized side-trips. The Bence Tourist Co. of New York for example, did much to create new business in Chile in the 1920s, arranging side-trips in the beautiful Valdivia–Lake Llanquihue region, encouraging passengers to make a special point of seeing what had been achieved there by the German–Chilean settlers, and generally helping to pioneer the Chilean Lake District's tourist industry.

Lack of Pullman service The preference for British rolling stock meant that the British railway companies in Argentina long resisted the introduction of Pullman cars. As one railway manager in Buenos Aires replied briskly to a request for Pullman service in the late 1880s: 'There is not a Pullman Car, nor a Baldwin locomotive, running out of this city on *any* railway line.'

This in itself would not have mattered if British manufacturers had produced an equally good Pullman-type car of their own, but this was not the case. In the United States, George Pullman had patented and developed his stylish 'Parlor, Sleeping, and Dining Cars' in Chicago between 1864 and 1868, 'hotels on wheels' ready for the new era of transcontinental railroad travel across the West. Indeed, one British journalist, relaxing in a Pullman car on his first visit to California in 1869, was astounded to discover the West's pioneering contribution to long-distance travel: 'the *Western* States are teaching those of the East to carry passengers in perfect comfort'. And not only the Eastern States; when comparisons were made with England in this respect, it was clear that 'the English railway companies have been surpassed by Chicago'. Pullman, and Pullman-type services developed more slowly in Europe. Although the de-luxe Grand European Expresses appeared in the 1880s, there was not the same willingness to widen the market and bring Pullman-style service more cheaply to the travelling public that characterized the policy of every major railroad company in the American West, without exception, in the 1880s and 1890s.

Americans found passenger service in the Southern Cone decades behind the times. In Argentina, it was the state-owned *Andino* railway that had introduced the first Pullman cars in 1885, and state railways consistently bought a proportion of their rolling stock from the USA. As for the English sleeping-cars on the Buenos Ayres & Pacific Railway, one traveller from Cincinnati in 1905 thought the accommodation cramped and uncomfortable. Moreover, he was annoyed to find that in addition to the standard supplement, 'there were extra charges, too, for such things as sheets, and towels, and soap'.

Some of the severest criticism of the British companies' neglect of passenger services was reserved for the dust-covered coach interiors. While allowances were made for the severest dust storms, the persistent disregard for passenger comfort under 'normal' conditions was considered outrageous. 'Choose a wet day to travel on the Great Southern,' advised one sufferer, 'or you will be as black as a tinker ere you reach, say, Mar del Plata or Azul. As for clothes, don the oldest and shabbiest in your wardrobe, for they will be fit for little else but the rag-shop by the time you get to your journey's end.'[54] Conditions were even worse on the Buenos Ayres & Pacific where, *inside the carriage*, the early twentieth-century traveller was still expected to endure both the dust and the rain: 'Rain came through the shut windows, bubbling like fountains through the sashes. The *mozos* rushed about stuffing dusters in the windows, and throwing sawdust on the floor to soak up the water, which dripped through the roof of the car.'[55] Dust was the regular grievance, however, not merely under storm conditions but as part of everyday living: 'Dust poured thick into the train,' wrote May Crommelin, 'as if bucketfuls were being sifted over us. . . . It lay inch-deep, and gray everywhere save under my head on the pillow.'[56] Yet dust control had been one of the priorities on America's Midwestern and Western railroads since the 1850s. Travelling by rail over the prairies in 1858, a British Member of Parliament on an investigative mission reported:

> Though the weather was extremely dry, and we travelled with open windows over 280 miles of dusty country at good speed, no passenger was annoyed with dust. A simple contrivance is adopted on this line . . . a thick canvas cover stretched on a frame along the bottom of the whole train, covering the wheels and all the open space between the carriage and the rail, so that the dust as it rises is carried off and out at the end of the train in a constant stream. There is no practical difficulty in it, and the additional comfort to passengers is so great, that I can confidently commend the plan to railway directors in this country.[57]

The British railway companies in Argentina, however, gave no priority to improving the quality and range of passenger services. Only in the years just before the First World War did the Great Southern add a better equipped 'Pullman' saloon and restaurant car to the Buenos Aires–Mar del Plata run, or the Central Argentine do likewise on the Buenos Aires–Rosario line. But, complained one *porteño* businessman in 1916, anxious to promote travel in Argentina, 'we still have no heating apparatus in the coaches during winter, no Pullman Vestibule Cars, and no Observation Decks attached to the trains even in regions of picturesque scenery'.

One visitor, fresh from an extensive tour of the American West, summed up the problem as he explored the Southern Cone in 1912–13: 'Here, travelling for pleasure is almost out of the question.'[58]

Poor hotels It was a pity, observed a New Yorker in 1913, that British investors in South America had not been more interested in the hotel industry. By the First World War, Americans were no longer alone in deploring 'the utter lack of a modern hotel worthy of the name in Rio de Janeiro, Montevideo, Valparaiso and Santiago'. In Buenos Aires, Americans recognized only one first-class hotel, the Plaza, financed by banker Ernesto Tornquist in 1908, and run by the Ritz-Carlton Co. of London. Even the Plaza Hotel had been built amid widespread local doubts that it would ever be filled: 'Condemned as a white elephant, the experiment was promised a very rapid extinction. For the first year the result remained in doubt. Now, however, the establishment is turning would-be guests from its doors.'[59]

No other country in the world consistently made such general use of its hotels in everyday business and social affairs as did the United States. Indeed, the first-class hotel, offering a wide range of services both to its guests and to the surrounding community, soon became a peculiarly American institution. The 'hotel habit' in the American sense was alien to European and South American society, but first-class hotels had played a pioneering role in the development of the American West since the 1870s, and were widely acknowledged by the international travelling public as offering not only some of the best, but also some of the most reasonably priced hotel facilities in the world. Around many of them clustered smaller hotels, boarding houses, and ancillary services of a type that in South America were normally only found among a few French or German family businesses, including the small German inns in south Chile. Backed by their experience and success in the American West, North American investigators in the early twentieth century identified the construction of new hotels as a virtually untouched field of enterprise for American investors and entrepreneurs. In a few cases, wrote one of them, the existing hotel building is impressive (even if over-furnished and over-priced), but an understanding of modern hotel management is almost totally lacking – poor food, poor staff, poor standards.

The failure of the 'tourist frontier' as a development mechanism in the Southern Cone was revealed by the disarmingly frank comment of an Argentine writer in 1916: 'Very few know that there are marvellous sights in the region of the Andes. ... It is true that to reach them there are no sleeping cars, and to serve them, there are no hotels, but if the tourist sacrifices himself a little, he will no doubt be largely rewarded.'[60]

Notes

1 M. Jefferson, *Recent Colonization in Chile*, American Geographical Society Research Series, No. 6, New York, 1921 (extract quoted above, p. 12); *Peopling the Argentine Pampa*, American Geographical Society Research Series, No. 16, New York, 1926; 'Pictures from Southern Brazil', *Geographical Review*, XVI, 1926, pp. 521–47. Studies on rainfall and temperature were also published.

2 M. Walker, *Germany and the Emigration, 1816–1885*, Cambridge, Mass., 1964, pp. 119–20; G. F. W. Young, *The Germans in Chile: Immigration and Colonization, 1849–1914*, New York, 1974, pp. 47–8.

3 W. R. Roberts to US Sec. of State, Santiago, 22 Mar. 1888, *Diplomatic Despatches from U.S. Ministers to Chile, General Records of the Dept. of State, Record Group 59*, Washington, D.C.

4 Young, *The Germans in Chile*, pp. 11–13. German immigration: to *Brazil* (1826–1920), 131,441; to *Argentina* (1856–1920) 69,696; to *Uruguay* (1881–1920), 8,767; to *Paraguay* (1881–1905), 1,952. (Source; I. Ferenczi, *International Migrations*, New York, 1929, I, pp. 261–72.)

5 Jefferson, *Recent Colonization in Chile*, p. 28.

6 Young, *The Germans in Chile*, pp. 136–40. Problems and conflicts of interest in colonizing the *Frontera*, are also discussed by G. M. McBride, *Chile: Land and Society*, American Geographical Society Research Series, No. 19, New York, 1936, pp. 292–307.

7 H. L. Wilson to US Sec. of State, Santiago, 26 June 1900, *Diplomatic Despatches from U.S. Ministers to Chile, General Records of the Dept. of State, Record Group 59*, Washington, D.C.

8 Jefferson, *Recent Colonization in Chile*, pp. 8–12. See also W. M. Collier to US Sec. of State, Santiago, 31 Aug. 1925.

9 Jefferson, 'Pictures from Southern Brazil', pp. 525–6, 534. See also US Vice-Consul W. A. Preller to State Department, Rio Grande do Sul, 30 Sept. 1881; *Despatches from U.S. Consuls in Rio Grande do Sul, Brazil, General Records of the Dept. of State, Record Group 59*, Washington, D.C.; and *Letter Books of Officers of the U.S. Navy*, Confidential Communications, South Atlantic, I, 1902–04 (National Archives Manuscript Collection).

10 P. E. James, 'The expanding settlements of Southern Brazil', *Geographical Review*, XXX, 1940, pp. 609, 612–13, 626.

11 W. A. Smith, *Temperate Chile*, London, 1899, pp. 268–9.

12 C. E. Akers, *Argentine, Patagonian, and Chilian Sketches, with a few notes on Uruguay*, London, 1893, pp. 150, 165.

13 B. Willis, *A Yanqui in Patagonia*, pp. 108, 64.

14 C. F. Jones, *Commerce of South America*, Boston, 1928, p. 194.

15 N. Palacios, *Comisión Parlamentaria de Colonización*, Santiago, 1912,

Anexo XVII, pp. 386–91 (see Young, *The Germans in Chile*, p. 148); and C. Solberg, *Immigration and Nationalism: Argentina and Chile, 1890–1914*, Austin, Texas, 1970, pp. 23–4.

16 C. F. Jones, *South America*, New York, 1930, pp. 360–1.

17 T. H. Holdich, *The Countries of the King's Award*, London, 1904, pp. 215–16, 219–22.

18 Solberg, *Immigration and Nationalism*, pp. 52, 132–4, 164–6.

19 For a summary of the conflicting arguments advanced by the estancia and the colonizing interests, see G. J. Butland, *The Human Geography of Southern Chile*, Institute of British Geographers Publication No. 24, London, 1957, pp. 70, 102-9. See also McBride, *Chile: Land and Society*, pp. 339–48.

20 E. L. Baker to State Department, Buenos Aires, 14 Dec. 1874, *Despatches from U.S. Consuls in Buenos Aires, Argentina, General Records of the Dept. of State, Record Group 59*, Washington, D.C.

21 J. E. Wappäus, *German Emigration and Colonization*, Leipzig, 1846; extract from quotation by Young, *The Germans in Chile*, pp. 51–2.

22 A. E. Bunge and C. Garcia Mata, *International Migrations*, II, New York, 1931, 'Argentina', pp. 153, 155.

23 G. S. Messersmith to US Sec. of State, Buenos Aires, 23 Feb. 1929, 'Economic Matters (Immigration and Emigration)' in *Records of the Department of State relating to the Internal Affairs of Argentina, Record Group 59*, Washington, D.C.

24 B. Willis, *A Yanqui in Patagonia*, pp. 117–18.

25 Holdich, *The Countries of the King's Award*, pp. 344, 346–7, 350–1. In contrast, a long but largely uncritical survey of Welsh achievement in the Chubut is to be found in J. E. Baur, 'The Welsh in Patagonia: an example of nationalistic migration', *Hispanic American Historical Review*, XXXIV, 1954, pp. 468–92.

26 J. B. Hatcher, *Reports of the Princeton University Expeditions to Patagonia, 1896–1899*, ed. W. B. Scott, Princeton, New Jersey and Stuttgart, 1903, I, p. 14.

27 *Ibid.*, p. 283. (My italics).

28 *Ibid.*, p. 288.

29 B. Willis, director, *Northern Patagonia: character and resources*, 2 vols., New York, 1914.

30 *Ibid.*, I, pp. 373–7.

31 'Correspondence respecting the treatment of British subjects in the Argentine Republic: 1870–72', *Parliamentary Papers*, LXX, 1872, pp. 87–119. H. G. MacDonell, British Chargé d'Affaires at Buenos Aires, received a copy of the letter to President Sarmiento signed by twenty of the California Colonists. Since the Colony contained a few British farmers, MacDonell included the letter, dated 11 Oct. 1871 (p. 99), in correspondence forwarded to the Foreign Office.

32 T. O. Osborn to US Sec. of State, Buenos Aires, 21 July 1877, *Diplomatic Despatches from U.S. Ministers to Argentina, General Records of the Dept. of State, Record Group 59*, Washington, D.C.

33 C. A. Logan to US Sec. of State, Santiago, 10 Sept. 1873, *Diplomatic Despatches from U.S. Ministers to Chile, General Records of the Dept. of State, Record Group 59*, Washington, D.C.

34 B. W. Hanna to US Sec. of State, Buenos Aires, 11 Jan. 1888, *Diplomatic Despatches from U.S. Ministers to Argentina, General Records of the Dept. of State, ibid.*

35 R. Nash, *The Conquest of Brazil*, New York, 1926, p. 397.

36 J. Madison, *Annals of the Congress of the United States*, 1st Congress, I, p. 1111 (House of Representatives, 3 Feb. 1790).

37 E. L. Baker to US State Department, Buenos Aires, 30 Sept. 1882; and Report, Nov. 1886; *Despatches from U.S. Consuls in Buenos Aires, Argentina, General Records of the Dept. of State, Record Group 59*, Washington, D.C.

38 Argentine Republic, *3rd National Census, 1914*, II, pp. 403–17; Solberg, *Immigration and Nationalism*, p. 42.

39 G. S. Messersmith to US Sec. of State, Buenos Aires, 23 Feb. 1929, 'Economic Matters (Immigration and Emigration)' in *Records of the Department of State relating to the Internal Affairs of Argentina, Record Group 59*, Washington, D.C.

40 *Immigration Commissioners Reports*, Washington, D.C., 1892, I, pp. 259–60. Also *Annual Report of the Commissioner-General of Immigration for the Fiscal Year ended June 30, 1907*, Washington, D.C., 1907, p. 136. The very high levels of immigration to the United States in the early years of the twentieth century were also marked by increased emigration, which, for 1906, was estimated at 16 per cent of the immigration figure. The number of returning aliens could not be estimated 'with any degree of definiteness'. In 1914, departures were 25 per cent of the immigration figure.

41 D. E. Clapp to US State Department, Buenos Aires, 12 Feb. 1873, report enclosed in *Diplomatic Despatches from U.S. Ministers to Argentina, General Records of the Dept. of State, Record Group 59*, Washington, D.C.

42 J. E. Bacon to US Sec. of State, Montevideo, 29 Mar. 1886, *Diplomatic Despatches from U.S. Ministers to Paraguay and Uruguay, General Records of the Dept. of State, Record Group 59*, Washington, D.C.

43 W. R. Roberts to US Sec. of State, Santiago, 30 Sept. 1885; 29 Sept. 1886; *Diplomatic Despatches from U.S. Ministers to Chile, General Records of the Dept. of State, Record Group 59*, Washington, D.C.

44 E. L. Baker to US State Department, Buenos Aires, 8 Nov. 1878; 30 Sept. 1879; 5 May 1880; *Despatches from U.S. Consuls in Buenos Aires, Argentina, General Records of the Dept. of State, Record Group 59*, Washington, D.C.

45 *Reports of the Commission Appointed under an Act of Congress Approved*

July 7, 1884 'To Ascertain and Report Upon the Best Modes of Securing More Intimate International and Commercial Relations Between the United States and the Several Countries of Central and South America' (published as a Separate of the House of Representatives, 49th Congress, 1st Session, Ex. Doc. No. 50), Washington, D.C., 1886.

46 W. E. Curtis, *Trade and Transportation between the United States and Spanish America*, Washington, D.C., 1889, p. 8. A supplement on Brazil was also included.

47 F. G. Carpenter, *South America: Social, Industrial, and Political*, Akron, Ohio, 1900; New York and Chicago, 1901, pp. 600–1.

48 T. Roosevelt, *Through the Brazilian Wilderness*, New York, 1914, p. 2.

49 J. V. Fifer, *American Progress*, Chester, Connecticut, 1988, pp. 4–15.

50 J. V. Fifer, 'Transcontinental: the political word', *Geographical Journal*, CXLIV, 1978, p. 449.

51 J. A. Hammerton, *The Real Argentine. Notes and Impressions of a Year in the Argentine and Uruguay*, New York, 1915, p. 325.

52 W. H. Koebel, *Argentina: Past and Present*, London, 1910, p. 233.

53 After years of intermittent closure, the Transandine Railway was finally closed in 1978. The only section still in use is in Argentina, where a tourist service is available between Mendoza and Puente del Inca.

54 T. A. Turner, *Argentina and the Argentines. Notes and Impressions of a Five Years' Sojourn in the Argentine Republic, 1885–90*, London, 1892, p. 177.

55 E. F. Noel, *Travel Journals: vol. 22, South America, 1907–1908*, p. 9. (Royal Geographical Society Archives).

56 M. Crommelin, *Over the Andes from the Argentine to Chili and Peru*, New York and London, 1896, pp. 15, 143.

57 J. Caird, MP, *Prairie Farming in America, with notes by the way on Canada and the United States*, London, 1859, p. 30.

58 C. R. Enock, *The Republics of Central and South America*, London, 1913, New York, 1922, p. 338.

59 W. H. Koebel, *Modern Chile*, London, 1913, p. 233.

60 A. B. Martínez, *Baedeker of the Argentine Republic*, New York, 1916, pp. 359–60.

4
The new fact-finders

The post-Civil War period in the United States saw the resumption of the great mapping and fact-finding surveys of the American West, and the start of one of the fastest and most ambitious regional promotions the world has ever seen. There had been a huge increase in the demand for information about the American West in the early 1870s, as more transcontinental railroads began to make their way to the Pacific; farmers, miners, tourists, traders, clerks, artisans, speculators, storekeepers and a host of others clamoured for facts and figures, and devoured what was offered. South America, by comparison, was still *terra incognita*.

The role of the Pan American Union

Aside from such sources as census records and British company reports, data collection even in the Southern Cone had been patchy in its coverage and limited in its distribution, reinforcing the United States own ignorance about the region. A key role for the Pan American Union, therefore, so far as the USA was concerned, was the creation of a Latin American information industry. It would collect and process background material on Mexico, Central and South America, applying the skills and know-how so recently employed in the American West. Indeed, the link was a direct one, since with the establishing of the International Union of American Republics in 1890, William Eleroy Curtis was appointed the first Director of its official agency, the International Bureau, known after 1910 as the Pan American Union. His success in organizing the information assembled by the Special Commissioners in 1884–85, and the speed with which he published *The Capitals of Spanish America* and *Trade and Transportation*, had made Curtis the obvious choice for the post, initially offsetting the disadvantage of his inability to speak Spanish or Portuguese. One can trace the continuity of Curtis's approach from his early reporting on the American West to his perception of the role of the International Bureau – that of making Latin America better known to the average American citizen. The valuable but undramatic task of providing and exchanging reliable information on the subcontinent is often totally obscured by the attention given to the more emotive events in Pan American history. Yet Curtis carried the spirit of his 'Bright and Breezy Little Books' from the American West into the Southern Hemisphere. During his term as Director (1890–93), Curtis began publication in January 1891 of the first *Hand Book of the American Republics* (as the monthly *Bulletin* was originally known). He laid the groundwork for the information service, wrote numerous booklets himself, and rounded off his term of office by organizing the spectacular exhibition on Latin America at the World Fair in Chicago.

Major expansion of information-gathering and distribution: the work of William A. Reid The appointment of John Barrett as Director in 1907 reinvigorated the work of the Bureau. Among his earlier appointments, Barrett had been US Minister to Argentina, Colombia, and Panama. In 1904, construction work had at last begun on the Panama Canal, and this, together with Secretary of State Elihu Root's successful three-month visit to South America in 1906, had resulted in fresh demands for accurate, up-to-date information on the region. Congressional reports were recirculated, and US Consulates required to produce ever more detailed returns. Barrett was a powerful speaker and a persuasive lobbyist. His determination to consolidate and expand the role of the Bureau was matched by formidable fund-raising skills, well displayed in the prestigious permanent new home for the Pan American Union (Barrett's preferred title for the Bureau), which opened in Washington in 1910 with substantial financial support from Andrew Carnegie.

Meanwhile, a young American, William Alfred Reid, had been working his way round Latin America since 1902, travelling in his own words 'from the Rio Grande to the Magellan Strait' to gain business experience, and learn Spanish and Portuguese. He agreed with a fellow commercial traveller in South America in 1905 that it was no longer sufficient to rely on the growth of the US domestic market:

'Even if today we have all we can do at home, it behooves us to prepare for tomorrow. The law of business life is growth or decay ... a flourishing business at a standstill is a contradiction in terms.' Americans were now being bombarded with the slogan 'Get Ready For The Panama Canal'. Back in Washington in 1908 with a job at the US Department of Commerce, Reid was soon appointed, under John Barrett's overhaul of the Bureau, to reorganize and head the publications department of the Pan American Union. The range of his work became outstanding, and Reid himself one of the quietly dedicated pioneers of the new information frontier.

He began in 1910 with the handbooks in the *Commerce Series*, later known as the *Foreign Trade Series*, annual publications on each of the Latin American states designed to present facts, market analyses, statistics and diagrams in manageable form. Widely distributed and highly successful, they paved the way for a major expansion of publications, including the *American Nation Series* and the *American Cities Series*, annually updated with basic statistics, illustrations and maps. Reid wrote several of the handbooks in all three series, including fifteen of the thirty titles in the *Cities* set.

With the opening of the Panama Canal in 1914, the United States inaugurated its first regular steamship route to the West Coast of South America in 1918; Valparaiso was regarded as the economic limit of the line. Passage through the Panama Canal halved the 8,000-mile journey from New York to Valparaiso via the Magellan Strait, and reduced the costs in fuel, insurance, and wear-and-tear to about one-tenth. Valparaiso's importance to the north-eastern United States at this time was reinforced by its location on South America's only transcontinental railroad. The future success of this railroad was assumed provided improvements were made, and Americans now called Valparaiso 'the San Francisco of South America'. New series of handbooks were added by William Reid – *Ports and Harbors of South America*, the *Commodity Series*, the *Agricultural & Forestry Series* and the *Communications Series* – as the Pan American Union rushed to cater for the increasing demands of the business community.

Enlarging the budget and the range of services in the 1920s Gaining ground by 1909–10, the greatest burst of United States investment in Chile and Argentina was in the 1920s. It was matched by an information explosion, much of it sponsored and co-ordinated in Washington by the Pan American Union. Reid had now assembled a team of writers, compilers, editors, librarians, and statisticians who, between them, were producing about 100 publications a year, one-third of them in Spanish and Portuguese, some also in French. In addition to the monthly *Bulletin of the Pan American Union* (in English, Spanish and Portuguese), which included first-hand accounts by businessmen and economists, the Columbus Memorial Library had expanded its collection from 30,000 volumes in 1914 to nearly double that by 1924. Since its creation in 1890, the Library was now well on the way to becoming one of the world's major collections on Latin America.

(*a*) *Illustrations* At this stage, the Pan American Union established a new photographic department, employing a full-time photographer, and equipping the section with motion-picture equipment, films and slides. By the mid–1920s, the department housed a collection of 25,000 photographs which aimed at a balanced coverage of urban and rural life, agriculture, industry, transportation, and, for the first time, a comprehensive record of Latin America's scenery and vegetation. Permanent and travelling exhibitions were mounted. Films and slide sets were freely available for hire, complete with lecture notes and commentaries.

(*b*) *Teaching material* The publications and photographic depart-ments now made improved teaching on Latin America a top priority. New maps were commissioned from Rand McNally in Chicago. Boxes of books, pamphlets, posters, slides, and a range of other display material were sent to teachers in both the USA and Latin America, as part of the drive to place the latter firmly in the school and college curriculum. Publishers in the 1920s drew freely on the picture col-lection so that many books of this period are noticeably better illustrated. Publishers also found books of facts and figures more marketable than pure adventure yarns. One best-seller in New York was *Cities and Towns Worthy of a Visit by American Commercial Travelers Canvassing the Pan-American Countries*, which identified places to be visited by *all* salesmen, *most* salesmen, small places recommended for close canvassing and hints on best visiting times. A Boston publisher, on the other hand, was equally successful with his 'Boys and Girls Travel Series' – *Traveller Tales of the Pan-American Countries*. Boston, and particularly the Boston Chamber of Commerce, was now showing the same type of interest in South America, particularly the Southern Cone, that the old Boston Board of Trade had shown in the American West. The members' twentieth-century expedition to South America recalls the 1870 Boston Board of

Trade Transcontinental Excursion to San Francisco, a trail-blazing trip to open up the Western market to New England-manufactured goods.

William Reid now purged the literature of the last traces of Western-style boosterism. The ebullience of Curtis and Barrett, vital in the early phases, disappeared. Writing in 1924, Reid reported: 'The over-optimistic and somewhat exaggerated nature of some of the Union's literature in past years has been replaced by more conservative statements and the desire to place before the reader the actual facts as they exist'.[1]

Helping to promote a new interest in tourism Fostering travel between North and South America had been an essential part of the Pan American Union's activities. By the mid–1920s, for example, there were 6,000 Latin American students in the United States on advanced study scholarships. As Chief Foreign Trade Adviser to the PAU, Reid toured schools and colleges in the United States to lecture on genuine career opportunities in Latin America, and to dispose of the 'El Dorado' image. Thousands wrote to the Pan American Union annually, he told his listeners, asking advice as to which of the 'wonderful lands and marvelous opportunities' they should head for in Latin America. But for those with few skills and limited means, Reid warned, Latin America was not like the American West in its great nineteenth-century heyday of frontier expansion.

Tourist travel, like business travel, held out better prospects. In the event, it was not the railroads, the hoteliers, or the tour operators who did most to promote tourism in South America, but the Pan American Union. It prepared individual and group itineraries, and arranged special side-tours for business visitors, or for sightseers. John Barrett had already made a start on commissioning guidebooks – the first by Albert Hale in Boston in 1909: *Practical Guide to Latin America; preparation, cost, routes, and sight-seeing*. Other travellers were soon encouraged to do the same, none more successfully than the mountaineer and lecturer Annie Peck, whose *South American Tour*, first published in 1913, went through several editions in the next ten years. In 1916, one of the leading American guidebook publishers, Appleton's of New York, produced a new 'Baedeker' to Argentina. In the 1920s, the Pan American Union's own team, under Reid's direction, enlarged and elaborated its popular *American Cities Series*, and introduced a new 200-page annual publication: *Seeing South America – Routes, Rates, Cities, Climate, Wonders*. Much of this literature was distributed free, some for 25 cents. With new discoveries and growing interest in antiquities, the new *American Archaeology Series* was launched in 1926.

All this left one British writer in the Southern Cone marvelling at the speed and success of the USA's new information industry. 'The Americans have come down late in the day,' observed William Koebel in 1917, 'but ... the importance of the work which the United States is already achieving in extending the knowledge of South America may be gauged from the "Bulletin of the Pan American Union", an admirably edited organ, with which we in England, to our loss, have nothing to compare.' Determined to take on the competition, Koebel produced his first *Anglo-South American Handbook* in London in 1921, a detailed annual guide for traders and travellers which in 1924 became *The South American Handbook*, adopting more of the guidebook format and tourist orientation it has retained to this day.

Expanding the information frontier: the contribution of the two major geographical societies in the United States

The American Geographical Society was founded in New York in 1851, a significant date both for the opening of the trans-Mississippi West and for new United States interest in South America. Not by chance did the Society's first *Bulletin*, published in 1852, contain papers on the planned Pacific Railroad Surveys across the West, the comparative advantages of rail and ship canal transportation across the Isthmus of Panama, and the future development of American commerce in southern South America made possible by the opening of the River Plate system to free navigation.

The flurry of initial activity, however, was followed by a lull. The surge of exploration and development within the United States, coupled with the decline of America's merchant marine, helped to reduce the personnel and resources available for work in South America, particularly, outside the exotic, unfamiliar regions of the Tropics. In addition to the American West, Europe, Africa, Asia, the Pacific, and the Arctic also demanded attention. Although shorter notices on Latin America kept members, libraries, editors, and institutions well informed about such items as boundary disputes, exploration, and in due course the work of the new International Union of American Republics, only Chile attracted more continued attention in the Temperate South. Lectures and published papers in the 1870s and 1880s reviewed its progress, and its growing economic and political power on the Pacific after the 'Nitrate War'.

The position was transformed at the turn of the century. New emphasis on Latin America began in the early 1900s and was forcefully underlined in 1915 with the appointment of Isaiah Bowman as Director of the American Geographical Society. Bowman had studied at Harvard and taught at Yale. In the newly awakened spirit of enquiry into Latin America in the United States, and with his own research interests stimulated by expeditions to the Central Andes and Atacama Desert in 1907, 1911 and 1913, Bowman was determined to make a Latin American Research Program a key element in the work of the Society. By 1918, a master plan comprising nineteen research categories for Latin America had been established, and to launch the project that same year, Bowman invited Mark Jefferson to lead the Society's ABC Expedition to South America in order to investigate selected aspects of European colonization and settlement in Argentina, Brazil and Chile.[2] Bowman had been both a student and an associate of Jefferson's in Michigan between 1901 and 1904, and had been inspired by Jefferson's teaching and first-hand knowledge of South America. Bowman's fascination with the region was increased during his years at Yale; among his three research expeditions, that in 1911 was led by Hiram Bingham and notable for the famous rediscovery of Machu Picchu. With an already formidable reputation as a lecturer, writer, researcher, and not least, as an organizer of Latin American studies, Bowman had an electrifying effect on the scale and diversity of the American Geographical Society's research publications and mapping projects after his appointment as Director, a position he held in the critical twenty-year period from 1915 to 1935.

In 1916, the Society's *Bulletin* was reborn as *The Geographical Review*, the purpose, wrote Bowman, 'to broaden the range and deepen the intellectual interest of its articles, and to give its notes and reviews a more critical and scholarly quality'.[3] Mark Jefferson's own memoirs and papers on the findings of the ABC expedition did much to establish the Society's national and international reputation in the Latin American research field in the 1920s, as Bowman and the American Geographical Society assembled an outstanding team to prepare and publish authoritative work on Latin America. Some was commissioned from outside professionals; other studies were completed by scholars appointed to the Society's staff, including Raye

Roberts Platt, Alan Ogilvie, and George McBride. In addition, as part of the Latin American Research Program formally approved in 1920, Bowman had also included his ambitious plan for the production of a *Map of Hispanic America on the Scale of 1:1,000,000* – 'the Society's greatest single undertaking in the field of geographical research', as Wright later reported in his centenary study.[4] For some, the project recalled the perspectives of the early 1850s, when it was decided that 'one of the first labors of our infant Society' would be to produce a new map of the American West. The imminent opening of the West had demanded fresh knowledge and accurate base maps. The thought behind that early cartographic undertaking for the West, observed Gladys Wrigley nearly a century later, was identical with the thinking behind the 'Millionth Map of Hispanic America'.[5] The last of the 107 sheets of the great 1:1,000,000 map were eventually completed in 1945, and linked with those produced by Brazil on the same scale.

Bowman combined two invaluable attributes, wrote one of his colleagues – at once 'the dreamer and the doer, the idealist and the realist'. Neither Bowman nor the American Geographical Society confined their interests to Latin America, but the thrust given by the Society to the detailed geographical study of the subcontinent, and the large number of research publications and articles it produced, were unmatched elsewhere in the English-speaking world. By the 1920s, *The Geographical Review* had become the first choice among many Latinamericanists as the most prestigious and widely read academic journal for presenting significant new findings, and promoting fresh discussion about the region. As a stimulus to university teaching and research programmes on Latin America in the United States, the Society's influence was incalculable.

During the 1930s, as research and publication on Latin America increased within a number of different disciplines, US academics saw the need for a comprehensive annual guide to the latest work on the region by North and South American, and European scholars. The first *Handbook of Latin American Studies* appeared in 1936, edited by the historian Lewis Hanke, and published by Harvard University Press. Initially *A Guide to the Material published in 1935 on Anthropology, Archaeology, Economics, Geography, History, Law, and Literature*, the Handbook's scope was soon widened, and with the assistance of the Pan American Union Library, the American Geographical Society, and the Library of Congress, among other sources, the *Handbook* quickly became a standard selective bibliographic reference for Latin American studies.

The National Geographic Society was formed in 1888 in Washington, D.C., and included among its founding members such distinguished explorers and surveyors of the American West as Major John Wesley Powell and Henry Gannett. Membership in the early years contained many associated with the US Government Bureaux and Agencies, and the *National Geographic Magazine*, despite its imposing title, was simply a small technical journal, publishing reports and monographs, together with a few maps and charts. Sales were low and the Society was soon in financial difficulties.

The great turning-point in the focus and the fortunes of the National Geographic Society came at the end of the nineteenth century. In 1898, Alexander Graham Bell became President and at once demanded a new approach to the Society's task of 'increasing and diffusing geographic knowledge'. Without further delay, Bell appointed his son-in-law, Gilbert H. Grosvenor, as the new editor of the *National Geographic Magazine*, and the transformation which followed, one of the most remarkable success stories in the history of publishing, thus coincided with the new wave of interest in the United States in Latin America.

Grosvenor immediately set about replacing reliance on a small technical readership with an appeal to the general public; henceforth, he announced, 'the Society's key to success would be a *popular* approach to geography'. Membership fees were lowered to $2 in 1900, and Grosvenor began to make fuller use of his Washington location by persuading government agencies to lend him some of their most spectacular photographic plates from the Western Surveys, and from other official publications. Illustrations became a major feature of the *National Geographic* in 1905, and by 1908, over half the magazine's pages were devoted to photographs. When, in 1910, the first hand-tinted photographs appeared, the results were sensational. Membership soared from 3,400 in 1905 to 107,000 in 1912. 'Better and better pictures' was the rule – varied, up-to-date, and integrated with a clear, readable text. 'What was the secret of the great travel journals?', Grosvenor asked himself. 'Each was a vivid eye-witness account; each contained simple, straightforward writing that sought to make pictures in the reader's mind.'[6]

Vivid eye-witness accounts of southern South America received their full share of the *National Geographic's* worldwide coverage.

Secretary of State Elihu Root set the scene with his 'An Awakened Continent to the South of Us' (January 1907), and the demand for more information about South America now helped to pack the pages of the magazine. Although Grosvenor's insistence on accuracy meant that the subcontinent's regional problems and constraints were not glossed over, the public perception of new opportunities and growth capacity, above all in the Far South, was strengthened by a series of major articles. Harriet Adams's journey on 'The First Transandine Railroad from Buenos Aires to Valparaiso' appeared in May 1910, just as the line was opened – 'a new era in the continent's commercial history, and in our own'. Her splendidly illustrated 'Longitudinal Journey through Chile' (September 1922) was another of the popular, well observed accounts by this Californian traveller with wide experience of South America. Robert Ward's 'Visit to the Brazilian Coffee Country' (October 1911), J. B. Hatcher's account of the Princeton University Expeditions to Patagonia (February 1900), Bailey Willis on 'The Awakening of Argentina and Chile; progress in the lands that lie below Capricorn' (August 1916), William Barbour's 'Buenos Aires ... and a Journey up the Paraná and Paraguay to the Chaco Cattle Country' (October 1921), and W. J. Showalter's 'Valparaiso and Santiago: Key Cities with a Progressive Present and a Romantic Past' (February 1929) were only some of the long, profusely illustrated articles that monitored the changes taking place in southern South America.

The National Geographic Society pioneered many new techniques in photography, but its use of colour in particular enabled readers to appreciate contrasts in terrain, vegetation and land use as never before. While colour enriched the striking illustrations of natural history in which the Society also specialized, as well as those of national costume, the variations, for example, in forest cover, in desert landscapes, and in irrigated agriculture, revealed in colour, now added new knowledge and appreciation of the environment. In 1907, the improved financial position enabled the Society to introduce annual grants for exploration and research. Hiram Bingham's series of expeditions to Peru in 1912–16 were jointly financed by Yale University and the National Geographic Society, and several dramatically illustrated articles on the follow-up work at Machu Picchu appeared in the magazine between 1912 and 1916. The Society established its own Cartographic Department in 1915, and map supplements went out to members with the magazine. In 1921, a large 'New Map of South America' was distributed – in colour, with detailed border insets on the economic regions, topography, and climate, and available mounted for wall display in offices and schoolrooms.

Thus, in the early years of the twentieth century, the two major geographical societies in the United States had identified their own particular markets and were responding vigorously to the demands of the information industry. The American Geographical Society's foundation had coincided with the opening of the trans-Mississippi West, that of the National Geographic Society, by contrast, with the imminent closure of the West's great frontier age. New initiatives and reorganization in both Societies, however, had coincided with the United States desire for reliable information in depth on the hitherto largely neglected field of South America. Under Isaiah Bowman, the American Geographical Society's focus on a primarily academic readership was stimulating fieldwork in Latin America, and encouraging the growth of other research journals such as Clark University's *Economic Geography*, whose first issue in 1925 included Preston James's 'Geographic Factors in the development of transportation in South America'. Between 1926 and 1929, seminal studies on the Agricultural Regions of the United States by O. E. Baker were accompanied by an important new series on the Trade and Agricultural Regions of South America by C. F. Jones, starting with detailed analyses of the Southern Cone.

Meanwhile, the *National Geographic Magazine* under Gilbert Grosvenor had built ever more successfully on the initial advice he had received at the beginning of the century from Alexander Graham Bell: 'Leave Science to others, and give us details of living interest beautifully illustrated by photographs.' Grosvenor, however, knew how to combine the two. He did not retire from the editorship, later the presidency, of the National Geographic Society until 1954, by which time the *National Geographic Magazine* had long since achieved one of the greatest monthly circulations in the world. Between 1900 and 1930, it had made an outstanding contribution to the expansion of the information frontier in Latin America, including substantial coverage of the lands and the people south of Capricorn. Years later, Grosvenor was to restate one of the fundamental American beliefs in pursuing the successful approach to development, whatever the field: 'To some people the word "promoter" is an unattractive designation, but I have been one all my life. Promotion in good taste and for a good cause is a creative enterprise.'[7]

Notes

1 Material for this section is based on the Archive collection, Columbus Memorial Library, Organization of American States, Washington, D.C.
2 For background to the work of the ABC Expedition, see G. J. Martin, *Mark Jefferson: Geographer*, Ypsilanti, Michigan, 1968, ch. 7.
3 *Geographical Review*, I, 1916, p. 1.
4 J. K. Wright, *Geography in the Making: The American Geographical Society, 1851–1951*, New York, 1952, p. 206.
5 G. M. Wrigley, *Geographical Review*, XXXIX, 1949, p. 524.
6 G. H. Grosvenor, *National Geographic Magazine*, CXXIV, October 1963, p. 563.
7 *Ibid.*, p. 525.

Conclusion
'A world moved on, a chance gone by'

Many Argentines, usually of the older generation, may be inclined to regard the wealth and importance of the United States as due solely to the happy accident of great natural resources, and to extraordinary luck in its international relations – and to nothing else.

(C. H. Haring, 1928)[1]

The widespread failure in the Southern Cone to grasp the scale of the effort the United States had put into its national and economic development in the second half of the nineteenth century was noted increasingly by American commentators in the 1920s. The trans-Mississippi West had presented daunting problems – huge size (greater than the whole of Temperate South America), a high proportion of mountain and desert, climatic extremes, and immense distances from the Eastern markets and the Atlantic seaboard. Despite these obstacles, the United States had completed the task of introducing sufficient permanent settlement into the void between Midwest and Pacific in a single generation to bring the frontier phase officially to a close. These hard facts were rarely acknowledged in the Southland. Nor, Americans concluded, was the degree of persistence and political will required to cope with them successfully ever fully understood.

Argentina's ownership of two-thirds of the Temperate South gave it a key role in regional development, and its early vision had apparently been real enough. Explicit comparisons between future frontier expansion in the American West and in Argentina were characteristic of the 1850s, 1860s, and early 1870s. Statements by Alberdi and Urquiza, Sarmiento's symbolism of 'school, telegraph, and railway', Avellaneda's 'homestead' legislation – all had encouraged initial optimism, before Argentina's inability to put policy into practice became more evident, and references to the United States model more rhetorical. By the early 1880s, Argentina had scaled down the comparison of its own frontier expansion with what it called the 'astounding' thrust of the United States across the arid and semi-arid West. As the American Minister noted in transmitting President Roca's Message to Congress in May 1882, only the Pampa Territory was now identified in Argentina as 'our own "Far West"'.

It soon became clear that Buenos Aires was not in the least interested in being part or parcel of a new South American USA. It was the Interior, not the Littoral, that stood to gain from the application of the United States development model to Argentina; in practice, Buenos Aires and the Humid Pampa moved increasingly towards the European, and away from the American approach to the economic and technological development of new lands.

The continued perception of wasted resources in the lands south of Capricorn

The perception of waste is the most persistent of the American economic assessments of the Southland throughout the nineteenth and early twentieth centuries. The US Naval Expeditions of the 1850s had sketched the potential wealth of mineral and agricultural resources in the Far South, and assumed that a purposeful start would be made on their systematic exploitation. It was true that most of the land lay idle, buried by centuries of isolation and neglect. Progress would be slower than in the United States, but the region was extremely well endowed geographically, and promising economic growth points were already in place in Chile, Argentina, and southern Brazil.

When Americans came in larger numbers fifty to sixty years later, the scale of underdevelopment still afflicting the Southland left them genuinely astonished. As one Bostonian noted in 1915, after examining the region as a whole: 'The first impression received by a close student of conditions is one of surprise that so small a proportion of the natural resources has yet been exploited.'[2] So far as Argentina was concerned, Americans increasingly perceived it as 'a meagerly developed land'. The reasons? Bad railroad policy, bad land policy, and failure by both Argentina and Chile to make the forest–grassland zone in the southern Andes and Patagonia a major frontier of expansion by North Europeans.

Conclusion

'What have Argentine railroads lacked? Resiliency, mobility, and the disposition to perceive business opportunity and to do something about it.' The fact that railroads in the United States and in Argentina had both been major recipients of British investment capital prompted the American historian, Leland Jenks, to begin an examination in the 1920s of the contrasts in their handling of the situation. In the United States, British capital had been used as a convenience; in Argentina, it came to dominate a considerable sector of the economy:

> The British railways came into being as an intrinsic part of a special kind of economic system in Argentina. ... The British did not invent the system or its parts. They did not invent large land grants or the preference of Argentinians to invest in land, to abjure trade, or to spend conspicuously abroad. But they were not so horrified at this sort of thing as so many Americans tend to be when they venture abroad. ... British activity aided and abetted the tendencies that were already there, and, in the case of Argentina, seemed for a time to have given them renewed strength.[3]

The mid–1880s had marked the beginning of a worldwide expansion of British investment. Much of the phenomenal growth of the United States railroad network in the eighties was financed by Britain, which, at the end of the ninetenth century, had more than five times as much investment in American railroads as Germany and the Netherlands combined – the next highest foreign investors.[4] British investment in American railroads, however, was not accompanied by business control. American management went its own way. As Mark Jefferson observed in 1926, having toured Argentina's 'English railways': 'English money was invested in railways in the United States, too, but imagine a company calling itself English there!'[5]

American criticism of the British railways in Argentina transcended market rivalry. US salesmen and government officials had come to terms with the fact that British railways would favour British locomotives and other equipment, even though specially commissioned studies by the State Department revealed that the bids of the British manufacturers were generally much higher than those of the American, which in turn were often underbid by German firms and by Skoda in Czechoslovakia.[6] Major criticism, however, was reserved for the fact that management of the British railways acted in unison and remained centred in London, an intolerable restriction on their flexibility and initiative. Condemnation of this practice is a feature of every major

American report on British railway operation in Argentina from the 1880s onwards, becoming even stronger in the 1920s as American business and technical evaluation of the Southland increased. Governors and management in Buenos Aires simply carried out instructions received from afar. No American railroad manager, one visitor observed, would believe the extent to which his power in a British railway company in Argentina would be confined to administration rather than to making decisions.

> In order to meet local prejudices the British railways have a Spanish name, have a local board of directors made up largely of Argentines, and apparently function as Argentine companies. In fact, the corporate name of these railways is English, the controlling corporations themselves are British companies, and the boards of directors which actually control are made up almost exclusively of British subjects residing in England. All control of the British railways in the Argentine, even in comparatively small matters, is in London.[7]

Despite claims to the contrary, British railway management in Argentina had remained unresponsive to local needs for improved services and new business opportunity. Why was it for example, one American railroadman asked, that even well into the twentieth century, *porteño* officials could complain that 'the fresh-fruit trade is not, in the Argentine, as it is in the United States, favoured by the existence of refrigerator cars, placed at the disposal of the producers by the railway companies'?[8] But this was just one of many standard improvements that were long overdue.

There was no dispute among American observers that British railways had played a vital part in the economic development of Argentina, only that the United States would have played it differently, and better, if they had had the resources available and been given the opportunity. A British economic historian viewing Latin America as a whole maintained that 'the general level of return on productive investments in trade, railways, and public utilities was not extravagant. At 6 to 7 per cent. ... Latin America would have found difficulty in obtaining the same services elsewhere on better terms.'[9] The US argument was that it could have.provided better services on the same terms.

Only in the years immediately before the First World War had Americans seen a new and revolutionary approach to railroad organization in southern South America. It was spearheaded by Percival

Conclusion

Farquhar, an American company promoter who in 1906 introduced the first stage of a spectacular continental strategy for integrated transport and regional development. He began with the intention of unifying the railways of southern Brazil, a scheme which foreshadowed a huge unification plan for the railroads of Brazil, Uruguay, Paraguay, Argentina, and Chile through a series of concessions, takeovers, and new lines.[10] In addition to a transcontinental railway network, Farquhar's plans also included the improvement of docks, bridges, and river navigation, land-grant railroads, colonization, lumber and cattle companies, *frigoríficos*, public utilities, and hotel development.

Farquhar, born in Pennsylvania and an engineering graduate of Yale, became a New York financier whose lifelong interest in railroads had been triggered by America's own rail expansion across the West in the 1880s. At the turn of the century, Farquhar had looked at South America's enormous growth potential and found only patchy and unco-ordinated development. His aim was to improve international connections, reduce high freight rates, boost immigration into the interior, and above all, to create new business in the regions and new traffic for the railroads. He made an immediate start on standardizing operations, and on introducing gauge, track and branch-line improvements. To study a map of Farquhar's long-term plans for the railroads is to see the closest South America ever approached to a North American land-with-transport development model on the continental scale.

Many Americans found that their greatest criticism of the Grand Design was not that it was too ambitious but that it had come too late. Although the Farquhar Syndicate was registered in the USA in November 1906, most of the funding was obtained in Europe, and by 1913–14 the money market was tightening. While the fear of 'Yankee imperialism' roused opposition in both London and South America, this most dramatic phase of Farquhar's career was in fact ended by the First World War, much to the relief of the British Antofagasta (Chili) and Bolivia Railway Co., and of the 'Big Four' British railway companies in Argentina who saw themselves increasingly threatened by Farquhar's skill and audacity. By 1912, the Syndicate's new Argentine Railway Co. had established working agreements with the Argentine North Eastern Railway, the Entre Rios Railway, the Central Córdoba group, the Province of Santa Fe Railway, and the Rosario to Puerto Belgrano line, thereby creating a co-ordinated system of operation and business promotion in the standard- and narrow-gauge zones of the Northeast on a scale not previously attempted. Not since the days of William Wheelwright's confrontation with the Buenos Ayres Great Southern fifty years before had conservative British railway interests been challenged by the more daring and innovative American approach to railroading – its transcontinental perspective, its capacity for business promotion and diversification, and its co-ordination of activity on a grand scale.

Lack of small towns Americans were less impressed by bald statistics of railway mileage than the majority of Europeans. By 1914, Argentina possessed over 40 per cent of South America's railways, yet, wrote Nevin Winter, unlike the United States, 'the railroad maps are no criterion of the actual settlement of the country. Names will be seen in abundance, but most of them are only stations for freight upon big *estancias*.'[11] The great landowners had welcomed railroad construction through foreign investment as the means of increasing their economic and political power, but neither they nor the railway companies had encouraged the type of agricultural and commercial settlement along the tracks that generated freight, attracted small entrepreneurs, diversified the traffic, and created strong internal markets. The American land-grant railroads had always pursued an aggressive policy towards the settlement of their own sections, besides acting as a focus of attraction for homesteaders who settled outside the land-grant banding. Renewed criticism by American investigators of Argentina's failure to develop a vigorous land-grant railroad policy is common in early twentieth-century reports. The Argentines chose to service foreign investment and imports by increased specialization on a limited range of pastoral and agricultural exports, placing such emphasis on direct rail transport to the seaports that Americans and others were frequently struck by the paucity and isolation of the intervening rural settlement.

There was a quality of 'still life' about the railroad landscape of Argentina. Architecture replaced action. Americans in search of illustrations for their publications at the turn of the century found little of the popular artistry of their own Western frontier age, few scenes of the tumultuously changing world of the railroad – swirling crowds, trains on the move, new towns bursting with business. Instead, there were endless pictures of railway *stations*, solid and sure, but often bare against a distant horizon.

The failure of the railroads to produce a network of small towns surprised Americans in different ways. Francis Herron, an Iowa journalist, was struck in the early 1940s by the dearth of lively, small-town newspapers in the Argentine. There was no 'killing pace' even on the larger provincial papers. The reason he concluded, after much poking around, was that Argentina lacked the diversified business enterprise that invigorated small communities, and encouraged the local press in their role as regional boosters. Every little frontier community in the American West had had its own *Chronicle*, *Clarion*, or *Gazette*. The trouble was that Argentina had the *city* but it did not have the *town*.[12]

Southern Chile as the key to the development of the Southern Cone; Americans emphasize the need to expand beyond the forest frontier into the dry zone 'Of all the parts of South America that we visited, southern Chile stands out to me as the land where one would choose to make a home.'[13] James Bryce, already praised for his perceptive comments on the American West, echoed the favourable opinion held by many visitors to southern Chile. Germans and German-Chileans were 'hammering away' whether as traders or colonists, but new core settlements were needed, so that while German pioneers continued to expand into the forests, further immigration could transform Temperate Chile 'into a well-stocked library of many tongues'.[14]

The need to forge strong links between the forest and the grassland frontiers had been a key element in the economic development of the American West, and the same approach was evident in American assessments of the needs of the Southern Cone in the nineteenth and early twentieth centuries. Argentina, however, had shown that it lacked the political will and the experienced manpower to tackle the dry lands. The whole of southern Argentina requires attention, wrote the US Minister in 1897, 'but it is reasonable to conclude that four-fifths of whatever immigration comes here will remain in the central zone'. The failure to take purposeful action to attract and distribute immigrants more widely was by now a constant criticism; 'they come crowding Buenos Aires instead of making Argentina'.

The importance of attracting more German colonists to the Southern Cone was emphasized by American observers throughout the 1850–1930 period. Three reasons were given:

1 The skill, hard work, and persistence of German immigrants, both in rural and urban environments.

2 Their ability to pioneer successfully in heavily forested regions, as well as to upgrade zones of low agricultural productivity such as poorly drained bogland, or dry, windswept heath.

3 Their thrift in business and farm management which, Americans stressed, would counterbalance the mindless extravagance bedevilling Argentina and parts of Chile.

German immigrants had acquired an outstandingly successful reputation as farmers in the United States, not least for their careful conservation of resources which often contrasted starkly with the more wasteful practices of some other pioneers. In common with the smaller numbers of Scandinavian, Swiss, and Dutch settlers, for example, German immigrants as a whole were prized for the unstinting labour they poured into the family farm. Throughout the 1850s, 1860s, 1870s, and 1880s, American railroad agents, and State and Territorial Commissioners, had kept up the pressure to attract German immigrants to the West, many of whom showed an unrivalled understanding of soil conditions and a sound grasp of varied agricultural techniques. Americans watched with satisfaction their skill in helping to develop the grain and livestock industries of the Great Plains, in extending irrigation along the Rocky Mountain Front, and in promoting the lumber industry, and land drainage and cultivation in the Pacific Northwest. Unlike the Irish, German immigrants made a remarkable contribution to the growth of small rural communities, and to improving farming and livestock management, as well as having a profound impact on the labour force, industry and commerce in the large cities.

Back in the 1860s, William Perkins had been the first North American to remind the Argentine authorities that they should be moving heaven and earth to attract German agricultural immigrants:

> For the Argentine Republic there is no class of immigration that ought to be fostered with greater assiduity and constancy than the German. ... The Italians and Basques establish themselves in the towns, the English and Irish take themselves off to the estancias. ... In the mean time, we are receiving none of that emigration which may be termed the bone and sinew of a country.
>
> The North Americans have always been alive to the great advantages of German immigration, and have exerted themselves in order to secure it. ...

Conclusion

They are active and indefatigable in spreading knowledge about the United States ... The Argentines have made and are making so much noise in their own country that they probably fancy it is heard throughout the world, ... but the world is not thoroughly acquainted with every hole and corner of the region of the River Plate. Ninety-nine out of a hundred German emigrants would not be able to tell to what quarter of the globe the River Plate belonged.[15]

Argentina's response to such advice over the years, however, was fitful and inadequate. Not until the very end of the 1850–1930 period were Argentines reminded of the traditional German skills in pioneering forested country. After the First World War, Germans from southern Brazil or direct from Germany, Austria and Switzerland had been encouraged by the Argentine Government to colonize the tropical hardwood forests in the isolated hill country of Misiones province in north-east Argentina. The newcomers' outstanding success led many Argentines to believe that the pioneers who colonized the Alto Paraná region were all experienced farmers. This was not the case, however; between 60 and 80 per cent of the Germans in the major settlements had come from the highly urbanized areas of Berlin, Hamburg, Leipzig, and Stuttgart, and even the equally flourishing colonies established by German–Brazilians had a significant proportion with an urban background. 'The farming success of these "city" residents is explained by cultural factors', Robert Eidt reported after field investigation – organizational experience, powers of innovation, and the determination to succeed. It was also underpinned by a German heritage of forest colonization reaching back into medieval times, when the German *waldhufendorf* (forest settlement) had become a model of frontier expansion into the forested regions of central Europe.[16]

As it was, Americans in Argentina praised the German contribution to urban business and commerce in the nineteenth century, but drew attention to the fact that German immigrants had lacked any steady incentives to settle in Argentina and expand the agricultural frontier. German rural colonization remained peripheral in the Southland, isolated for the most part in southern Chile, southern Brazil, and north-east Argentina. Yet southern Chile had been perceived as the key for a regional development based on the eastward movement of colonists from the Concepción–Valdivia–Puerto Montt growth zone. They would cross the 'supposed impassable mountains' into the continental interior, as the American Minister to Chile observed in

1870, and encourage the integration of the economy of the coast, the cordillera, and Patagonia. Aided by northward expansion from Magellanes, eastward passage through the forests and lake country into the headwater region of the Neuquén, Limay, and Chubut was regarded as the most practicable way to tackle the dry lands, and bring essential irrigation, flood control, and power generation to the central plateaux and plains. It represented passage from a water surplus to a water deficient region, pioneered by colonists skilled in the techniques needed to develop such environments, and capable of attracting others to follow their lead. Such a movement, preparing the way for greater economic co-operation and east-west trade across the Southland, had been envisaged in reports by American officials and fieldworkers ever since Lieutenant Gilliss's survey in the 1850s. Characteristically, one of the few American colonists who settled in the cordillera near Lake Nahuel Huapí in the 1880s (a region already containing a sprinkling of German pioneers from Chile) had prepared plans to extend irrigation in the upper Limay valley, and develop business both downriver and into Chile.[17]

Failure to expand irrigation in western Argentina had been a frequent criticism since the 1870s, and by the early 1900s it was listed by Americans as one of the specific indicators of Argentina's under-development. Comparisons were now often made with the American West. 'Much of what we once called the Great American Desert was, *and is still being* made more fertile and fruitful,' wrote one investigator in 1906; 'there is no more reason for supposing that even the most forbidding parts of Argentina are doomed to perpetual infertility.' Work along the Río Negro, long overdue, was still in its preliminary stages years after the first wide-ranging national legislation on irrigation in 1909.[18] As C. F. Jones noted in 1930, the irrigated oases of Western Argentina remained 'mere specks in a vast area of arid plains and mountains'. Carl Taylor, seconded from the US Department of Agriculture in 1942–43, reported on the dry western pampa between Mendoza and the Río Negro: 'One crosses the Río Colorado, a beautiful, large river running through a quite flat, untilled area, and wonders why so much needed water is not tapped for irrigation.'[19]

Chile v. Argentina As the nineteenth century progressed, Chile was increasingly perceived by American observers as more vigorous and more innovative than Argentina. 'Chile has the energy, Argentina has the space', concluded William Lord in 1900, a former Governor of

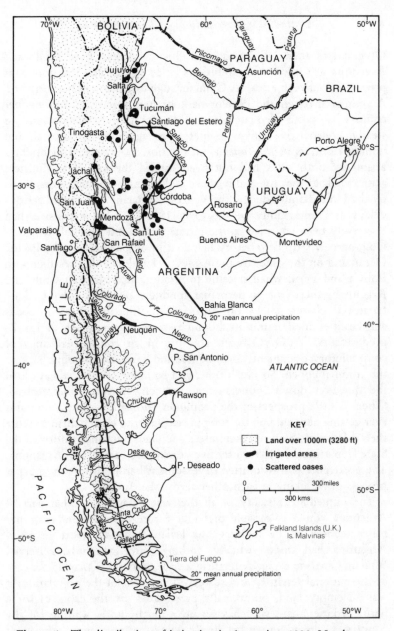

Figure 6 The distribution of irrigation in Argentina, 1930. North Americans criticized the very limited development of irrigation in west and south Argentina. (Based on the 1:500,000 map series, Argentine National Survey, Instituto Geográfico Militar, 1928–32 edition; and on other sources)

Oregon and then US Minister in Buenos Aires. 'Both Chile and Argentina are filled with ambitious pride to become the dominant power of South America, ... Chile through expansion of her territory, Argentina through the development of her resources.' But neither country had taken adequate practical steps to fulfil these ambitions, no steady, constructive moves to merge the agricultural, pastoral, and mining frontiers *in the continental interior*. Even threats of military action by both sides had not been carried through. US Ministers acknowledged that the ambivalence and clumsy diplomacy displayed by the United States during the War of the Pacific had caused serious delays and uncertainty in the early 1880s. Chile's expansion had effectively been confined to the nitrate desert and now left her as 'a long, narrow strip of territory hemmed in on one side by the Pacific Ocean and on the other by the Andes'.[20] Unlike Chile's conflict with Bolivia and Peru, when it came to relationships between Chile and Argentina, there was a perpetual fondness on both sides to base territorial claims solely on historical justification. Present needs and realities in determining boundaries, complained one of Lord's predecessors, T. O. Osborn, are lost in an endless exchange of contradictory documents, despatches, and antecedents going back to the colonial epoch. So much time, and so many treaties, always load the question down. Fundamental problems remained unresolved. 'There is little prospect of the people on both sides of the mountains ever getting near enough together in sentiment to enable them to settle their differences between themselves', William Buchanan informed the State Department in 1899, after five years as US Minister to Argentina. The great potential of unified development had been lost in 'a paper process of shrieking at each other across the Andes'.

The immediate casualty of all this was Patagonia – 'that part of Argentina which is capable of larger future development than any other section of the country', as Isaiah Bowman wrote in 1915. Argentina had done virtually nothing with Patagonia, observed William Curtis in typically forthright style; with more than 25 per cent of the national territory and scarcely 1 per cent of the population, it was an empty land, occasionally punctuated 'by the cabin of some hardy frontiersman, who has set up a ranch and is waiting for the country to grow down to him'. All Americans who concerned themselves with the matter agreed that the frenzied and protracted dispute between Chile and Argentina over the ownership of Patagonia had destroyed both the concept and the reality of a co-ordinated economic development that tied the Pacific Slope to the eastern plains. 'Between them, Chile and Argentina have rubbed Patagonia off the map', said one observer, and with it had gone a new and challenging focus for the Southland. Settlers, surveyors, and others working in the region experienced the advantages of freer east–west movement between the Pacific and Atlantic, but they lived in a world of .their own. Unable or unwilling to take decisive action to remove the political divide, Buenos Aires and Santiago developed an obsession with the maintenance of the Andes Mountains as a 'natural' boundary between them, despite the fact that such a 'natural' role was not performed by the Andes anywhere else in South America save where the line was extended into Bolivia. More flexible in the colonial period,[21] the boundary's existence was reinforced by the politics and transport technology of independence – to such an extent, observed one American engineer, as to drain the Southland of its meaning. It was a verdict supported by Colonel T. H. Holdich as he surveyed part of the disputed boundary between Chile and Argentina in the southern Andes in 1903. Was not the positioning of the line 'comparatively immaterial'? 'There will gradually yet surely arise *the far more important question whether there ever need have been an international boundary at all.*'[22]

An end to comparison

'We have seen an astounding number of agreeable but visionary articles written on the subject of the strong logical tie, geographical, political and mental, between North and South America', wrote L. E. Elliott, editor of New York's *Pan-American Magazine* in 1917. But the truth was, she continued, that more genuine understanding would be achieved with the realization that there was little similarity between them.[23]

American confidence in Chile's future leadership of Hispanic America was shaken by the downfall of Balmaceda in 1891. Diplomatic reports from Santiago to the State Department in the 1870s and 1880s commented on a drive and growth potential that might well place Chile second only to Brazil. In Balmaceda's plans for accelerated regional development and new infrastructure, including roads, railroads, and colonization, Americans saw signs of forward planning and hope for continued progress. Chile's state railways were undoubtedly hindered by political interference and inexperienced management, US investigators reported, but the extension of the central railroad northwards into the Atacama desert and southwards into the forests as far as Puerto Montt (reached in 1913) was nearer to American ideas of the railroad's role in frontier development than anything seen in Argentina. If the abandonment of Balmaceda's policies led to a faltering of purpose in Chile, and to a more dominant position for Argentina, then in the view of many American observers, Argentina was inadequate for the task of leadership – it remained an extraordinary blend of opulence and backwardness: 'The country amazes me: I expected to find it not unlike the United States. It is, however, as different as lemons are different from pumpkins. We have in the United States a booming country. Things also boom in the Argentine, but the character and conditions of prosperity are entirely different.'[24]

The practice of superimposing the map of Argentina over a map of the west-central United States became less popular now, both in the USA and in Argentina, which, at the turn of the century, had been swept by a new wave of anti-American and anti-Pan American sentiment. The superimposed map fell out of favour with American authors for a different reason – the gradual realization that the two countries had little in common. The extent of their divergent development could not be masked by a neat cartographic exercise in latitude and longitude. Argentina's earlier designation as 'the United States of South America' was recognized by both as one of the most misleading titles ever applied. 'Let us cease making idle comparisons,' advised a correspondent in *The World's Work*; 'Let us cease exchanging compliments or insults in newspapers, in diplomacy, in international conferences. ... Let us simply get down to business.'

Not a 'New West' but an 'Old South' Argentina had 'grown old before its time', observed a New Yorker investigating the Southland after the First World War. Comparisons with the antebellum South were a feature of the 1920s, when more Americans than ever before visited the Southern Cone. Argentina was much better known by North Americans than Uruguay, indeed many Americans did not (and could not) distinguish them. Yankees frequently reported that Argentina focused the image of the 'Old South' – a landowning aristocracy, concerned with preserving the rights of a small number of property-holders, and absorbed in maintaining close trading and cultural ties with Europe. Americans saw a landscape of tenants and sharecroppers, where the dream remained 'to buy a farm'.[25] Even Chile had lost something of its perceived 'U.S.-style'; 'Here we are in Chile's portion of this great continent,' wrote a visitor from Wisconsin in 1905, 'yet everything is European and very little is either Chilean or American.'

Argentine extravagance was roundly condemned by those who saw an undeveloped country still in the frontier stage. Katherine Dreier was dismayed by the scale and luxury of many of the *estancias* – 'enormous houses which remind one of hotels, so large and spacious are they. I suppose one ought to say palaces, but they never seemed so to me. I cannot associate palaces with new countries.'[26] The lavishness and dominance of Buenos Aires now attracted more gloom than praise among American visitors. The city was apparently unconcerned that to be the New York, Chicago, and New Orleans of Argentina simultaneously at this late stage was no compliment; it reflected more the restricted growth of the rest of the country than the fundamental strength of Buenos Aires. The contrast between British and American perceptions of Buenos Aires was observed by Sir John Hammerton: 'I was continually meeting Britishers who would ... contrast the Argentine capital with the cities of their Homeland, to the total eclipse of the latter, proclaiming that there was but one place on earth for them, and that was Buenos Ayres. But I never met an American there who preferred it to any of the cities of his own country.'[27] Americans often identified more readily with Brazil in the 1920s. Brazil had displayed determination in the nineteenth century to expand its frontiers in search of new land and new resources, despite the historical claims of the Hispanic states. Brazil showed less jealousy and less fear of the United States than Argentina, observed Haring, less interest in American intervention in Central America and the Caribbean, less arrogance and sense of 'superiority'. Part of the reason of course was that 'Brazil is economically a supplement, not a competitor of the United States. She is a producer of the commodities we need.'[28] C. S. Cooper agreed; Tropical Brazil provided essential foodstuffs and raw materials, but there were also special opportunities in the Temperate South: 'Southern Brazil is our Far West of the last generation.'[29]

Americans who were Westerners by birth or by experience were generally the most knowledgeable about the possibilities of regional development in the Southern Cone, and the most critical of the poor and uneven results. This was as true of the diplomat and the consular official as it was of the merchant and the engineer. A significant proportion of the most competent US representatives to Chile and Argentina in the nineteenth and early twentieth centuries had the backing of many years' experience in the American West. John Bigler, an early Minister to Chile, had interrupted his career as a lawyer and made the overland journey to California as a goldrush 'forty-niner'. Highly successful as a freighter and trader, he had subsequently been elected State Governor. He was keenly aware of the basic needs of new settlers in any frontier region, and of the vital importance of attracting them to the Southland. Three other Ministers to Chile, lawyers or doctors from Massachusetts and Pennsylvania, had pioneered into Kansas in the 1850s, and spent many years helping to establish frontier communities. Ministers and Consuls appointed to Argentina included lawyers, agricultural experts, editors, and businessmen from Chicago and the Midwest, Oregon, and California. What Westerners tended to comment upon most frequently was the lack of any sense of urgency in developing the land. In Argentina particularly, reported one in 1920, 'there exists a heavy atmosphere of indifference'. A few Argentine voices cried in the wilderness, but there was no widespread interest in making the challenge of new frontier expansion into the West and the South a new way forward for a state increasingly characterized by uncertainty and lack of direction. These regions had failed to become a national workshop of development and change. As the world moved on, Argentina appeared to think that time was always on its side. It had tended to attract those who shunned the more challenging, more competitive, more disturbing environment of the United States.

Clinging to the past had skewed the entire perspective of the Southland. By the early years of the twentieth century, Americans observed that the majority of Chileans and Argentines would rather squabble amicably together about the future of Bolivia than address themselves to preparing constructive new development projects with each other. Indeed, the American Minister in Buenos Aires noted with impatience that the height of Argentina's ambition appeared to be no more than the dream of resurrecting the old viceregal boundary of the Río de la Plata – of once more incorporating Uruguay, Paraguay and Upper Peru (Bolivia) within its borders. As a result, added the US Commercial Attaché in the mid–1920s, there was more enthusiasm in Argentina for extending existing railroads to the north and east than for building new transcontinental railroads west into Chile. Continuity with the colonial past remained a factor in the attitudes of the successor states; Chile had been a remote captaincy-general in the

Viceroyalty of Peru, Argentina a late but important addition to the viceregal hierarchy. The opening of the Transandine Railway in 1910 had cut the 3,000-mile journey round the Horn between Santiago and Buenos Aires to a mere 890 miles. At best the two cities had been placed within thirty-six hours of each other, but Americans reported little sign of improved communication, mental or physical. Growing antagonism between Chile and Argentina increased the concern of both states to keep their territorial interests clearly defined and well separated.[30] After Chile's enthusiasm for transcontinental railroads was stifled by Argentina, projects for regional co-operation and integration along the foothill zone and in Patagonia attracted no support. It was significant, wrote one Western American bluntly, that in such a region the United States presence would be typified by an *engineer*, the Spanish American by a *lawyer*.

The Pacific Rim Emphasis on the future importance of the Pacific Rim grew strongly in the late nineteenth and early twentieth centuries. By 1909, C. R. Enock, a British civil and mining engineer with many years' experience in North and South America, had recently completed an extensive tour through the American West and the Southern Cone; in *The Great Pacific Coast*, he presented a bold attempt to analyse the trading potential of the West Coast of the Americas, and the future economic importance of the Pacific Rim. Some writers had already suggested that the Pacific Ocean was destined to become the main centre of human activity in the future. Full participation by Chile and Argentina in the great opportunities for expanded commerce in this region, Enock stressed, would depend largely, as in Canada and the United States, on good transcontinental rail linkage, and on a co-ordinated development plan, unhampered by political barriers, to exploit the virtually untouched resources of the Andes – minerals, forests, irrigation waters, and hydroelectric power. 'A good many years experience in Spanish-America has adduced that one of the qualities of the Spanish-American is "failure to make connections".'[31]

When American writers underlined Argentina's proximity to the Pacific, it was not simply self-interest in the form of increased market penetration by American manufacturers after the opening of the Panama Canal. Americans also saw the lack of transcontinental railroads in the Southern Cone as a fundamental restriction on the Southland's own regional development. This is because, throughout the Americas, increasingly efficient linkage of the settlements along the *eastern* base of the Cordillera to the *West Coast* has been a primary factor of sustained regional and national growth. Linkage of these eastern settlements solely to the core settlements on the Atlantic seaboard has never been an adequate long-term substitute for location on a routeway linking the Atlantic and Pacific Oceans. The most successful Cordilleran marginal zones in the New World have invariably gained from the transcontinental connection. Without it, the interior 'edge-settlements' at the junction of the plains and the mountains tend to become the most restricted of all in terms of potential development.

Paradoxically, restricted movement in the Southland was intensified by the proximity of the Chile–Argentine boundary to the West Coast – a continuous 3,000-mile line closer to the Pacific than any other international boundary in North or South America except the Chile–Bolivia frontier and the Alaska panhandle. Failure to remove the boundary between Chile and Argentina allowed the railroad age to come and go with its unique potential for creating new settlement patterns and new economic growth over much of the interior lost at a crucial turning-point in the development of South America. The real obstacle was never the Andes, only the political boundary running through them. The statue of Christ at the Uspallata Pass, helping to symbolize the permanence of the line, is a reminder not of political achievement but of lost political and economic opportunity. In many ways, the survival of the boundary between Chile and Argentina has been South America's most serious boundary problem, and one of the greatest impediments to the successful political and economic development of the entire subcontinent.

Chile, the dynamic western edge of the Southern Cone, failed to expand eastwards and develop the interior. Argentina remained preoccupied with the concept of territorial ownership rather than with an appreciation of the land's resources, and the unique role that their exploitation could play in creating new economic and political momentum. Argentina has continued to pay the price of its neglect of the land and transport development strategies devised by the United States and imitated by Canada. Geographical isolation characterizes the Southern Cone. Its failure to offset this disadvantage by developing fully the rich physical and human resources of the Temperate South, and becoming one of the world's most flourishing and forward-looking regions, remains one of the great disappointments of the twentieth century.

Conclusion

The final irony was that for the United States, it was the Temperate South, not the Tropics, that exposed the extent of the gulf between Anglo-America and Latin America. The exotic worlds of tropical rain forest and Inca empire were predictably different, but the Temperate South had earlier been perceived as similar in its possibilities to the trans-Mississippi West – the setting for 'Manifest Destiny', for fundamental cultural and boundary changes, for rapid technological advance throughout the region, and for increasing adjustment to the dry-land frontier. Development south of Capricorn, however, had not produced a South American 'West'. If what initially had appeared to be so like the United States was not like it at all, then even the Southern Cone – the bulk of the Southland – was as Latin American as Bolivia or Peru. The reality and the geographical extent of the Latin American culture region were finally understood.

Notes

1 C. H. Haring, *South America looks at the United States*, New York, 1928, p. 196.
2 R. W. Babson, *The Future of South America*, Boston, 1915, p. 229.
3 L. H. Jenks, *The Migration of British Capital to 1875*, New York and London, 1927, p. 169; 'Britain and American railway development', *Journal of Economic History*, XI, 1951, pp. 387–8.
4 W. Z. Ripley, *Railroads: Finance and Organization*, New York, 1915, pp. 5–7.
5 M. Jefferson, *Peopling the Argentine Pampa*, p. 137.
6 For example, see report by S. W. Washington to the State Department, Buenos Aires, 21 Feb. 1929, 'Communication and Transportation (Railway)' in *Records of the Department of State relating to the Internal Affairs of Argentina, Record Group 59*, Washington, D.C.
7 From a confidential report by G. S. Messersmith to US Secretary of State, Buenos Aires, 10 Aug. 1929, *ibid.*
8 A point made by A. B. Martínez and M. Lewandowski, *The Argentine in the Twentieth Century*, London and Leipzig, 1911, p. 206.
9 D. C. M. Platt, ed., *Business Imperialism, 1840–1930: An Inquiry based on British Experience in Latin America*, Oxford, 1977, p. 12.
10 Farquhar's projects were widely reported in the press, in Pan American Union publications, and in British and American railroad journals of the period. See also S. G. Hanson, 'The Farquhar Syndicate in South America', *Hispanic American Historical Review*, XVII, 1937, pp. 314–26; and C. A. Gauld, *The Last Titan: Percival Farquhar, American Entrepreneur in Latin*

America, Institute of Hispanic American and Luso-Brazilian Studies, Stanford, California, 1964. Gauld also includes an account of Farquhar's projects in Amazonia – port works, the Amazon Navigation Co., and construction of the Madeira-Mamoré Railway (1909–12).

11 N. O. Winter, *Argentina and her people of today*, Boston, 1911, p. 392.

12 F. Herron, *Letters from the Argentine*, New York, 1943, pp. 41, 106-7, 113.

13 J. Bryce, *South America: Observations and Impressions*, New York, rev. edn 1917, p. 242.

14 W. A. Smith, *Temperate Chile*, pp. 174, 220.

15 W. Perkins, 'German Immigration', *Artículos Varios*, Rosario, 18 May 1867 (Archive Collection, Biblioteca Argentina).

16 R. C. Eidt, *Pioneer Settlement in Northeast Argentina*, Madison, Wisconsin, 1971, pp. 161–2, 122–5.

17 G. H. Newbery, *Pampa Grass. The Argentine Story as told by an American Pioneer to his son*, Buenos Aires, 1953, pp. 228–9, 231.

18 Law # 6546 (28 Sept. 1909), *'Irrigation in the zone served by the national railways'*. See ch. 2, n.60.

19 C. F. Jones, *South America*, New York, 1930, p. 336; C. C. Taylor, *Rural Life in Argentina*, Baton Rouge, Louisiana, 1948, p. 40.

20 W. P. Lord to US Sec. of State, Buenos Aires, 3 Oct. 1900; C. A. Logan to US Sec. of State, Santiago, 7 April 1883; *Diplomatic Despatches from US Ministers to Argentina/to Chile, General Records of the Dept. of State, Record Group 59*, Washington, D.C.

21 The earliest Spanish settlements in Argentina had been founded along the eastern foothills of the Andes by transandean expeditions from Peru (Santiago del Estero, Tucumán, Córdoba, Salta, Jujuy and La Rioja) and from Chile (Mendoza, San Juan and San Luis). Transandean trade remained important to these towns, and as further promotion, a decision 'to improve direct communication and commerce' between the Pacific and the Atlantic by a new road from Concepción to Buenos Aires was made in the late colonial period. See *Extracts from the Journal of Don Luís de la Cruz employed by the Government of Buenos Ayres in conjunction with that of Chili to open a communication between the two Viceroyalties through the intermediate Indian Tribes, 1806*, with map (Royal Geographical Society Archives). See also D. J. Robinson, 'Trade and trading links in Western Argentina during the Viceroyalty', *Geographical Journal*, CXXXVI, 1970, p. 38.

22 T. H. Holdich, *The Countries of the King's Award*, London, 1904, pp. 410, 411 (my italics).

23 L. E. Elliott, *Brazil: Today and Tomorrow*, New York, 1917, pp. 7–8.

24 F. G. Carpenter, *South America: Social, Industrial, and Political*, Akron, Ohio, 1900; New York and Chicago, 1901, p. 294.

25 Taylor, *Rural Life in Argentina*, p. 292. See also Jefferson, *Peopling the Argentine Pampa*, pp. 106, 124, 175–8.

26 K. S. Dreier, *Five Months in the Argentine From a Woman's Point of View, 1918 to 1919*, New York, 1920, p. 83.

27 J. A. Hammerton, *The Real Argentine. Notes and Impressions of a Year in the Argentine and Uruguay*, New York, 1915, p. 195.

28 Haring, *South America*, pp. 212–13. Also ch. 9, *passim*. F. B. Pike (*Chile and the United States, 1880–1962*, University of Notre Dame, Indiana, 1963, p. 84) has suggested that the United States welcomed animosity between Argentina and Chile as it was a significant factor in allowing Washington largely to dominate the Pan American movement from 1889 to 1933. But this stresses political relationships and tends to overestimate the long-term influence of Argentina and Chile, united or divided. US interest and successful penetration in the Far South were overwhelmingly commercial and resource-based, not political.

29 C. S. Cooper, *Latin America – Men and Markets*, Boston, New York, etc., 1927, p. 239.

30 Opposition to joint projects was marked among the educated classes, an attitude which became more entrenched with the passage of time. In examining Argentine Gallup Institute data of the mid–1980s, for example, C. Escudé concluded that an obsession with territory seemed to be more serious within the better-educated segments of the population, with the educational system and the mass media appearing 'to operate in a way which is counterproductive for regional co-operation'. See 'Argentine Territorial Nationalism', *Journal of Latin American Studies*, XX, 1988, p. 164.

31 C. R. Enock, *The Great Pacific Coast*, London, 1909, New York, 1910. Also *Some Notes on a Trans-Andean Excursion, 1903* (Royal Geographical Society Archives).

Sources and bibliography

I Principal sources of manuscript and printed collections

National Archives, Washington, D.C.:
   Diplomatic Despatches and Consular Despatches, *in* the General Records of the Department of State.
   Letter Books of Officers of the US Navy, *in* the General Records of the Department of the Navy.
   General Records of the Department of Commerce.
   Records of the United States House of Representatives.

Library of Congress, Washington, D.C.

Columbus Memorial Library and Archive Collections, Organization of American States, Washington, D.C.

Public Record Office, Kew:
   Board of Trade Company Records.
   Transport journal collections.

British Library Newspaper Library, Colindale:
   Commercial newspaper collections, 1850–1930 (London, New York, Buenos Aires).

University College London Library, Manuscript and Rare Books collection.

Royal Geographical Society, London, Library, Archives, and Map Collection.

Biblioteca Congreso de la Nación, Buenos Aires.

Biblioteca Nacional, Buenos Aires.

Archivo General de la Nación, Buenos Aires.

Museo Nacional y Centro de Estudios Históricos Ferroviarios, Library and Archives, Buenos Aires.

Biblioteca Argentina, Rosario.

Sources and bibliography

Biblioteca del Consejo de Mujeres, Rosario.

Biblioteca Popular, Cañada de Gómez, prov. Santa Fe.

Biblioteca Nacional, Santiago de Chile.

Museo Histórico Nacional, Library and Archives, Santiago de Chile.

Museo Histórico, Universidad Austral de Chile, Valdivia.

II Books and articles

This list includes references cited in the notes to the text, and other selected material having a bearing on the theme.

Abel, C. and Lewis, C. M. (eds.), *Latin America, Economic Imperialism and the State: The Political Economy of the External Connection from Independence to the Present*, London, 1985.

Adler, Dorothy R., *British Investment in American Railways, 1834–1898*, Charlottesville, Virginia, 1970.

Akers, Charles E., *Argentine, Patagonian, and Chilian Sketches, with a few notes on Uruguay*, London, 1893.

Alberdi, Juan B., *Bases y Puntos de Partida para la Organización Política de la República Argentina*, Buenos Aires, 1852.

—— *The Life and Industrial Labors of William Wheelwright in South America*, Boston, 1877. (First publ. in Spanish, Buenos Aires, 1875.)

Ammen, Daniel, USN, *The Old Navy and the New*, Philadelphia, 1891.

Aubertin, John J., *By Order of the Sun to Chile to see his total eclipse*, London, 1894.

Babson, Roger W., *The Future of South America*, Boston, 1915.

Barclay, William S., 'The first transandine railway',*Geographical Journal*, XXXVI, 1910, pp. 553–62.

—— 'The geography of South American railways', *Geographical Journal*, XLIX, 1917, pp. 161–201, 241–81.

Barrett, John, *Latin America, the Land of Opportunity*, Washington, D.C., 1909.

Bates, Hendy & Co. (publ.), *The River Plate (South America) as a Field for Emigration*, London, 1867, 1872.

Baur, John E., 'The Welsh in Patagonia: an example of nationalist migration', *Hispanic American Historical Review*, XXXIV, 1945, pp. 468–92.

Bishop, Nathaniel H., *The Pampas and the Andes: A Thousand Miles' Walk Across South America*, Boston, 1869.

Boyce, William D., *Illustrated South America. A Chicago Publisher's Travels* and *Investigations in the Republics of South America, with 500 Photographs of People and Scenes from the Isthmus of Panama to the Straits of Magellan*, Chicago and New York, 1912.

Boyd, R. Nelson, *Chili: Sketches of Chili and the Chilians during the War, 1879–80*, London, 1881.

Bryce, James, *South America: Observations and Impressions*, London and New York, 1912, rev. edns 1914, 1917, 1920, ... 1929.

Bunge, Alejandro E., *Ferrocarriles Argentinos: Contribución al Estudio del Patrimonio Nacional*, Buenos Aires, 1918.

—— and Garcia Mata, C., 'Argentina' in *International Migrations*, II, New York, 1931.

Burr, Robert N., *By Reason or Force: Chile and the Balancing of Power in South America, 1830–1905*, University of California Publications in History, Berkeley and Los Angeles, LXXVII, 1965.

Butland, Gilbert J., *The Human Geography of Southern Chile*, Institute of British Geographers Publication No. 24, London, 1957.

Butterworth, Hezekiah, *Traveller Tales of the Pan-American Countries*, Boston, 1902.

Caird, James, *Prairie Farming in America, with Notes by the way on Canada and the United States*, London, 1859.

Campbell, Allan, *Documentos Relativos al Projecto de un Ferro-Carril entre Santiago i Valparaiso*, Santiago, 1852.

—— *Report to His Excellency Dr. Don Santiago Derqui, Minister of the Interior, on the Survey of the Paraná and Córdova Railway, with estimates, maps, plans, and profiles*, Rosario, Argentine Confederation, 30 November 1855.

—— *Report on the Paraná and Córdova Railway*, London, 1857, 1861.

Cárcaño, Miguel A., *Evolución Histórica del Régimen de la Tierra Pública, 1810–1916*, Buenos Aires, 1917, 2nd edn 1925, 3rd edn 1972.

Carpenter, Frank G., *South America: Social, Industrial, and Political*, Akron, Ohio, 1900; New York and Chicago, 1901.

Carter, J. R., *South American Railways: Argentina*, London, 1890; *Argentina and Uruguay*, London, 1891.

Castro, Juan J., *Treatise on the South American Railways and the great International Lines*, Montevideo, 1893.

Cattell, Edward J. *et al.*, *Commercial Guide to South America*, Philadelphia, 1906.

Caviedes, César, *The Southern Cone: Realities of the Authoritarian State in South America*, Totowa, New Jersey, 1984.

Child, Theodore, *The Spanish American Republics*, New York, 1891.

Clarke, Thomas C., 'The building of a railway', in *The Railways of America: their Construction, Development, Management, and Appliances*, London and New York, 1890.

Clemens, Eliza J. M., *La Plata Countries of South America*, Philadelphia, 1886.

Cleveland, F. A. and Powell, F. W., *Railroad Promotion and Capitalization in the United States*, New York, 1909.

Connell-Smith, Gordon, *The United States and Latin America: an historical analysis of Inter-American Relations*, London, 1974.

Cooper, Clayton Sedgwick, *Understanding South America*, New York, 1918.

—— *Latin America – Men and Markets*, Boston, New York, etc., 1927.

Corliss, Carlton J., *Main Line of Mid-America: the story of the Illinois Central*, New York, 1950.

Corthell, Elmer L., *Argentina Past, Present and Future*, New York, 1903.

Crawford, Robert, *Across the Pampas and the Andes*, London, 1884.

—— *South American Sketches, and Reminiscences of Foreign Travel*, London, 1898.

Crommelin, May, *Over the Andes from the Argentine to Chili and Peru*, New York and London, 1896.

Currier, Charles W., *Lands of the Southern Cross: a visit to South America*, Washington, D.C. 1911.

Curtis, William E., *The Capitals of Spanish America*, New York, 1888.

—— *Trade and Transportation between the United States and Spanish America* (with a supplement on Brazil), Washington, D.C., 1889.

—— *Illustrated and Descriptive Catalogue of the Exhibition of the Bureau of the American Republics*, World's Columbian Exposition, Chicago, 1893.

—— *Between the Andes and the Ocean: an account of an interesting journey down the west coast of South America from the Isthmus of Panama to the Straits of Magellan*, Chicago, 1900; New York, 1907.

Dahlgren (Goddard), Sarah Madeleine V., *South Sea Sketches. A Narrative*, Boston, 1881.

Denis, Pierre, *The Argentine Republic: its development and progress*, English edn, New York and London, 1922.

Díaz Alejandro, Carlos F., *Essays on the Economic History of the Argentine Republic*, New Haven, Connecticut, 1970.

Dorsey, Edward B., 'English and American railroads compared', *Transactions of the American Society of Civil Engineers*, XV, 1886, pp. 1–78.

Drees, Charles W., *Americans in Argentina: a record of past and present activities of Americans in Argentina*, Buenos Aires, 1922.

Dreier, Katherine S., *Five Months in the Argentine from a Woman's Point of View, 1918 to 1919*, New York, 1920.

Duncan, Julian S., 'British railways in Argentina', *Political Science Quarterly*, LII, 1937, pp. 559–82.

Eidt, Robert C., *Pioneer Settlement in Northeast Argentina*, Madison, Wisconsin, 1971.

Elliott, Lilian E., *Brazil: Today and Tomorrow*, New York, 1917.

—— *Chile: Today and Tomorrow*, New York, 1922.

—— *The Argentina of Today*, London, 1926.

Enock, C. Reginald, *The Great Pacific Coast. Twelve Thousand Miles in the*

Golden West. Being an account of life and travel in the western states of North and South America, from California, British Columbia, and Alaska: to Mexico, Panama, Peru and Chile; and a study of their physical and political conditions, London, 1909; New York, 1910.

—— *The Republics of Central and South America*, London, 1913; New York, 1922.

Ernesto Tornquist & Co., *The Economic Development of the Argentine Republic in the last Fifty Years*, Buenos Aires, 1919.

Escudé, Carlos, 'Argentine territorial nationalism', *Journal of Latin American Studies*, XX, 1988, pp. 139–65.

Etcheguía, Gregorio, *Los Ferrocarriles Argentinos vistos por Ojos Argentinos*, Buenos Aires, 1938.

Evans, Henry C., *Chile and its relations with the United States*, Durham, North Carolina, 1927.

Fair, John, *Some Notes on my earlier connection with the Buenos Ayres Great Southern Railway*, Bournemouth, 1899.

Ferenczi, Imre (comp.), *International Migrations*, I. New York, 1929.

Ferns, Henry S., *Britain and Argentina in the Nineteenth Century*, Oxford, 1960.

—— *Argentina*, London and New York, 1969.

Fifer, J. Valerie, *Bolivia: Land, Location, and Politics since 1825*, Cambridge, 1972.

—— 'Transcontinental: the political word', *Geographical Journal*, CXLIV, 1978, pp. 438–49.

—— *American Progress*, Chester, Connecticut, 1988.

Foster, Harry L., *If You Go to South America*, London, 1928.

Fraser, John F., *The Amazing Argentina: a new land of enterprise*, London and New York, 1914.

Galton, Douglas, *Report to the Lords of the Committee of Privy Council for Trade and Foreign Plantations, on the Railways of the United States*, presented to both Houses of Parliament by Command of Her Majesty, London, 1857.

Gates, Paul W., *The Illinois Central Railroad and its Colonization Work*, Cambridge, Massachusetts, 1934.

Gauld, Charles A., *The Last Titan: Percival Farquhar, American entrepreneur in Latin America*, Institute of Hispanic and Luso-Brazilian Studies, Stanford, California, 1964.

Gibbon, Lardner, USN, *Exploration of the Valley of the Amazon*, II, Washington, D.C., 1854.

Gilliss, James M., USN, *The US Naval Astronomical Expedition to the Southern Hemisphere during the Years 1849– '50– '51– '52*, 6 vols., Washington, D.C., 1855.

Goodwin, Paul B., 'The Central Argentine Railway and the economic development of Argentina, 1854–1881', *Hispanic American Historical Review*, LVII, 1977, pp. 613–32.

Sources and bibliography

Grahame, Leopold, *Argentine Railways. A Review of their Position, Conditions, and Prospects*, New York, 1916.

Grandpierre, Charles, *What May We Learn from the Other Americans?*, printed as manuscript while at sea (returning to New York) aboard SS *Verdi*, 1912.

Gravil, Roger, *The Anglo-Argentine Connection, 1900–1939*, Dellplain Latin American Studies, No. 16, Boulder, Colorado, 1985.

Grosvenor, Gilbert Hovey, 'The romance of the Geographic', *National Geographic Magazine*, CXXIV, 1963, pp. 516–85.

Gschwind, Juan Jorge, *Guillermo Perkins, su contribución al progreso económico argentino*, Rosario, 1936.

Hadfield, William, *Brazil, the River Plate, and the Falkland Islands*, London, 1854.

—— *Brazil and the River Plate in 1868*, London, 1869.

—— *Brazil and the River Plate, 1870–76*, Sutton, Surrey and London, 1877.

Hadley, Arthur T., *Railroad Transportation: its history and its laws*, New York, 1885, 19th impr. 1909.

Hale, Albert B., *The South Americans; the story of the South American Republics, their characteristics, progress and tendencies; with special reference to their commercial relations with the United States*, Indianapolis, 1907.

—— *Practical Guide to Latin America; preparation, cost, routes, and sight-seeing*, Boston, 1909.

Halsey, Frederic M. *The Railways of South and Central America*, New York, 1914.

—— *Railway Expansion in Latin America*, New York and Chicago, 1916.

Hammerton, John A., *The Real Argentine. Notes and Impressions of a Year in the Argentine and Uruguay*, New York, 1915.

Hanson, Simon G., 'The Farquhar Syndicate in South America', *Hispanic American Historical Review*, XVII, 1937, pp. 314–26.

Haring, Clarence H., *South America Looks at the United States*, New York, 1928.

Hatcher, John B., *Reports of the Princeton University Expeditions to Patagonia, 1896–1899*, ed. William B. Scott, Princeton, New Jersey and Stuttgart, 1903 (I, Narrative and Geography.)

Helps, Arthur, *Life and Labours of Mr. Brassey, 1805–1870*, London, 1872.

Herndon, William L., USN, *Exploration of the Valley of the Amazon*, I, Washington, D.C., 1853, 1854.

Herron, Francis, *Letters from the Argentine*, New York, 1943.

Hirst, William A., *Argentina*, London, New York and Leipzig, 1910.

—— *A Guide to South America*, London and New York, 1915.

Holdich, Thomas A., *The Countries of the King's Award*, London, 1904.

Holland, William J., *To the River Plate and Back*, New York, 1913.

Hopkins, Edward A., 'A Memoir on the geography, history, productions, and trade of Paraguay', *Bulletin of the American Geographical and Statistical Society*, I, 1852, pp. 14–42.

Hungerford, Edward, *The Story of the Baltimore and Ohio Railroad, 1827–1927*, 2 vols., New York and London, 1928.

Hunter, Daniel J. *pseud.* (B. Vicuña Mackenna), *A Sketch of Chili, expressly prepared for the use of emigrants from the United States and Europe to that country*, New York, 1866.

Hunter, J. *et al.*, *Letters from Settlers in Chile*, London, 1887.

Hutchinson, Thomas J., *Buenos Ayres and Argentine Gleanings*, London, 1865.

—— *The Paraná; with incidents of the Paraguayan War, and South American Recollections, from 1861 to 1868*, London, 1868.

—— *Up the Rivers and through some Territories of the Río de la Plata districts of South America*, London, 1868.

James, Preston E., 'Geographic factors in the development of transportation in South America', *Economic Geography*, I, 1925, pp. 247–61.

—— 'The expanding settlements of Southern Brazil', *Geographical Review*, XXX, 1940, pp. 601–26.

—— 'The process of pastoral and agricultural settlement on the Argentine Humid Pampa', *Journal of Geography*, XL, 1941, pp. 121–37.

——'Expanding frontiers of settlement in Latin America – a project for future study', *Hispanic American Historical Review*, XXI, 1941, pp. 183–95.

Jefferson, Mark, *Recent Colonization in Chile*, American Geographical Society Research Series, No. 6, New York, 1921.

—— *Peopling the Argentine Pampa*, American Geographical Society Research Series, No. 16, New York, 1926.

—— 'Pictures from Southern Brazil', *Geographical Review*, XVI, 1926, pp. 521–47.

Jenks, Leland H., *The Migration of British Capital to 1875*, New York and London, 1927.

—— 'Britain and American railway development', *Journal of Economic History*, XI, 1951, pp. 375–88.

Johnson, Hildegard B., 'The location of German immigrants in the Middle West', *Annals of the Association of American Geographers*, XLI, 1951, pp. 1–41.

Johnson, H. C. Ross, *A Long Vacation in the Argentine Alps, or Where to Settle in the River Plate States*, London, 1868.

Jones, Clarence F., *Commerce of South America*, Boston, 1928.

—— *South America*, New York, 1930.

Jones, Tom B., *South America Rediscovered*, Minneapolis, Minnesota, 1949.

Koebel, William H., *Modern Argentina, with notes on Uruguay and Chile*, London, 1907; Boston, 1912.

—— *Argentina: Past and Present*, London, 1910; New York, 1911; 2nd edn 1914.

—— *Uruguay*, London and New York, 1911.

—— *Modern Chile*, London, 1913.

—— *Paraguay*, New York, 1916; London, 1917.

—— *British Exploits in South America*, New York, 1917.

—— *The Great South Land: the River Plate and Southern Brazil of Today*, London, 1919; New York, 1920.

—— (ed.) *Anglo-South American Handbook for 1921*, Federation of British Industries, London, 1921; annual publ. 1922, 1923 (cont. as *The South American Handbook*.)

—— *The New Argentina*, London and New York, 1923.

Kunz, Hugo, *Chile und die Deutschen Colonien*, Leipzig, 1891.

Latham, Wilfred, *The States of the River Plate: their Industries and Commerce*, London, 1866, 2nd edn 1868.

Lewis, Colin M., 'Problems of railway development in Argentina, 1857–1890', *Inter-American Economic Affairs*, XXII, 1968, pp. 55–75.

—— *British Railways in Argentina, 1857–1914: a case study of foreign investment*, London, 1983.

Lloyd, Reginald, *Twentieth-Century Impressions of Argentina: its history, people, commerce, industries, and resources*, London, 1911.

—— *Twentieth-Century Impressions of Uruguay. Its history, people, commerce, industries, and resources*, London, 1912.

—— *Twentieth-Century Impressions of Chile. Its history, people, commerce, industries, and resources*, London, 1915.

Long, Stephen H., 'On the principles which should govern the location and construction of rail-roads', *Journal of the Franklin Institute of the State of Pennsylvania*, VI, 1830, pp. 178–93.

Ludewig, Charles K., *Developments in Inter-American Transportation and Communications, 1890–1940*, Washington, D.C., 1940.

Mabragaña, H. (comp.), *Los Mensajes, 1810–1910*, 6 vols., Buenos Aires, 1910.

McBride, George M., *Chile: Land and Society*, American Geographical Society Research Series, No. 19, New York, 1936.

MacCann, William, *Two Thousand Miles' Ride through the Argentine Provinces*, 2 vols., London, 1853.

MacDonell, H. G., 'Remarks on the River Plate Republics as a field for British emigration', *Parliamentary Papers*, LXX, 1872, pp. 1–47.

—— Correspondence respecting the treatment of British subjects in the Argentine Republic: 1870–72; *Parliamentary Papers*, LXX, 1872, pp. 87–119.

McGann, Thomas F., *Argentina, the United States, and the Inter-American System, 1880–1914*, Harvard Historical Studies II, 1957.

Mackellar, C. D., *A Pleasure Pilgrim in South America*, London, 1908.

McLean, I. W., 'Anglo-American engineering competition, 1870–1914: some third market evidence', *Economic History Review*, XXIX, 1976, pp. 452–64.

MacRae, Archibald, USN, *The U.S. Naval Astronomical Expedition to the Southern Hemisphere during the Years 1849– '50 – '51 – '52*, II, Washington, D.C., 1855.

Maitland, Francis J. G., *Chile: its Land and People*, London, 1914.

Mansfield, Robert E., *Progressive Chile*, New York, 1913.

Marshall, Alfred S., *A Glimpse of South America. A 15,000-mile trip in 1914. Hints to Tourists and Business Men*, Woodbury, New Jersey, 1914.

Martin, Geoffrey J., *Mark Jefferson: Geographer*, Ypsilanti, Michigan, 1968.

—— *The Life and Thought of Isaiah Bowman*, Hamden, Connecticut, 1980.

Martin de Moussy, J. A. V., *Description Géographique et Statistique de la Confédération Argentine*, 3 vols., Paris, 1860–73.

Martínez, Albert B., *Manuel du Voyageur. Baedeker de la République Argentine*, Barcelona, 1907.

—— *The Argentine Republic in its first centennial year, 1810–1910*, Buenos Aires, 1910.

—— *Baedeker of the Argentine Republic*, 4th edn, rev., New York and London, 1916.

—— and Lewandowski, M., *The Argentine in the Twentieth Century*, London and Leipzig, rev. edn 1911.

Maury, Matthew F., USN, 'On extending the commerce of the South and West by sea', *De Bow's Southern and Western Review*, XII, 1852, pp. 381–99.

—— *The Amazon, and the Atlantic Slopes of South America*, Washington, D.C., 1853.

May, Earl C., *Two Thousand Miles through Chile*, New York and London, 1924.

Merwin (Wood), Loretta L., *Three Years in Chili, By a Lady of Ohio*, Columbus, Ohio, 1861; New York, 1863. (Also as *Chili through American Spectacles*, New York, 1863.)

Molinas, Florencio F., *La Colonización Argentina y las Indústrias Agropecuarias*, Buenos Aires, 1910.

Morant, George C., *Chili and the River Plate in 1891. Reminiscences of Travel in South America*, London, 1891.

Morris, Arthur S., 'The development of the irrigation economy of Mendoza, Argentina', *Annals of the Association of American Geographers*, LIX, 1969, pp. 97–115.

Mulhall, Michael G., *Rio Grande do Sul, and its German Colonies*, London, 1873.

—— *The English in South America*, Buenos Aires and London, 1878.

—— and Mulhall, E. T., *Handbook of the River Plate*, Buenos Aires, 1869; 5th edn Buenos Aires and London, 1885; 6th edn Buenos Aires and London, 1892.

Nash, Roy, *The Conquest of Brazil*, New York, 1926.

Newbery, George H., *Pampa Grass. The Argentine Story as told by an American Pioneer to his son*, Buenos Aires, 1953.

Noa, Frederic M., 'William Wheelwright: the Yankee pioneer of modern industry in South America', *The Arena* (Boston), XXXVI, 1906, pp. 591–602; XXXVII, 1907, pp. 31–8.

'Our Gulf States and the Amazon', *De Bow's Review and Industrial Resources, Statistics, etc.*, XVIII, 1855, pp. 91–3, 364–6.

Page, Thomas J., USN, *Report of the Exploration and Survey of the River 'La Plata' and Tributaries*, Washington, D.C., 1856.

—— *La Plata, the Argentine Confederation, and Paraguay*, New York, 1859; 2nd edn 1873.

Palacios, Nicolás, *Comisión Parlamentaria de Colonización*, Anexo XVII, Santiago de Chile, 1912.

Peck, Annie S., *The South American Tour*, New York, 1913, 1914, rev. edn 1916; new edn 1924.

—— *Industrial and Commercial South America*, New York, 1922; rev. edn 1927.

Pennington, A. Stuart, *The Argentine Republic*, London and New York, 1910.

Pepper, Charles M., *Panama to Patagonia; the Isthmian Canal and the West Coast Countries of South America*, Chicago, 1906.

Perkins, William, *The Colonies of Santa Fe; their origin, progress, and present condition, with general observations on emigration to the Argentine Republic*, Rosario, 1864. (Also in Spanish and German.)

—— *The Journal of William Perkins, life at Sonora, 1849–52*, ed. D. L. Morgan and J. R. Scobie, Berkeley, California, 196. (First publ. in Spanish, Buenos Aires, 1937.)

—— *Artículos Varios*, Biblioteca Argentina Archive Collection, Rosario.

Peterson, Harold F., *Argentina and the United States, 1810–1960*, Albany, New York, 1964.

Pike, Fredrick B., *Chile and the United States, 1880–1962*, Notre Dame, Indiana, 1963.

Platt, D.C.M. (ed.), *Business Imperialism, 1840–1930: An Inquiry based on British Experience in Latin America*, Oxford, 1977.

—— and di Tella, G., *Argentina, Australia and Canada. Studies in Comparative Development, 1870–1965*, New York, 1985.

Prichard, Hesketh V. H., *Through the heart of Patagonia*, New York and London, 1902.

Pulley, Raymond H., 'The railroad and Argentine national development, 1852–1914', *The Americas*, XXIII, 1967, pp. 63–75.

'Railway-engineering in the United States', *Atlantic Monthly*, II, 1858, pp. 641–56.

Ray, G. Whitfield, *Through Five Republics on Horseback, being an account of many wanderings in South America from 1889 to 1901*, Brantford, Ontario, 1903; 5th edn Toronto, 1911.

Regalsky, Andrés M., 'Foreign capital, local interests, and railway development in Argentina: French investments in railways, 1900–1914', *Journal of Latin American Studies*, XXI, 1989, pp. 425–52.

Rennie, Ysabel F., *The Argentine Republic*, New York, 1945.

Report of the Secretary of War on the Pacific Railroad Surveys, 27 Feb. 1855,

Washington, D.C., 1855, House Executive Document No. 129, XVIII, Part I, 33rd Congress, 1st Session.

Reports of the Commission Appointed under an Act of Congress Approved July 7, 1884 'To Ascertain and Report Upon the Best Modes of Securing More Intimate International and Commercial Relations Between the United States and the Several Countries of Central and South America.' Submitted 1885; publ. as a Separate of the House of Representatives, 49th Congress, 1st Session, Executive Document, No. 50, Washington, D.C., 1886.

Reyes, Rafael, *The Two Americas*, New York, 1914.

Rickard, F. Ignacio, *The Mineral and Other Resources of the Argentine Republic (La Plata) in 1869*, London, 1870.

Ringwalt, John L., *Development of Transportation Systems in the United States*, Philadelphia, 1888.

Ripley, William Z., *Railroads: Finance and Organization*, New York, 1915.

Rippy, J. Fred, *British Investments in Latin America, 1822–1949*, Minneapolis, Minnesota, 1959.

Robertson, William S., *Hispanic American Relations with the United States*, New York, London, etc., 1923.

Robinson, David J., 'Trade and trading links in Western Argentina during the Viceroyalty', *Geographical Journal*, CXXXVI, 1970, pp. 24–41.

Rögind, William, *Historia del Ferrocarril del Sud, 1861–1936*, Buenos Aires, 1937.

Roosevelt, Theodore, *Through the Brazilian Wilderness*, New York, 1914.

Root, Elihu, *Addresses on Government and Citizenship*, Cambridge, Massachusetts, 1916.

Ross, Gordon, *Argentina and Uruguay*, New York, 1916; London, 1917.

Rudolph, William E., 'The new territorial divisions of Chile with special reference to Chiloé', *Geographical Review*, XIX, 1929, pp. 61–77.

—— 'Southern Patagonia as portrayed in recent literature', *Geographical Review*, XXIV, 1934, pp. 251–71.

Rumbold, Horace, *The Great Silver River. Notes of a Residence in Buenos Ayres in 1880 and 1881*, London, 1887.

Scalabrini Ortiz, Raul, *Historia de los Ferrocarriles Argentinos*, Buenos Aires, 1940.

Scobie, James R., *Revolution on the Pampas. A Social History of Argentine Wheat, 1860–1910*, Austin, Texas, 1964.

—— *Argentina: a City and a Nation*, Oxford, 1964; 2nd edn 1971.

Sears, Anna W., *Two on a Tour in South America*, New York, 1913.

Sell, Lewis L., *Pan American Dictionary and Travel Guide for Tourists, Commercial Travelers, Motorists*, New York, 1935.

Seymour, Richard A., *Pioneering in the Pampas, or, The First Four Years of a Settler's Experience in the La Plata Camps*, London, 1869, 1870.

Smith, J. Russell, 'The economic geography of the Argentine Republic', *Bulletin of the American Geographical Society*, XXXV, 1903, pp. 130–43.

Sources and bibliography

Smith, W. Anderson, *Temperate Chile*, London, 1899.

Solberg, Carl E., *Immigration and Nationalism: Argentina and Chile, 1890–1914*, Austin, Texas, 1970.

—— *The Prairies and the Pampas: agrarian policy in Canada and Argentina, 1880–1930*, Stanford, California, 1987.

Stephens, Henry, *Illustrated Descriptive Argentina*, New York, 1917.

Stevenson, David, *Sketch of the Civil Engineering of North America*, London, 1838.

Strain, Isaac G., USN, *Cordillera and Pampa, Mountain and Plain. Sketches of a Journey in Chili, and the Argentine Provinces, in 1849*, New York, 1853.

Talbott, Elisha H., *Railway Land Grants in the United States: their History, Economy and Influence upon the Development and Prosperity of the Country*, Chicago, 1880.

Taylor, Carl C., *Rural Life in Argentina*, Baton Rouge, Louisiana, 1948.

Taylor, G. R. and Neu, I. D., *The American Railroad Network, 1861–1890*, Cambridge, Massachusetts, 1956.

The Times Book on Argentina, London, 1927.

Tower, Walter S., 'The Pampa of Argentina', *Geographical Review*, V, 1918, pp. 293–315.

Turner, Thomas A., *Argentina and the Argentines. Notes and Impressions of a Five Years' Sojourn in the Argentine Republic, 1885–90*, London, 1892.

Ugarte, Manuel, *The Destiny of a Continent*, Madrid, 1923; English trans. New York, 1925.

US Bureau of Foreign and Domestic Commerce, Trade Promotion Series, *Railways of South America*; Part 1, Argentina, George S. Brady; Part 2, incl. Paraguay and Uruguay, and Part 3, Chile, W. Rodney Long, Washington, D.C., 1926–30.

US Department of Commerce, *The Railways of Argentina*, Emerson R. Johnson, Washington, D.C., 1943.

US Department of Labor, Bureau of Immigration, *Annual Reports of the Superintendent (Commissioner-General) of Immigration*, Washington, D.C., 1892–1905; becomes Bureau of Immigration and Naturalization, 1906–1913; divides into Bureau of Immigration and Bureau of Naturalization, 1913–1934.

Vincent, Frank, *Around and About in South America; Twenty Months of Quest and Query*, New York, 1890.

Waibel, Leo, 'European colonization in Southern Brazil', *Geographical Review*, XL, 1950, pp. 529–47.

Walker, Mack, *Germany and the Emigration, 1816–1885*, Cambridge, Massachusetts, 1964.

Wappäus, Johann E., *Deutsche Auswanderung und Colonisation*, Leipzig, 1846.

Warren, Harris G., 'The Paraguay Central Railway, 1856–1889', *Inter-American Economic Affairs*, XX, 1967, pp. 3–22.

—— 'The Paraguay Central Railway, 1889–1907, *Inter-American Economic Affairs*, XXI, 1967–68, pp. 31–48.

Washburn, Charles A., *The History of Paraguay, with Notes of Personal Observations, and Reminiscences of Diplomacy under Difficulties*, 2 vols., Boston and New York, 1871.

Watkin, Edward W., *A Trip to the United States and Canada*, London, 1852.

Wellington, Arthur M., *The Economic Theory of the Location of Railways*, New York, 1877; rev. and enlarged edn 1887; 4th edn 1889; 5th edn 1891; 6th edn 1899, . . . 1915.

Wheelwright, William, *Remarks and Observations on Mr. Allan Campbell's Report on the Paraná and Córdova Railway*, London, 1857.

—— 'Proposed railway route across the Andes, from Caldera in Chile to Rosario on the Paraná, via Córdova', *Journal of the Royal Geographical Society*, XXXI, 1861, pp. 154–62.

—— *Ferro-carril a la Ensenada : Recopilación. Memorandum sobre el Ferro-carril y Puerto de la Ensenada*, Buenos Aires, 1870.

Whitaker, Arthur P., *The United States and Argentina*, Cambridge, Massachusetts, 1954.

—— *The Western Hemisphere Idea: its Rise and Decline*, Ithaca, New York, 1954.

—— *The United States and the Southern Cone: Argentina, Chile, and Uruguay*, Cambridge, Massachusetts, 1976.

Wiborg, Frank, *A Commercial Traveller in South America*, New York, 1905.

Wilcken, Guillermo, *Las Colonias. Informe sobre el estado actual de las Colonias Agrícolas de la República Argentina, presentado a la Comisión Central de Inmigración por el Inspector Nacional de ellas, 1872*, Buenos Aires, 1873.

Wilkes, Charles, USN, *Narrative of the United States' Exploring Expedition during the Years 1838, 1839, 1840, 1841, 1842*, 5 vols., Philadelphia, 1845.

Williams, John H., *Argentine International Trade under Inconvertible Paper Money, 1880–1900*, Cambridge, Massachusetts, 1920.

Willis, Bailey, *Northern Patagonia: character and resources. Report for the Ministry of Public Works, Argentina*, 2 vols., New York, 1914.

—— *A Yanqui in Patagonia*, Stanford, California, 1947.

Winter, Nevin O., *Brazil and her people of today*, Boston, 1910.

—— *Argentina and her people of today*, Boston, 1911.

—— *Chile and her people of today*, Boston, 1912.

Wright, John K., *Geography in the Making: The American Geographical Society, 1851–1951*, New York, 1952.

Wright, Winthrop R., *British-Owned Railways in Argentina: their effect on economic nationalism, 1854–1948*, Austin, Texas, 1974.

Wrigley, Gladys M., 'Ubique: a challenge', *Geographical Review*, XXXIX, 1949, pp. 523–5.

Young, George F. W., *The Germans in Chile: Immigration and Colonization, 1849–1914*, New York, 1974.

Zahm, John A., *Through South America's Southland*, New York, 1916.

Index

Index

in USA, 45, 52–60, 79–80
Llanquihue (lake and prov.), Chile,
    113–15, 119, 145
Long, Major/Col. Stephen Harriman,
    37–8
López, President Carlos Antonio, 17

MacRae, Lieut. Archibald, USN, 7,
    19, 20, 24–5
Maury, Lieut. Matthew Fontaine,
    USN, 9–10, 11–12, 26
Mendoza, Argentina
    as centre of irrigated agriculture,
    24, 112–13
    rail links to, 24, 78, 94–5, 97, 98,
    152 n.53
Mississippi (river), 1, 7–8, 9–11
Mitre, President Bartolomé, 45, 51,
    52
Mitre, Emilio, 88

Nahuel Huapí (lake), Argentina, 91,
    100, 127, 174
National Geographic Society,
    Washington, D.C., 161–3
Negro (river), Argentina, 21, 77, 87,
    108 n.60, 174
Neuquén (river, town, prov.),
    Argentina, 87, 93, 100, 174

Osorno, Chile
    as centre of German colonization,
    115, 119–20
    on proposed transcontinental
    railway, 100

Pacific Railroad Surveys, USA (1853–
    55), 1, 28, 51
Pacific Steam Navigation Co., 22,
    113, 144
Page, Lieut. Thomas Jefferson, USN,
    7, 14–19, 25
Pan American Union (1910)
    (formerly International Bureau of
    the American Republics), 153–8,
    160, 178
Panama Canal, 99, 102, 104, 145, 155
Panama Railroad, 9, 24

Paraguay Central Railway
    (construction started 1854), gauge,
    45, 92
Paraná (city), Argentina, 16–18
Paraná-Paraguay (rivers)
    explored by US Navy expeditions
    (1853–55, 1859–60), 13–19
    opened to free navigation (1852),
    13
Patagonia
    conflicting claims to, 126, 176–7
    potential of, 91–2, 120–2, 125–8,
    174
Pérez Rosales, Vicente, 114
Perkins, William
    in California, 61
    promotes land-grant railroad and
    colonization in Argentina, 61–8,
    70, 128, 172–3
Peto, Sir Morton, 47
Philippi, Bernhard, 113–14
Pino Hachado Pass, Andes Mts, 100,
    101
Planchón Pass, Andes Mts, 21, 93,
    101
Portillo Pass, Andes Mts, 21, 25
Puerto Montt, Chile, 113, 115, 119,
    173, 178
Punta Arenas, Chile, 113, 121

railways
    conflicting US–British approach
    to, 34–40, 46–7, 50, 80–1, 88–91
    contrasted costs of, 38–40, 43,
    46–7
    distinguishing features of US
    construction, 35–8, 43, 91
    gauge variations on, 74–6, 88, 92,
    108 n.59
    US criticisms of Argentine, 3–4, 77,
    78–93, 96, 167–8; of Chilean, 96,
    177–8
    Individual railway companies or
    systems:
    Andino, 74, 94, 95, 108 n.60
    Antofagasta (Chili) and Bolivia, 99,
    103, 110n.100, 169
    Argentine Great Western, 95

Index